Happy Purim!
Rabbi Leivi Sudak
and all at
Lubavitch of Edgware

הגדה של פסח

Haggadah Shel Pesach

כי ישאלך בנך מחר לאמר

Ki Yishalcha Bincha

When Your Child Asks...?

A COMPILATION OF SELECTED
TORAH INSIGHTS,
THOUGHT-PROVOKING IDEAS,
HOMILIES AND EXPLANATIONS
OF HAGGADAH PASSAGES

by

Rabbi Moshe Bogomilsky

New Expanded Edition

5766 • 2006

KI YISHALCHA BINCHA —
WHEN YOUR CHILD ASKS...?

Published and Copyrighted © by
Rabbi Moshe Bogomilsky
1382 President Street
Brooklyn, New York 11213

First Impression — 5759-1999
Second Impression — 5760-2000
Third Impression — 5761-2001
Fourth Impression — 5764-2004
Fifth Impression — 5766-2006

ISBN 1-8808-8028-8

Dedicated to the memory
of our beloved father

Moshe Yaakov Grunfeld

ר' **משה יעקב** ב"ר **אהרן** ע"ה

נפטר ביום ב' דר"ח אלול תש"מ

He went through the Holocaust and suffered greatly, but it did not affect his loyalty to Hashem.

He came to Los Angeles, California when it was popularly known as a spiritual wasteland, and thanks to his efforts and those of a few other members of his generation, it is today a flourishing oasis of Torah and *Yiddishkeit*.

The growth of *yeshivot*, expansion of *kashrut*, and the prolification of Chabad in California are just some of the many merits in which he has a share.

Through the Rebbe's emissary to the West Coast, Rabbi Menachem Shmuel Dovid זצ"ל Raichik, he became a Lubavitcher *chassid* and was attached to the Rebbe זי"ע with heart and soul.

He was an *oheiv shalom* and a *rodeif shalom,* and it earned him the admiration, respect, and love of all who knew him.

May his memory be an inspiration to us, and may we faithfully continue his legacy.

Avraham Aaron and Peninah Chavah Grunfeld
Batya, Tzvi, Yehoshua and Chaya Tzivyah

Yosef and Nurit Amalya Grunfeld
Daniella, Deena and Donna Miriam

TABLE OF CONTENTS

Ki Yishalcha Bincha

FOREWORD

Is there a need for yet another *Haggadah*? This question may be asked by many who will take this *sefer* in their hands, for in the past 500 years the *Haggadah* has been printed throughout the world, in thousands of editions and millions upon millions of copies. It has been translated into the language of almost every country where Jews have sojourned, and it has become so popular that it can be found in many a home that does not even have a complete set of *Chumashim*.

If so, why am I going through the effort and expense to print another one? The reason is the following: A most eagerly anticipated event in a Jewish home is the *Seder* table. The parents have an opportunity to *shep* — derive — *nachas* from their children, and the children have a chance to demonstrate their knowledge and intelligence. Permeated with joy, the parents listen to their little ones say the *"Mah Nishtanah,"* and with excitement and awe the children tune in to the wisdom of the parents and relish every nuance of family history they may convey. The experience leaves an indelible mark on all present. As the children grow up and are blessed with families of their own, they nostalgically reminisce about *Zeidy* and *Bubby's Seder*.

According to King David it is a blissful experience when, "Your children will be like olive shoots surrounding your table" (Psalms 128:3). Although the commentaries give deep and profound interpretation to this, literally it means that it is the traditional blessing in the eyes of every parent to have his children sitting together with him around the table.

Like any other *Zeidy* and *Bubby*, we would love to have all our children and grandchildren around our *Seder* table, but unfortunately, geographic distances, lack of adequate space and facilities, etc., make this a virtual impossibility.

In a sense, we can achieve our desire of having our entire family with us at the *Seder* table through publishing this *Haggadah*, in which they will find many of the thoughts they heard in their

younger years when they were with us. While reading it, their imaginative powers will bring them to our *Seder*, and hopefully it will also help them share with their children and spouses the Torah thoughts and memories of the wonderful times they experienced around *Zeidy* and *Bubby's Seder* table, and thus, they will all be together with us in spirit.

This *Haggadah*, however, is not only limited to our family. It is customary to have guests at the *Seder*, and the more the merrier. Dear readers, I would love to also have all of you join us *Pesach* night for the *Seder*. Thus, I invite you to read this *Haggadah*, and through dwelling on the thoughts therein, the unifying power of Torah will unite us all.

* * *

This *Haggadah* follows the same style as the five volumes of *Vedibarta Bam* on the Torah. Every thought is presented in a question and answer format in order to facilitate comprehension and encourage lively conversation and discussion. I hope that this will be particularly appropriate on *Pesach*, when the Torah says, *"Ki yishalcha bincha"* — "When your child asks you," and *"Vehigadeta lebincha"* — "You shall tell your child."

* * *

As mentioned in the introduction to *Vedibarta Bam*, my primary intention in publishing *sefarim*, is to link my family with my predecessors through Torah. Consequently, in this volume too, some Torah thoughts from my grandfather, Rabbi Tzvi *Hakohen z"l* Kaplan and my father, Rabbi Shmuel Pesach *z"l* Bogomilsky, are included.

* * *

WHY THE NAME *KI YISHALCHA BINCHA* — *WHEN YOUR CHILD ASKS...?*

When I told Rabbi Yonah Avtzon, of Sichos In English, that I plan to call the *Haggadah, "Ki Yishalcha Bincha..."* — *"When Your Child Asks...?"* — his immediate reaction was, "There must already be numerous *Haggadot* with that name; why not pick something more original?" My curiosity took me to the Rebbe's library

(which is one of the most extensive private libraries in the world and which is now under the auspices of Agudat Chassidei Chabad and open to the public).

There I saw *"Otzar Haggadot"* — a bibliography of Passover *Haggadot* from the beginning of Hebrew printing until 1960 by Isaac Yudlov, which list 4,715 *Haggadot* — and how interesting, not one had the name *"Ki Yishalcha Bincha."*

But it was not a seeking for originality that prompted me to choose this name. And in fact, how can anyone, except Hashem, claim originality to a *pasuk* in the Torah? This name was chosen for a general reason and also a very personal one.

The Torah tells parents to anticipate their child's questions on *Pesach*. Thus, not only is the practice of asking questions appreciated, but encouraged. Taking into consideration the question and answer style used throughout this *sefer*, it was deemed appropriate to name it *Ki Yishalcha Bincha — When Your Child Asks*. This is the preface in *Devarim* (6:20) to the questions asked by the *chacham* — wise child — and it is possible that many a wise child asks his father some of the questions in the book or the father would deem it appropriate to discuss these questions with his wise son. As King Shlomo says, "Give the wise man [knowledge] and he will become even wiser" (Proverbs 9:9).

After analyzing the *pasuk "Ki yishalcha bincha machor leimor"* (כי ישאלך בנך מחר לאמר) — "When your child asks you tomorrow saying" — it struck me that the numerical value of these words in *mispar katan* (singular numerals, not counting tens and hundreds) is 46, which is also exactly the *mispar katan* of my name — Moshe — my wife's name — Bracha — and our family name — Bogomilsky (משה, ברכה, באגאמילסקי).

Taking this a step further, the number 46 is also the numerical value of the two words לב and יד — heart — hand. Our family name, Bogomilsky, is of Polish-Russian origin. The first four letters of the name is the Polish-Russian version for G-d. And Bogomil, I was told, means "dear to G-d" or "precious to G-d." The last three letters — sky — are a common suffix in Polish-Russian names.

The way to be dear and precious to G-d is by, "Love G-d, your G-d, with all your heart," and "Serve Him with all your heart" (*Devarim* 6:5, 11:13). It is our fervent wish and prayer that we and our offspring always conduct ourselves in such a way which will make all of us be worthy of the meaning of the name Bogomilsky: Dear and precious to G-d, and that He reciprocate with bestowing upon us and them from His open, holy, and generous "*yad*" — "hand" — materially and spiritually.

ACKNOWLEDGEMENTS

To say that everything connected with this *sefer* is my doing would be presumptuous and somewhat removed from the truth.

Like *Vedibarta Bam*, it originated from the booklets on the *Haggadah* I made annually at the United Lubavitcher Yeshivoth before *Pesach*. Of great assistance in this venture was my assistant Principal, Rabbi Sholom Baras. I liked him many years ago when he was a student in my class and appreciated his qualities even more when I was fortunate to have him as a co-worker. May he enjoy much success in his *avodat hakodesh* and merit to go from strength to strength.

This is the sixth *sefer* I am publishing with the editorial assistance of Dr. Binyamin Kaplan of New Orleans, LA. To work with a person of his stature is a highly rewarding experience. In addition to his expertise in his respective field of English, his knowledge of Torah matters enhances his skill. To say that his pen and patience enriched this book is an understatement. He deserves profuse thanks and I wish him much success in all his endeavors to accomplish in his field. May he and his wife enjoy an abundance of *Yiddish* and *chassidish nachas* from their family.

To my daughter, Yehudis Leiter, who was my secretary in the making of this book, I say of her the words of King Shlomo, "Many daughters have done valiantly but you surpassed them all" (Proverbs 131:24). Our Sages say of the mother of Rabbi Yehoshua ben Chananya, "*Ashrei yoladeto*" — "Happy is she who bore him" — because when she was pregnant she would visit places of Torah study and ask the scholars to pray that her child

be a *talmid chacham* (*Pirkei Avot* 2:9, Rashi). She, too, during all the months of pregnancy sat in front of me to hear and write up all the *Divrei Torah* in this volume. May she together with her husband, Shimon, merit to see in good health a *"Dor yeshorim yevorach"* (Psalms 112:2) — a generation of upright who shall be blessed — children and children's children, etc., who will be engaged in Torah study and *yirat shamayim*.

Rabbi Yonah Avtzon, Director of Sichos In English, has most generously extended to me the services of his organization and worked indefatigably to disseminate my *sefarim* to the broad public. May all his efforts for Torah and *chassidut* be crowned with success, and may he be rewarded with the heavenly blessing reserved for those who are *"oskim betzarchei tzibur be'emunah"* — "involved faithfully in the needs of the community."

A major key to the success of Sichos In English is having on their staff Yosef Yitzchok Turner, a master of computer graphics. The layout of this volume was not like all others. It required much skill, innovation, and patience. He has been blessed with these qualities and indeed the work of his hands praises him. His patience, easy-going attitude and *mentchlichkeit* made it a pleasure to work with him. He is not a person of many words and shies away from honors, so I just say "thank you," and pray that he knows that I really mean it.

"Acharon acharon chaviv" — "The most beloved are put at the end" (*Bereishit* 32:2, Rashi). I thank Hashem for giving me my wife Bracha. As her name indicates, she is a true blessing to me and our family. Her understanding and encouragement were valuable assets in the making of this volume, and also the many other milestones I have reached. She is a great source of inspiration to our family, and has assisted in making *Pesach* and many other events memorable and inspiring. I pray to Hashem, that *"biz 120"* He grant us good health in which to reap much *Yiddish* and *chassidish nachas*, materially and spiritually, from our dear children and their families, to all of whom this volume of *Ki Yishalcha Bincha* on the *Haggadah* is a gift from us.

Rabbi Moshe Bogomilsky

INTRODUCTION

NUSACH ARI HAGGADAH

Rabbi Shneur Zalman of Liadi, founder of *Chabad Chassidut* and first *Rebbe* of the Lubavitch dynasty, also known as the *Alter Rebbe*, published many *sefarim* which earned him much acclaim for his erudition in all parts of the revealed and esoteric teachings of Torah. Among his universally popular works are the *Tanya* and *Shulchan Aruch*. In addition, in 1803 he published a *Siddur* which became known as the *Nusach Ari Siddur*.

There were numerous editions of *Nusach Ari Siddurim* prior to his, but this one differed in that while others emphasized the Lurianic *kavanot* — meditations — and were intended solely for *Kabbalistic* scholars, his was geared to serve as a prayer book for laymen who were not well-versed in the *Kabbalah* teachings. The text was developed after a careful review of sixty other *Siddurim* and he edited it to make it consistently conform to the Lurianic *Kabbalah* as well as Talmudic and halachic rulings concerning the prayers.*

In the *Siddur* he also included the *Haggadah* together with relevant instructions of the procedure to follow in conducting the *Seder*.

In 1946 the *Haggadah* was published separately with a comprehensive commentary by the Rebbe. It was received with much praise by Torah scholars throughout the world and many, then for the first time, had a chance to recognize his illustrious genius. In addition to the profoundly scholarly notes, he included *Chabad* customs in general, and the tradition observed by the *Rabbeim* of *Chabad* (*Minhag Beit Harav*) in particular.

---

* For the advantages and superiority of *Nusach Ari* over other forms of liturgy, see Introduction to *Sha'ar Hakolel*, Rabbi Avraham Lavut; *Responsa Maharashdam, Orach Chaim*; *Minchat Elozer* vol. 1, #2; *Chatam Sofer*, vol. 1, #15; *Divrei Chaim* vol. 2, #8.

To retain the completeness of the *Alter Rebbe's* work, the Hebrew part of the *Haggadah* was reprinted exactly as it appeared in the original form. However, in the English section, there are elaborations on *halachah*, custom, and particularly the prevailing Lubavitch custom.

ABOUT THE TRANSLATION

The *Haggadah* is a compilation of passages related to the Exodus, explanations offered by the Sages of the *Talmud* to Biblical verses, Psalms, passages from the *Shabbat* morning prayers, and various *berachot* — blessings.

All of these were written originally in *Lashon Hakodesh* — the Holy Language — which is a beautiful and multi-faceted language. Commentaries often offer many interpretations for the same word, some of which appear to be mutually contradictory. Nevertheless, all the interpretations are true, and the great number of interpretations gives us an insight into the profundity and deep thinking of the author of a particular piece.

Indeed, our Sages state that there are "70 countenances to Torah" (*Zohar* 1:47b), which means the Torah can be interpreted and elucidated in 70 different ways, and all are correct and part of Hashem's wisdom.

Unfortunately, regardless of which language Torah is translated into, it is impossible really to bring out the grandeur and varied nuances of the original text. The most one can achieve in a translation is to assist the reader to a superficial comprehension of the text as it is explained by *one* of the many commentaries.

For this reason, it is strongly recommended that one use the translation only as a means to gain insight but not for actual prayer.

* * *

In contemporary times we are witness to a tremendous awakening. Many of our brethren are expressing an interest in *Yiddishkeit* and returning to the authentic Torah way of life. Their

limited knowledge, or at times complete illiteracy of Hebrew, compels them to pray in the language of their native tongue.

To accommodate this need, I have endeavored to offer them an accurate and clear text, which hopefully they will find comprehendible and accessible. I am indebted to Sichos In English for granting me access to the translation of the *Haggadah* which was made for their *Haggadah, "At our Rebbe's Seder Table"* by Rabbi Eli Touger. He is an articulate and prolific writer and has done a superb job. Nevertheless, after reviewing it and the other translations which were made by Rabbi Jacob Immanuel Schochet, Rabbi Nissan Mangel, plus many other *Haggadah* and *Siddur* translations, I saw fit to make a number of changes. Some of these reflect halachic issues (see p. 61) about which there are legitimate differences of opinion, and others were geared towards producing an aesthetically pleasing text. It is hoped that the present translation will help the reader to see, at least somewhat, the beauty and profundity of our prayers.

TRANSLATING HIS NAME

A dilemma with which all translators grapple is how to translate the Ineffable Name or the Tetragrammaton — the Holy four letter Name, which refers to His Holy essence.

It is not acceptable to translate the Name as "Hashem" because if one prays reciting the translated text, he must either recite His Name correctly or use a word that means "G-d" in another language.

To translate it as "Lord" is also not a solution because according to *halachah* (*Orach Chaim* 214) any *berachah* in which there is no mention of His Name is not a valid *berachah*, and it is highly questionable whether using the term "Lord" meets the requirement to be considered His Name.

My esteemed brother, Rabbi Shmuel Pesach Bogomilsky, of Maplewood, New Jersey, has written and published extensively on the subject and concludes that it is definitely insufficient. Many renowned halachic authorities have corroborated his opinion,

including the universally accepted halachic authority of our generation, Rabbi Moshe *z"l* Feinstein, who agrees with my brother in a letter dated 15 *Elul*, 5741.

Another alternative under consideration was to translate it as "G-d." However, I refrained from doing so because in a *berachah* where the Tetragrammaton is mentioned together with the Name *Elokeinu*, even though it would be correct to say "G-d, our G-d," there would be no distinction for the reader if both Names were translated in this way.

Thus, in the English section of this *Haggadah*, for the Holy four letter Name the authentic pronunciation of *A-donai*, is used, exactly the way the *Gemara* (*Pesachim* 50a) says His Name is pronounced.

The Name *"Elokim"* is translated as "G-d." And in accordance with (Rashi, *Bereishit* 31:29, Ramban 17:1) and *Siddur* commentaries (see *Eitz Yosef, Siddur Otzar Hatefilot* pg. 668) the Name *"Keil"* is translated as "Al-mighty."

NOTE ON TRANSLITERATION AND FORMAT

Transliteration generally employs the Sephardi accent, with the following usages:

1. Words with a final *hei* are spelled with a final "h."
2. "Ei" (the vowel-sound in "freight") is used for a *tzere.*
3. "Ai" is used for the vowel-sound in the word "tide."
4. An apostrophe is used between distinct consecutive vowels, as in *"Ba'al."*
5. An "e" is used for a vocalized *sheva*, i.e. *"bemeizid,"* not *"b'meizid."*
6. "F" is preferred to "ph."
7. "O" is used for *cholem.*
8. Doubling of consonants is generally avoided.

Use of Italics:

Transliterated Hebrew words are generally given in italics without capitalization, except for proper nouns, which are capitalized and, in the case of names, not italicized. Some exceptions are made for very familiar Hebrew words, such as "Torah."

English and Hebrew:

Names of Biblical persons and names of the books of the Pentateuch are given in Hebrew, but other books of *Tanach* are given in English; thus "Moshe" is preferred to "Moses," *"Bereishit"* to "Genesis," and "Proverbs" to *"Mishlei."* Generally English words are preferred to Hebrew ones, but often the content requires the use of the Hebrew.

Exceptions:

Exceptions to these rules most often involve forms already familiar to the English reader, forms that would otherwise be awkward, and ones likely to be mispronounced.

Halachot Uminhagim
Laws and Customs

1) Many have a custom not to eat *matzah* from *Rosh Chodesh Nissan*. The *Chabad* custom is not to eat *matzah* from thirty days before *Pesach*.

(באר היטב סי' תע"א, ה, אגרות כ"ק אדמו"ר ח"ח ע' שי"ט, אגרות משה או"ח ח"א סי' קנ"ה)

2) This stringency, however, does not apply to *chameitz matzot*.

(נטעי גבריאל הל' פסח ח"א פ"ב סעי' י"א בשם משנת יעקב ח"ג סי' תע"א, וכן מוכח משו"ע הרב סי' תע"א, ז)

3) *Tachanun*, *"Laminatzei'ach Ya'ancha"*, *"Av Harachamim,"* and *"Tzidkatecha Tzedek,"* are omitted in prayers throughout the *entire* month.

(שו"ע הרב סי' תכ"ט:י"ב וסידור נוסח אר"י-חב"ד)

4) Fasting is not permitted during the entire month except in the following cases:

A) A bad dream (and it is not necessary to fast an additional day afterward to make up for fasting in *Nissan*; except if the fast was on *Shabbat* or *Yom-Tov*).

B) A firstborn male on *Erev Pesach*.

C) A *chatan* and *kallah* on the day of their wedding even when it is on *Rosh Chodesh*.

(שו"ע הרב סי' תכ"ט:ט-י"א)

5) In the wilderness the altar in the Tabernacle was dedicated on *Rosh Chodesh Nissan*. During the 12 day period commencing with *Rosh Chodesh*, the *Nesi'im* — leaders of the twelve tribes — brought their own personal offering in celebration of the momentous event.

In commemoration of this, from *Rosh Chodesh* to the 12th of *Nissan*, every morning after *Shacharit*, the *Nasi* is read by each individual. On *Rosh Chodesh* the first *Nasi* is read starting with, *"Vayehi beyom kalot Moshe"* (*Bamidbar* 7:1).

(של"ה דף ק"מ ע"ב שו"ע הרב סי' תכ"ט:ט"ו)

6) On the 13th day we read from, *"Zot chanukat hamizbei'ach"* till *"Kein asah et hamenorah"* (ibid. 7:84 — 8:4) which corresponds to the tribe of Levi.

(שו"ע, שם)

7) After reading the *Nassi* corresponding to the day of the month, a *"yehi ratzon"* (see *Nusach Ari siddur*) is recited which is also said by *Kohanim* or *Levi'im*.

(היום יום ר"ח ניסן)

הגדה של פסח

BLESSING ON TREES — ברכת האילנות

One who goes out during the days of *Nissan* and sees trees in blossom says the following blessing:

בָּרוּךְ אַתָּה יְיָ אֱלֹהֵנוּ מֶלֶךְ הָעוֹלָם שֶׁלֹא חִסַּר בְּעוֹלָמוֹ כְּלוּם וּבָרָא בוֹ בְּרִיוֹת טוֹבוֹת וְאִילָנוֹת טוֹבוֹת לֵיהָנוֹת בָּהֶם בְּנֵי אָדָם.

Blessed are You *Adonai*, our God, King of the universe, Who has not made His world lacking anything and created in it goodly creatures and goodly trees to give pleasure to mankind.

(סדר ברכת הנהנין פי"ג - הלכה י"ד)

1) This *berachah* is said only the first time that one sees [this sight] each year.

(שם)

2) The *berachah* is recited only over fruit producing trees.

(שו"ע סי' רכ"ו באר היטב ומ"ב, ועי' חזון עובדיה על הגש"פ, ושערי הלכה ומנהג ע' רי"ט)

3) Although the *Kabbalists* hold that it should be said *only* in the month of *Nissan*, halachically, when the trees blossom early or late, it may be said also in the months of *Adar* or *Iyar*.

(קצות השלחן ח"ב סי' ס"ו, ט, ועי"ש בבדי השלחן, ועי' שערי הלכה ומנהג ח"א ע' ר"כ)

4) Preferably it should be made when one sees *two* trees, but halachically it may be recited even over one tree.

(בדי השלחן)

5) In Australia where the trees blossom around *Tishrei*, or countries in the Southern Hemisphere where the seasons are "reversed" relative to North America or *Eretz Yisrael*, the *berachah* should be made during the season in which the trees blossom.

(שו"ת מנחת יצחק ח"י סי' ט"ז)

6) There are halachic opinions that women, too, should make this *berachah* when seeing trees in blossom.

(שו"ת הר צבי או"ח סי' רכ"ו ועי' בחזון עובדיה על הגש"פ)

MA'OT CHITIM — מעות חטים

A long-standing tradition in all Jewish communities is to make a campaign for *ma'ot chitim* (*Shulchan Aruch* 429:1). Though *ma'ot chitim* literally means "money for wheat," it is not limited to the expense of *matzot* only. The intention is to assure that every family in the community have *all* that it needs for them to have a kosher and *freilach Pesach*.

Since it is customary to conduct appeals for this purpose, the following are some thoughts on the subject:

One *Erev Pesach* in the afternoon, a man asked Rabbi Yosef Ber Soloveitchik of Brisk, Poland whether it is permissible to use four cups of milk instead of wine at the *Seder*. The rabbi told him that he had asked a difficult question and that time did not permit him to look into it immediately. He then gave him 100 rubles and wished him a happy *Yom Tov*. The rabbi's wife, who observed this, asked, "Why did you give him so much money? Couldn't he buy wine for much less than that?" The Rabbi explained, "If he considered using milk, obviously he also does not have meat for the festive meal, and perhaps he is missing many other things also. Therefore, I gave him enough money to ensure that he and his family will have all their needs."

* * *

It is the custom in many congregations for the Rabbi to deliver a scholarly *derashah* on *Shabbat Hagadol*. The learned people of the city look forward to this event and immensely enjoy the Rabbi's erudition. One year a certain Rabbi stunned his listeners by telling them that he had been unable to sleep for the past week due to an exceptionally difficult Rambam he had come across.

The town scholars were eager to hear what was puzzling their Rabbi. The Rabbi went on to explain that the word "רמבם" ("Rambam") is an acronym for ראזינקעס (raisins), מצה (*matzah*), בולבעס (potatoes), and מרור (*maror*). During *Pesach* we need raisins for wine, *matzah* and *maror* to perform the *mitzvot*, and potatoes are a staple food on *Pesach*.

He continued, "As Rabbi of this city, I know that we have many needy people and families who are suffering from the recession; I cannot determine how they will deal with this difficult רמב"ם on *Pesach*. If anyone has an answer, please come forth."

The people were dumbfounded and unable to solve their Rabbi's dilemma. Finally, the Rabbi said, "Last night I managed to find a solution. When I opened my Rambam I noticed that the most popular commentary is the *Kesef Mishneh,* which literally means 'double money.' If the rich will double their contribution of last year, it will be easy for everyone to tackle this difficult Rambam and enjoy a kosher and *freilachen Pesach.*"

(שמעתי מהרב רפאל ע"ה שטיין)

* * *

In 1930 many religious families were unfortunately affected by the depression. The Young Israel of Brooklyn, on Bedford Avenue in Williamsburg, was giving out *Pesach* packages for needy families, and anyone who came and stood in line would receive one. My grandfather, Rabbi Tzvi *z"l HaKohen* Kaplan, was raising money to help a prominent needy family. Knowing that they would not stand on line he sent his oldest son, Shimon, to stand in line and get a package which he would give to the family. The line was very long, and after Shimon had stood there a long time, he felt very uncomfortable, and he went home.

When my grandfather asked, "Where is the package?" he responded, "The line was very long and I felt embarrassed, so I left." My grandfather said to him, "I do not understand you. You are a *yeshiva bachur* and you have already learned about a *'kal vechomer'* (a conclusion inferred from a lenient law to a strict one). If you are embarrassed, knowing it is not for you, how much more embarrassment would it be for them to stand in line for their own need. Go back and bring home a package so that we can help them for *Yom Tov.*"

(שמעתי מדודי ר' שמעון הכהן שי' קאפלאן)

"The Great *Shabbat*" — "שבת הגדול"

QUESTION: Why is the *Shabbat* before *Pesach* called *"Shabbat Hagadol"* — the **great** *Shabbat?*

ANSWER: Per Hashem's instructions, on the tenth of *Nissan*, which was *Shabbat (Gemara Shabbat* 87b), the Jews prepared lambs to be used as *Pesach*-offerings. When the Egyptian firstborn visited Jewish homes and asked what they were planning to do with the lamb, the Jews replied that they were preparing a *Pesach*-offering to G-d, who would kill the Egyptian firstborn. Upon hearing this they went to their parents and to Pharaoh begging them to send out the Jewish people. When they refused, the firstborn declared war against their parents and killed many of them, as it is written in Psalms (136:10), *"Lemakeh Mitzrayim bivchoreihem"* — "Who struck Egypt through its firstborn."

Because of the *"neis gadol"* — *"great* miracle" that occurred on this *Shabbat* day, the *Shabbat* before *Pesach* is called *Shabbat Hagadol* — the **great** *Shabbat.*

(שו״ע הרב סי׳ ת״ל:א)

What is so unique about this miracle that it should be described as a *"neis gadol"* — **"great** miracle"?

Throughout history the Jewish people have been confronted with numerous enemies. Fortunately, Hashem comes to our salvation and miraculously our enemies are destroyed. The uniqueness of the miracle of *Shabbat Hagadol* was that while Egypt and Pharoah were still in their fullest strength and glory, their *own* firstborn demanded compliance with G-d's will, and when they refused, an internal war erupted, fought *on behalf* of the Jewish people. Thus, the Egyptians killing Egyptians on behalf of the Jewish people was equivalent to *"ithapcha chashocha lenehora"* — "transforming darkness to light" — and the greatest miracle that the Jewish people have witnessed.

(לקוטי שיחות חלק י״ב)

* * *

Alternatively, on the 10th day of *Nissan*, which was a *Shabbat*, the Jewish people prepared lambs for the *Pesach*-offering as Hashem had commanded and tied them to the foot of their beds (*Tur Orach Chaim* 430). On Wednesday afternoon, the 14th day of *Nissan*, the Jews slaughtered the *Pesach*-offering, and left Egypt the following morning (Thursday), the 15th day of *Nissan* (*Shabbat* 87b).

The Egyptians visited the homes of their Jewish slaves and were horrified to see how the Jews were treating the lambs, which they worshipped as their god. The Egyptians asked, "What is the purpose of this, what are you were doing with the lambs?" The Jews did not try to evade the question and proudly proclaimed, "We have a G-d Who commanded us to slaughter these as an offering to Him."

A major difference between a *katan* — minor — and a *gadol* — adult — is that a minor is frequently timid and likely to obscure the truth with excuses. On the other hand, an mature adult, is not ashamed to forthrightly proclaim his convictions. On this *Shabbat* the Jews acted as *gedolim* — mature adults — and unhesitatingly proclaimed their allegiance to Hashem. Since they acted like *gedolim*, this *Shabbat* is known as *Shabbat Hagadol*.

* * *

Alternatively, after the first day of *Pesach*, the *mitzvah* of counting the *omer* commences. In commanding this *mitzvah*, the Torah writes "*Usefartem lachem mimacharat haShabbat*" — "You shall count for yourself from the morrow of the day of rest" (23:15).

In the days of the Talmud there was a sect known as the "*Tzedokim*" — "Sadducees/Boethusians." They believed in the Written Torah but did not accept the Oral Torah, and hence they interpreted the Torah literally. Thus, "*mimacharat haShabbat*" according to them means Sunday, and the *omer* is brought on "the morrow of *Shabbat*" — the first Sunday following *Pesach*.

The Sages of the Talmud vehemently opposed this view, and in the *Gemara* (*Menachot* 65a) they disproved their theory. Consequently, according to our authentic interpretation, when the

first day of *Pesach* falls in the middle of the week, the *omer* is offered the following day.

Since the Torah refers to the day the *omer* is brought as *"macharat haShabbat"* — "the morrow after *Shabbat*" — i.e. the *Yom Tov* of *Pesach*, which is a day of rest — the *Shabbat* before is called *Shabbat Hagadol* — the **great** *Shabbat* — to indicate that *during* this week there is also another *Shabbat* (*Yom Tov*) which takes place, and *Shabbat* is greater and holier than *Yom Tov*.

(שו"ת שמן המור יו"ד סי' סט"ו בשם ר' מרדכי נאב ז"ל הספרדי והובא בבני יששכר מאמר שבה"ג סעי' ב')

* * *

Alternatively, the first *mitzvah* the Jewish people were commanded prior to their leaving Egypt was to prepare the lamb for a *Pesach*-offering and other details pertaining to celebrating the *Pesach Yom Tov*. Our patriarchs Avraham, Yitzchak, and Yaakov fulfilled all the *mitzvot* of the Torah (see *Yoma* 28b), and undoubtedly they, too, made a *Pesach*-offering on the fourteenth of *Nissan* and celebrated *Pesach*.

Nevertheless, there is a big difference between us and them in regard to performing *mitzvot*. The *Gemara* (*Kiddushin* 31a) says that *"Gadol hametzuvah ve'oseh mimi she'eino metzuvah ve'oseh"* — "The one who is commanded and fulfills is greater than the one who fulfills without a command." The reason is that the one who is not commanded has the option of not performing the precept at all, while the one who is commanded is worried and under pressure due to his obligation (see *Tosafot*).

Thus, on this *Shabbat* the Jews exhibited the *greatness* of one who is commanded, and therefore this *Shabbat* is called *"Shabbat Hagadol"* — "the **great** *Shabbat*."

(עוללות אפרים)

* * *

Alternatively, the *Pesach*-offering and the *Yom Tov* of *Pesach* emphasize the *mitzvah* of *"ve'ahavta le'rei'acha kamocha"* — "Love your fellow as yourself" (*Vayikra* 19:18). The *Pesach*-offering is a communal get-together. Not only does the family share, but also neighbors gather to partake in the offering, as the Torah says "He

and a close neighbor shall take according to the number of people; everyone according to what he eats shall be counted for the lamb" (*Shemot* 12:4). *Ahavat Yisrael* is also demonstrated by the special *mitzvah* of *ma'ot chitim* — extending financial assistance for *Yom Tov* to enable everyone to celebrate the holiday properly.

Regarding the *mitzvah* of "Love your fellow as yourself" Rabbi Akiva says, "*Zehu klal* **gadol** *baTorah*" — "This is a **great** (major) rule in the Torah" (Jerusalem Talmud, *Nedarim* 9:4).

In Egypt, the taking of the lambs for the *Pesach* offering was on *Shabbat*, the tenth of *Nissan* (*Shemot* 12:3, *Shabbat* 87b). Hence, the *Shabbat* before *Pesach* is called "*Shabbat Hagadol*" — the "*great Shabbat*" — because it is associated with the *Shabbat* prior to the redemption, when the Jews prepared for the first *Pesach* and thus emphasized the **great** *mitzvah* of "loving your fellow as yourself."

(עיטורי תורה – ויקרא, שבה"ג)

* * *

Alternatively, the Jews were liberated from Egypt in the year 2448 after creation. They had their first real taste of freedom and felt *great* about being Jews on the *Shabbat* before *Pesach*, when they prepared the sheep for the *Pesach*-offering. The words "שבת הגדול" remind us lamb of the momentous *Shabbat* of the redemption: "ש" stands for *Shabbat*, "בי" = 2,000, "ת" = 400, and the word "הגדול" has the numerical value of 48.

THE SALE OF *CHAMEITZ* — מכירת חמץ

The prohibition against possessing *chameitz* on *Pesach* applies only to *chameitz* which is owned by a Jew. It is permitted to have *chameitz* owned by a gentile in one's home, provided it is kept in a closed place which is set aside for that purpose. Based on this principle, one may sell any *chameitz* which one desires to keep to a gentile and purchase it back after the holiday. Because of the intricacies involved in making such a sale, it has become customary for the Rabbis of the community to act as agents and sell the *chameitz* on behalf of those who desire to do so. The sale becomes effective by the conclusion of the fifth seasonal hour on the 14th of *Nissan*.

It is advisable that one not wait until *Erev Pesach* to make these arrangements. The Rabbi should be contacted a few days before *Pesach*, either in person, by telephone, or in writing.

Since the sale takes effect at the conclusion of the fifth seasonal hour, if one who lives in the United States is going to Israel for *Pesach*, or if a resident of California is coming to New York for *Pesach*, he should arrange with the Rabbis in the place where he is spending *Pesach* for the sale of his *chameitz*.

It is highly advisable to encourage people to sell their *chameitz*, so that they will thus avoid violating two Biblical transgressions. Even when, G-d forbid, one who sold his *chameitz* should use it during *Pesach*, it does not invalidate the sale.

In fact, when the Rabbi negotiates the sale to the non-Jew, he should tell him, "If anyone of the people involved in this sale uses any of the *chameitz* during *Pesach*, it shall not invalidate this sale, and the cost will be deducted from whatever you will have to pay for the *chameitz* when the accounting will be made. In the event anyone sells or gives away any of the *chameitz*, he will be acting as your agent, without any remuneration whatsoever, and it shall not invalidate the sale in any way."

(אגרות כ״ק אדמו״ר חי״ט ע׳ רמ״ו - מענה לשאלת אחי הרב שמואל פסח שי׳ באגאמילסקי)

EREV PESACH — THE 14TH DAY OF *NISSAN* — ערב פסח

The dates which follow are based on the Hebrew calendar. Each year, the corresponding dates of the secular calendar will vary. The hours mentioned with regard to the morning of the 14th of *Nissan* are *"sha'ot zemaniot"* — "seasonal hours." This term refers to one twelfth of the period from the beginning of the day (sunrise) until its conclusion (sunset). Thus, these times vary from year to year and are dependent on the latitude in which one lives and the date of the solar calendar. For example, if on the 14th of *Nissan* the sun rises at 5:42 and sets at 6:19, each seasonal hour would be 63 minutes. Hence, the conclusion of the fourth seasonal hour is 9:54 and the conclusion of the fifth seasonal hour 10:57.

(שו"ע הרב סי' תמ"ג:ד)

1) Upon *tzeit hakochavim* — nightfall — of the 14th day of *Nissan* we do *Bedikat Chameitz* — the search for *chameitz*. See page 47 for detailed instructions.

(שו"ע הרב סי' תל"א:ה)

2) If *Erev Pesach* is on *Shabbat*, it is done on Thursday night.

(או"ח סי' תמ"ד:א)

3) On the 14th day of *Nissan*, all firstborn males must fast or participate in a *se'udat mitzvah*, e.g. a *siyum mesechta* — a meal in honor of concluding a Talmud tractate.

(שו"ע הרב סי' ת"ע:א,ח)

4) It is forbidden to eat *matzah* on *Erev Pesach*.

(או"ח סי' תע"א:ב)

5) It is forbidden to eat any *chameitz* after the conclusion of the fourth seasonal hour.

(או"ח סי' תמ"ג:א)

6) There is a custom to eat *chameitz* on *Erev Pesach* before the conclusion of the fourth seasonal hour.

(עי' באוצר מנהגי חב"ד ע' צ"ב, ומהרב משה דובער ע"ה ריוקין שמעתי שכן מוכח משו"ע הרב סי' תכ"ט, ט"ז)

7) *Kashering* utensils should be done before the conclusion of the fourth seasonal hour.

(או"ח סי' תנ"ב:א)

8) The sale of *chameitz* must take place before the conclusion of the fifth seasonal hour.

9) Prior to the conclusion of the fifth seasonal hour, one must burn the *chameitz* found in the search as well as all *chameitz* in one's possession not included in the sale and nullify all undiscovered or un-removed *chameitz* which is possibly in one's possession. See detailed instructions on page 47.

10) From the morning of *Erev Pesach* until after *Koreich* (*matzah* and *maror* sandwich) of the second *Seder*, it is customary not to eat any *maror* or any of the ingredients of the *charoset*.

(שו״ע הרב תע״א: י״א, י״ב, ספר המנהגים - חב״ד)

11) From one half hour after *chatzot* — noonday (approximately 12:30 PM E.S.T.) — one may recite the *Minchah* services and afterwards one should study the *Seder karban Pesach*. (See p. 49.)

12) When the first day of *Pesach* is on a Thursday or a Friday, an *Eiruv Tavshilin* must be made on *Erev Pesach*. (See p. 31.)

13) When preparing food for the *Seder* meal, bear in mind that no roasted or broiled meat or chicken, or even pot roast, is to be eaten on the two *Seder* nights.

(שו״ע הרב סי׳ תע״ו:ג - ד׳)

14) It is customary not to perform work on *Erev Pesach* in the afternoon if it is not something required for the *Yom Tov*. One may do any work that is permissible to do on *Chol Hamo'eid*. Work that a Jew is prohibited from doing in the afternoon may be done for him by a non Jew.

(שו״ע הרב סי׳ תס״ח, ה)

15) The items necessary for the *Seder* plate and the salt water should all be prepared before *Yom Tov*.

(קיצשו״ע סי׳ קי״ח, ד. ועי׳ במסגרת השלחן)

16) The *Seder* table (except the *ke'arah* and *matzot*) should be set before *Yom Tov*.

(או״ח סי׳ תע״ב, א)

WHEN THE 14TH OF *NISSAN* FALLS ON A *SHABBAT*
ערב פסח שחל בשבת

When the fourteenth of *Nissan* falls on *Shabbat*, the practices regarding the search for the destruction of *chameitz* differ from those observed when this date falls on a weekday because it is forbidden to search for or burn *chameitz* on *Shabbat*. Instead of the search being held on the night of the 14th of *Nissan*, it is held on Thursday evening, the night of the 13th. The *chameitz* found in the search is burnt on Friday morning, the 13th of *Nissan*, at the same seasonal hour as it would be burnt in other years.

The accepted custom is that the entire house is prepared for *Pesach* on Friday, and the *Shabbat* meals are cooked in *Pesachdike* pots and pans and served in *Pesachdike* dishes. There is one exception: It is forbidden to eat *matzah* on the day before *Pesach*, but we are required to eat bread at our evening and morning *Shabbat* meals. Therefore, two small *challot* are used at the beginning of both the evening and morning meals. Generally, the practice is to eat them in a place slightly removed from the dinner table so that no crumbs will fall on the *Pesachdike* dishes.

We are forbidden to eat *chameitz* after the conclusion of the fourth seasonal hour on *Shabbat* morning. Hence, we must conclude eating the *challot* of the morning meal by that time. This may require starting the *Shabbat* morning services earlier in certain communities. Afterwards, before the conclusion of the fifth seasonal hour, the crumbs and any remaining *chameitz* should be disposed of by flushing it down the toilet or similar means and the nullification statement is recited in regard to all undiscovered and un-removed *chameitz* which is possibly in one's possession.

After the conclusion of *Shabbat*, the preparations for the *Seder* and the *Pesach* meal should not begin until the appearance of three stars. Before beginning these preparations, the women must recite the phrase *"Baruch hamavdil bein kodesh lekodesh"* — "Blessed is He Who made a distinction between the holy and the holy."

After this time, and after the recitation of this phrase, the women should light the *Yom Tov* candles.

The items necessary for the *Seder* plate and the salt water should all be prepared before *Shabbat*.

THE FAST OF THE FIRSTBORN — תענית בכורות

In commemoration of the miracle that the Jewish firstborn sons were spared while the Egyptian firstborn were slayed, our Sages require that every firstborn son of either parent, including firstborn of *Kohanim* and *Levi'im*, fast on the day preceding *Pesach* from *alot hashachar* — the rising of the morning star — until nightfall.

(שו"ע הרב סי' ת"ע:א, ואו"ח סי' תקס"ד)

If a woman has a miscarriage and then her first child after that is a boy (and the father has no firstborn from another marriage), the boy is considered a firstborn for the laws of inheritance and thus must fast *Erev Pesach*.

(שם, ב)

When a firstborn son is below the age of 13, his father is required to fast on his behalf.

(שם, ג-ד)

If *Erev Pesach* is on Friday, the fast takes place that day.

(שם, ז)

If *Pesach* begins Saturday night, the Fast of the Firstborn is held on the preceding Thursday.

(שם)

A fast of this nature may be broken for a *se'udat mitzvah* — a feast held in celebration of a *mitzvah* — e.g., a *brit* — circumcision — or a *siyum* — conclusion of a Talmud tractate. Once a person participates in such a feast, he may continue eating for the entire day. The popular practice is that the firstborn, or the father of the firstborn, attend a *siyum* which is usually held in *shul* after the morning services.

(עיי"ש, ח)

EIRUV TAVSHILIN — עֵרוּב תַּבְשִׁילִין

While it is permitted to cook and bake on *Yom Tov*, it is forbidden to do so on the first day for the second day, even if the second day is *Shabbat*. If, however, preparations were started before *Yom Tov* began, they may be continued on *Yom Tov*, and an *Eiruv Tavshilin* (lit. "mixture of cooked dishes") constitutes this preparation. Thus, when the first day of *Yom Tov* is either on a Thursday or a Friday, it is necessary to make an *Eiruv Tavshilin* on *Erev Yom Tov* in order to be able to cook and bake for *Shabbat*.

The following procedure should be followed. One should take an entire *shemurah matzah* (which is the equivalent in measure to an egg, i.e. two ounces), as well as a highly regarded cooked food, e.g., meat or fish (in the quantity of a *kezayit*, i.e. one ounce). He should hand the *matzah* and the cooked food to another person who is not a member of his household and say:

אֲנִי מְזַכֶּה לְכָל מִי שֶׁרוֹצֶה לִזְכּוֹת וְלִסְמוֹךְ עַל עֵרוּב זֶה

I hereby grant a share in this *eiruv* to anyone who wishes to participate in it and rely on it.

The person to whom the *matzah* and the cooked food was given raises them a handbreadth (in order to acquire a share in it for anyone else who may wish to rely on this *eiruv*) and then returns them to the person making the *eiruv*, who then says:

בָּרוּךְ אַתָּה יְהֹוָה, אֱלֹהֵינוּ מֶלֶךְ הָעוֹלָם, אֲשֶׁר קִדְּשָׁנוּ בְּמִצְוֹתָיו, וְצִוָּנוּ עַל מִצְוַת עֵרוּב.

בְּדֵין יְהֵא שָׁרֵא לָנָא לַאֲפוּיֵי וּלְבַשּׁוּלֵי וּלְאַטְמוּנֵי וּלְאַדְלוּקֵי שְׁרַגָּא וּלְתַקָּנָא וּלְמֶעֱבַד כָּל־צָרְכָנָא מִיּוֹמָא טָבָא לְשַׁבַּתָּא לָנָא וּלְכָל־יִשְׂרָאֵל הַדָּרִים בָּעִיר הַזֹּאת.

Blessed are You, *Adonai*, our God, King of the universe, Who has sanctified us with His commandments and commanded us concerning the *mitzvah* of *eiruv*.

"Through this it shall be permissible for us to bake, to cook, to kindle a light, and prepare and do on the festival all that is necessary for the *Shabbat*. [This dispensation is also granted] for all Israelites who dwell in this city."

* * *

1) With the *eiruv* one is permitted to cook or bake for *Shabbat*. However, all cooking or baking must be done *only* on Friday and completed while there is still much of the day left.

(שו"ע הרב סי' תקכ"ז: ח, כ"ג)

2) It is customary that the *eiruv matzah* (if whole) be used on *Shabbat* as *lechem mishnah* and eaten in the afternoon at the *Seudah Shelishit* — third meal.

(שם סעי' כ"ה והובא בבאר היטב סק"ב בשם מהרי"ל)

3) If one forgot to make an *eiruv tavshilin* or if it was eaten up before *Shabbat*, a competent halachic authority must be consulted.

EIRUV CHATZEIROT — ערוב חצירות

Although it is permitted to carry in one's private apartment or private home, Rabbinic law prohibits carrying from the apartment or private home into an *enclosed area* to which more than one apartment or home have access, such as a common hallway, lobby, or courtyard, if no *Eiruv Chatzeirot* (lit. "mixture of courtyards") was made. The reason for this injunction is concern that people might erroneously think that it is also permissible to carry from one's private apartment or home to a real public domain or an unenclosed courtyard.

The *eiruv* is accomplished through collecting a loaf of bread before *Shabbat* from each of the dwellings and placing it in one of the dwellings. Thus, all the residents, so to speak, establish their residency in one dwelling and the common area is therefore the province of only one dwelling (where the bread is deposited). Carrying is now permitted since it is permissible to carry from one's private dwelling to one's private hallway or courtyard.

In lieu of collecting loaves of bread from all the residents, one may make the *eiruv* with his own food and be *mezakeh* — give a share in it — to all the other residents.

1) An *eiruv* can be made with either bread or *matzah* equivalent to six eggs — approximately 12 ounces — (some require eight eggs — approximately 16 ounces).

(שו"ע הרב סי' שס"ח:ג)

2) If the breads or *matzot* are collected from each of the dwellings they must be whole.

If one is being *mezakeh* his food to all the residents, the bread or *matzah* need not be whole.

(שם, סי' שס"ו:י)

3) Because of *matzah's* resistance to spoilage, it is common to use it to make the *eiruv*. If one made an *eiruv* with *chameitz matzah*, a new one *must* be made before *Pesach*. Even if one made one last year with *Pesach matzah*, it is customary to make a new one before *Pesach*, since the old one may become rancid and inedible and since it was not protected from *chameitz* during the year.

(שם, סי' שס"ח: ד. ואגרות כ"ק אדמו"ר חי"א ע' מ)

4) If the area is shared by non-Jews, a competent halachic authority should be consulted.

The following procedure should be followed. The person takes a pound of *shemurah matzot* and hands it to another person who is not a member of his household and says:

אֲנִי מְזַכֶּה לְכָל מִי שֶׁרוֹצֶה לִזְכּוֹת וְלִסְמוֹךְ עַל עֵרוּב זֶה

I hereby grant a share in this *eiruv* to anyone who wishes to participate in it, and rely on it.

The person to whom the *matzot* were given, raises them a handbreadth (in order to acquire a share in it for anyone else who may wish to rely on this *eiruv*) and then returns them to the person making the *eiruv*. That person then says:

בָּרוּךְ אַתָּה יְהוָֹה, אֱלֹהֵינוּ מֶלֶךְ הָעוֹלָם, אֲשֶׁר קִדְּשָׁנוּ בְּמִצְוֹתָיו, וְצִוָּנוּ עַל מִצְוַת עֵרוּב.

בְּדֵין יְהֵא שָׁרָא לָנָא לְאַפּוּקֵי וּלְעַיּוּלֵי וּלְטַלְטוּלֵי מִבַּית לְבַית וּמֵחָצֵר לְחָצֵר וּמִבַּית לְחָצֵר וּמֵחָצֵר לְבַית וּמֵרְשׁוּת לִרְשׁוּת בֵּין בְּשַׁבָּת זוֹ וּבֵין בִּשְׁאָר שַׁבָּתוֹת הַשָּׁנָה לָנוּ וּלְכָל-הַדָּרִים בִּשְׁכוּנָה (נ"א בָּעִיר) הַזֹּאת.

Blessed are You, *Adonai*, our God, King of the universe, Who has sanctified us with His commandments and commanded us concerning the *mitzvah* of *eiruv*.

Through this it shall be permissible for us to take out, to bring in, to carry from house to house, from courtyard to courtyard, from house to courtyard, from courtyard to house, and from area to area, whether on this *Shabbat* or on any other *Shabbat* of the year — for us and for all who live in this neighborhood. (*Another version:* city.)

Halachot Uminhagim
Laws and Customs

Matzah
Wine
Maror
Zeroa
Charoset
Beitzah
Karpas
Custom of Not Eating Gebrokt
Four Cups
Candlelighting

SEDER PREPARATIONS
REQUIREMENTS, MEASUREMENTS, AND
RECOMMENDATIONS

MATZAH

It is a Biblical obligation upon men and women to eat *matzah* on the night of *Pesach*. In the Diaspora this refers also to the second night. At present there are two types of *matzot* available: Machine-made *matzot*, and hand-baked round *shemurah matzot*. One should make an effort to use the latter throughout the entire *Yom Tov* or at least for the *Sedarim*.

At three points in the *Seder* it is necessary to eat at least a *kezayit* — a measure formally described as the size of one olive and traditionally determined as one ounce, 27 grams. The prevailing Lubavitcher custom is to eat two *kezeitim* for the initial consumption, then one *kezayit* for *koreich* and again two *kezeitim* for the *afikoman*. This requires a large quantity of *matzah* to meet the needs of all those present at the *Seder* table, so ample provisions should be prepared before the *Seder* begins.

For the initial eating of *matzah*, a *kezayit* — one ounce — is one half of the average hand-baked *matzah*. If one finds it difficult to consume two *zeitim* of this size, one may use a smaller amount for the second *kezayit*; namely, two-thirds of an ounce, since it is only *miderabanan* — a Rabbinic precept.

The *matzah* used for *koreich* is also *miderabanan*; thus, here too, if it is difficult to follow the stricter measure of approximately one ounce, one may suffice with just two-thirds of an ounce of *matzah*.

For *afikoman*, one should ideally consume two *kezeitim* of one ounce each. If this is difficult, one may suffice with the smaller size of two-thirds of an ounce for each. If this, too, is difficult, one *kezayit* can suffice. (See p. 181.)

In each of the three cases, the consumption of the required amount should be completed in *less than four minutes*. If one

should find this difficult, the eating of *matzah* for *koreich* and *afikoman* can extend to a maximum of 6 or 7 minutes.

(שו"ת צמח צדק שער המילואים ח"א סי' ט, וספר שיעורי תורה להגרא"ח ז"ל נאה)

"*Matzah*, according to the *Zohar* (II, 183b) is '*meichla d'atvata*' and '*meichla demeheimenuta*' — the 'food of health' and the 'food of faith.' It is evidence of the absolute trust of our ancestors in Divine Providence, and our similar trust, and it has the quality of strengthening this faith. Observing this holy *mitzvah* in its true spirit, the *Zohar* states, increases the inner faith in Hashem which is in the heart of every Jew. Nowadays, more than ever, it is necessary to foster this faith, which is the basis of all the *mitzvot* and of true Jewish life in general. Fulfilling this *mitzvah* according to the best and fullest requirements of the Torah will surely bring increased vitality in the observance of Torah and *mitzvot* all year round; and a healthy year spiritually must also bring with it a healthy year physically and materially."

(כ"ק אדמו"ר, שבמ"ח ניסן תשי"ד)

WINE

During the *Seder* on both nights each of the participants, both men and women, are required to drink four cups of wine. Although some halachic authorities question the validity of grape juice for the *Seder*, according to most opinions it is acceptable, although mixing at least a small quantity of wine with the grape juice is suggested. Each cup must contain *at least* a *revi'it* (approximately 3.5 fluid ounces).

According to Rabbi Avraham Chaim z"l Noe in *Sefer Shiurei Torah*, a *revi'it* is 86 grams. Since 1 ounce equals .03527 grams a *revi'it* is equivalent to a bit more than 3 ounces. Incidentally, the numerical value of the word *kos* — cup (כוס) — is 86.

Ideally, one should drink the *whole* cup each time. If this is difficult, one should drink *at least* a little more than one half of a *revi'it* (approximately 2 ounces). For the fourth cup however, one must drink a full *revi'it* (3.5 ounces), even if one made do previously with less, in order to be able to recite the *Berachah Acharonah* — Concluding Blessing.

(שו"ע הרב סי' תע"ב, י"ט)

MAROR

Maror should be eaten by all participants, men and women, for the initial *mitzvah* and again for *koreich* ("the sandwich"). For *maror* it is popular to use either romaine lettuce or pure horseradish (*chrein*). It is important to carefully wash and check the romaine lettuce to assure that there are no bugs or insects on it. The Lubavitcher custom is to use romaine lettuce and horseradish together, on both occasions. In addition to the grated horseradish, some eat a whole piece.

Although preferably the amount consumed should be a *kezayit* — one ounce — if one finds it difficult, the smaller measure, namely two-thirds of an ounce, will suffice, since it is only *miderabanan* — a Rabbinic precept.

For both *maror* and *koreich* one should complete the consumption of the required amount in less than *four* minutes. If this should prove difficult, one can extend the time to a maximum of 6 or 7 minutes.

ZEROA — shankbone [lit., arm or shoulder bone]

The prevailing Lubavitcher custom is to use the neckbone of a chicken and to make a point of removing as much of the meat as possible in order to avoid any resemblance to the *Pesach*-offering, which it commemorates at the *Seder*.

CHAROSET

Charoset is a mixture of ground apples, pears, and nuts, which is placed on the *Seder* plate and to which red wine is added during the *Seder*. The prevailing Lubavitcher custom is not to mix in cinnamon or ginger.

BEITZAH

A hard boiled egg is used to commemorate the *Chagigah*-offering. It is the prevailing Lubavitcher custom that the egg be placed on the *Seder* plate unshelled and eaten at the beginning of the meal dipped into the salt water.

KARPAS

A vegetable placed on the *Seder* plate. The most commonly used are raw onion and boiled potato.

CUSTOM OF NOT EATING GEBROKT — מצה שרויה

Many have a custom of eating *shemurah matzah* on *Pesach*. "*Shemurah*" means "guarded." The wheat is guarded from any moisture from the time of harvest until it becomes the end product — the baked *matzah*. Some are careful to guard the finished product from moisture as well, in case a small amount of the flour was not mixed well and is still subject to becoming *chameitz*. Though this is highly unlikely, they go to great lengths to avoid the most remote possibility of *chameitz*. Thus, on *Pesach* the *matzah* is kept covered, and they are careful not to dip *matzah* into water or any liquid to which water has been added. In *Yiddish* it is called "*gebrokt*," which means "breaking up the *matzah* into pieces and dipping it in."

On the eighth day of *Pesach* the *matzah* is uncovered and dipped into water, soup, etc. The reason for this leniency is because in the Diaspora our Sages added this day to the seven Biblical days of *Pesach*. Since it is only *miderabanan* — a Rabbinic ordinance — therefore, for the sake of *simchat Yom Tov* — happily enjoying ourselves on *Yom Tov* — one may be lenient and not worry about stringencies based on highly unlikely possibilities.

(שו"ת בסוף שו"ע הרב סי' ו)

When the eighth day of *Yom Tov* falls on *Shabbat*, one may prepare *gebrokt*, e.g. cook soup with *kneidelach* — *matzah* balls — on Friday.

(עי' ספר נטעי גבריאל, ואוצר מנהגי חב"ד, ואודות שמהדרין לשרות
באחש"פ עי' לקוטי שיחות חכ"ב ע' 30)

FOUR CUPS — ארבע כוסות

QUESTION: Why do we drink four cups of wine at the *Seder*?

ANSWER: They correspond to the following:

1) The four expressions of redemption, "I shall *take you out* from under the burdens of Egypt, I shall *rescue you* from their service, I shall *redeem you* with an outstretched arm, I shall *take you to Me for a people* (*Shemot* 6:6-7).

2) The four times *"kos"* — "cup" — is mentioned in the conversation between Yosef and the butler (*Bereishit* 40:11, 13).

3) The four empires who subjugated the Jewish people — Babylon, Media-Persia, Greece, and Rome.

4) The four cups of retribution Hashem will make the nations of the world drink in the days of *Mashiach* for treating the Jews badly.

5) The four cups of consolation Hashem will give to the Jewish people. (ירושלמי פסחים פ"י הל"א, מדרש רבה בראשית פ"ח:ה)

Alternatively, the four cups correspond to the four matriarchs: Sarah, Rivkah, Rachel, and Leah.

The first cup corresponds to Sarah, who together with Avraham, converted many people and brought them close to Hashem (*Bereishit* 12:5, Rashi). Over this cup we recite *Kiddush* and say *"Asher bachar banu mikol am"* — "Who has chosen us from among all nations."

The second cup corresponds to Rivkah, who rose to spiritual heights, regardless of her family of idol worshippers. Over this cup we recite the passage in the *Haggadah* about the confrontation between Lavan (Rivkah's brother) and Yaakov.

The third cup corresponds to Rachel. It is filled at the conclusion of the meal, and we recite *Birkat Hamazon* (Grace After Meal) over it. It was Rachel's son Yosef, who supplied everyone with food in Egypt.

We say *Hallel* over the fourth cup, which corresponds to Leah. She was first to thank Hashem (*Berachot* 7b): Upon giving birth to Yehudah she declared *"Hapa'am odeh et Hashem"* — "This time I will offer praise to Hashem" (*Bereishit* 29:35). (של"ה)

* * *

QUESTION: 1) Why did Hashem utter four expressions of redemption when seemingly one would have been sufficient? 2) Why drink four cups because of the four expressions when basically they all concern one redemption — the Exodus from Egypt?

ANSWER: The four expressions represent four independent phases of the redemption.

"Vehotzeiti" — "I shall take you out" — means that the burden of slavery was removed before they were even permitted to leave the country. Slavery ended in *Tishrei* (*Rosh Hashanah* 11a) and the actual departure took place six months later in *Nissan*.

"Vehitzalti" — "I shall rescue you" — was a promise to the Jewish people that the subjugation to Egypt would be formally ended and that wherever they would be, they will be totally emancipated and free of any obligation, such as paying taxes, to the Egyptian government.

"Vega'alti" — "I shall redeem you" — alludes to the splitting of the sea when the Egyptians experienced their ultimate destruction. Until then the Jews feared that their former masters would pursue them and return them to slavery.

"Velakachti" — "I shall take you to Me for a people" — refers to Hashem making us His chosen people through the giving of the Torah on Mt. Sinai.

(רבינו בחיי)

Alternatively, in *Bereishit* we learn of four generations that angered Hashem with their behavior. The first was the generation of Enosh, who were the first to commit idolatry (*Bereishit* 4:26, Rashi). The second was the Generation of the Flood — *dor hamabul* — of which it is written, "Hashem saw the earth and behold it was corrupted for all flesh had corrupted its way upon the earth" (6:12). The third was the Generation of Dispersion — *dor haflagah* — with which Hashem was angered because they built the Tower of Babel and contemplated an ascent to heaven and revolt against Him. Hashem punished them by "dispersing them from there over the face of the whole earth" (11:8). The fourth was the generation of

Sodom, of which Hashem said, "The outcry of Sodom and Gemorrah has become great, and their sin has been very grave" (18:20).

These four generations were reincarnated in the people enslaved in Egypt, and the Egyptian bondage was a form of elevation for them. Thus, the four expressions of redemption are not just a redundancy; they correspond to the redemption of these four generations that needed to become spiritually elevated through being in Egypt.

In fact, the first letters of the words of the first expression of redemption, *"Hotzeiti etchem mitachat sivlot"* "[I] shall take you out from under the burdens" (הוצאתי אתכם מתחת סבלות) — are an acronym for Haflagah — dispersion — (הפלגה), Enosh (אנוש), *Mabul* — flood — (מבול), Sodom (סדום).

(מגלה עמוקות, ואתחנן אופן רל"ו)

* * *

QUESTION: Why are the four cups of *wine* necessarily?

ANSWER: Four times the words *"kos yayin"* (כוס יין) — "cup of wine" — equals six hundred and twenty-four, which is the same numerical value as the word *"cheirut"* (חירות) — "freedom."

(הגש"פ מוצל מאש – בית אהרן – בפי' פאר אהרן מר' אברהם אהרן ז"ל פריעדמאן, טשאפ, רוסיא, תש"ב)

CANDLELIGHTING — הדלקת נרות

On *Pesach*, as on the *Shabbat* throughout the year, Jewish women and girls are granted the privilege and the responsibility of lighting the candles to usher in the holiness of the holiday into their homes. Preferably, the holiday candles should be lit on the afternoon of the 14th of *Nissan*, 18 minutes before sunset. Unlike candlelighting on the *Shabbat*, however, if the candles are not lit before sunset, they may be lit afterwards. In such a situation, however, the candles must be lit from an existing flame, since it is forbidden to create a new fire by striking a match or lighter, etc., on the holiday.

The following two blessings are recited when lighting candles:

בָּרוּךְ אַתָּה יְהֹוָה, אֱלֹהֵינוּ מֶלֶךְ הָעוֹלָם, אֲשֶׁר קִדְּשָׁנוּ בְּמִצְוֹתָיו, וְצִוָּנוּ לְהַדְלִיק נֵר שֶׁל (שַׁבָּת וְשֶׁל) יוֹם טוֹב.

בָּרוּךְ אַתָּה יְהֹוָה אֱלֹהֵינוּ מֶלֶךְ הָעוֹלָם שֶׁהֶחֱיָנוּ וְקִיְּמָנוּ וְהִגִּיעָנוּ לִזְמַן הַזֶּה:

Blessed are You, *Adonai*, our God, King of the universe, Who has sanctified us with His commandments and commanded us to kindle the (*Shabbat* and) festival lights.

Blessed are You, *Adonai*, our God, King of the universe, Who has granted us life, sustained us, and enabled us to reach this occasion.

On the second night of *Pesach*, the candles are lit from an existing flame after the appearance of three stars, and the same two blessings are recited. When the 15th of *Nissan* (1st day of *Pesach*) falls on the *Shabbat*, candlelighting for the 2nd day is delayed until the appearance of three stars. Before lighting the candles, the women should recite the phrase, *"Baruch hamavdil bein kodesh lekodesh"* — "Blessed is He Who made a distinction between the holy and the holy." The candles are lit from an existing flame.

When there is a *Shabbat* among the intermediate days of *Pesach*, candlelighting is carried out before sunset, in the same manner as on *Shabbat* throughout the year.

For the seventh and eighth days of *Pesach*, the procedure is the same as for the first and second days, except that on these two days the blessing *"Shehechiyanu"* — "Who has granted us life..." — *is not recited.*

הגדה של פסח

Ki Yishalcha Bincha
When Your Child Asks...?

סדר בדיקת וביעור חמץ

המנהג להניח פתיתי חמץ קשה זמן מה קודם הבדיקה כדי שימצאם
הבודק וע״פ הקבלה יש להניח עשרה פתיתין וקודם שיתחיל לבדוק
יברך:

בָּרוּךְ אַתָּה יהוה אֱלֹהֵינוּ מֶלֶךְ הָעוֹלָם אֲשֶׁר
קִדְּשָׁנוּ בְּמִצְוֹתָיו וְצִוָּנוּ עַל בִּעוּר חָמֵץ:

וצריך לחפש לאור הנר בכל המחבואות גם בסדקים שבקרקע. ולא
ידבר בין הברכה לתחלת הבדיקה אפילו מעניני הבדיקה ונכון שלא
ישיח שלא מעניני הבדיקה כל זמן בדיקתו ויעמיד מב״ב אצלו לשמוע
הברכה שיבדקו איש במקומו ולא ישיחו בינתים ויזהרו לבדוק תחלה
בחדר הסמוך למקום ששמעו הברכה ולא ילכו לבדוק תיכף אחר
הברכה לחדר אחר. ואחר הבדיקה יזהר בחמץ שמשייר להצניעו למחר
לשרפה או לאכילה לשמרו שלא יוליכוהו אנה ואנה שלא יתפרר ויתגרר
ממנו ע״י תינוקות או עכברים. וגם צריך לבטל אחר הבדיקה ויאמר:

כָּל־חֲמִירָא וַחֲמִיעָא דְּאִכָּא בִרְשׁוּתִי דְּלָא
חֲמִיתֵיה וּדְלָא בְעַרְתֵּיה וּדְלָא יְדַעְנָא לֵיה
לִבָּטֵל וְלֶהֱוֵי הֶפְקֵר כְּעַפְרָא דְּאַרְעָא:

ביום יד בשעה ה׳ יעשה לו מדורה בפני עצמו וישרפנו ויבטלנו ובביטול
היום יאמר:

כָּל־חֲמִירָא וַחֲמִיעָא דְּאִכָּא בִרְשׁוּתִי
דַּחֲזִיתֵיה וּדְלָא חֲזִיתֵיה דַּחֲמִיתֵיה וּדְלָא
חֲמִיתֵיה דְּבִעַרְתֵּיה וּדְלָא בְעַרְתֵּיה לִבָּטֵל וְלֶהֱוֵי
הֶפְקֵר כְּעַפְרָא דְּאַרְעָא:

THE SEARCH FOR *CHAMEITZ*

It is customary to place ten pieces of hard bread wrapped in paper in various places around one's property. Before commencing the search, one should recite the following blessing:

ברוך Blessed are You, *Adonai,* **our God, King of the universe, Who has sanctified us with His commandments and commanded us concerning the removal of** *chameitz.*

Every person should search all the properties he owns in which *chameitz* is kept or carried. One searches by the light of a beeswax candle, using a feather and a wooden spoon to collect the *chameitz.*

One should not speak between the recitation of the blessing and the beginning of the search, even concerning the search. During the search, one should speak only concerning the search.

If the search is being conducted by several members of the household, the other members should first stand near the head of the household to hear the blessing. They should then begin searching in the room nearest to where the blessing was recited, proceeding afterward to their designated area, without speaking.

Any *chameitz* that is found should be placed in a small paper bag. This bag, together with the feather and any remnant of the candle, is placed together with the wooden spoon. All this is then wrapped in paper (except for the spoon handle, which protrudes) and tied securely with string.

This *chameitz* which is to be burnt, and any other *chameitz* left to be eaten in the morning, should be placed in a safe place where it will not be taken by children or rodents and spread throughout the house.

After the search, one should nullify one's ownership of *chameitz* by making the following declaration:

כל All leaven and leavened products that exist in my possession that I have not seen, have not removed, and do not know about, should be considered nullified and ownerless, like the dust of the earth.

On the following morning, before the conclusion of the fifth hour of the day, the *chameitz* collected in the search and any *chameitz* remaining in the house should be burned. A fire should be kindled especially for this purpose. The following declaration nullifying ownership of all *chameitz* should be recited:

כל All leaven and leavened products that exist in my possession — whether I have seen it or have not seen it, whether I have observed it or have not observed it, whether I have removed it or have not removed it, should be considered nullified and ownerless, like the dust of the earth.

יְהִי רָצוֹן מִלְּפָנֶיךָ יְהֹוָה אֱלֹהֵינוּ וֵאלֹהֵי אֲבוֹתֵינוּ כְּשֵׁם שֶׁאֲנִי מְבַעֵר חָמֵץ מִבֵּיתִי וּמֵרְשׁוּתִי כָּךְ תְּבַעֵר אֶת כָּל הַחִיצוֹנִים וְאֶת רוּחַ הַטֻּמְאָה תַּעֲבִיר מִן הָאָרֶץ וְאֶת יִצְרֵנוּ הָרַע תַּעֲבִירֵהוּ מֵאִתָּנוּ וְתִתֶּן לָנוּ לֵב בָּשָׂר לְעָבְדְּךָ בֶּאֱמֶת וְכָל סִיטְרָא אַחֲרָא וְכָל הַקְּלִיפוֹת וְכָל הָרִשְׁעָה בֶּעָשָׁן תִּכְלֶה וְתַעֲבִיר מֶמְשֶׁלֶת זָדוֹן מִן הָאָרֶץ וְכָל הַמְּעִיקִים לַשְּׁכִינָה תְּבַעֲרֵם בְּרוּחַ בָּעֵר וּבְרוּחַ מִשְׁפָּט כְּשֵׁם שֶׁבִּעַרְתָּ אֶת מִצְרַיִם וְאֶת אֱלֹהֵיהֶם בַּיָּמִים הָהֵם בַּזְּמַן הַזֶּה אָמֵן סֶלָה:

סדר קרבן פסח

וְנִשְׁלְמָה פָרִים שְׂפָתֵינוּ וּתְפִלַּת מִנְחָה הִיא בִּמְקוֹם תָּמִיד שֶׁל בֵּין הָעַרְבַּיִם וּבִזְמַן שֶׁבֵּית הַמִּקְדָּשׁ הָיָה קַיָּם הָיָה הַפֶּסַח נִשְׁחָט אַחַר תָּמִיד שֶׁל בֵּין הָעַרְבַּיִם כֵּן רָאוּי לַעֲסוֹק בְּסֵדֶר קָרְבַּן פֶּסַח אַחַר תְּפִלַּת הַמִּנְחָה וְיֹאמַר זֶה:

קָרְבַּן פֶּסַח מֵבִיא מִן הַכְּבָשִׂים אוֹ מִן הָעִזִּים זָכָר בֶּן שָׁנָה וְשׁוֹחֲטוֹ בָּעֲזָרָה בְּכָל מָקוֹם אַחַר חֲצוֹת אַרְבָּעָה עָשָׂר דַּוְקָא וְאַחַר שְׁחִיטַת תָּמִיד שֶׁל בֵּין הָעַרְבַּיִם וְאַחַר הֲטָבַת נֵרוֹת שֶׁל בֵּין הָעַרְבַּיִם וְאֵין שׁוֹחֲטִין אֶת הַפֶּסַח עַל הֶחָמֵץ וְאִם שָׁחַט קוֹדֶם לַתָּמִיד כָּשֵׁר וּבִלְבַד שֶׁיְּהֵא אַחֵר מְמָרֵס בְּדַם הַפֶּסַח כְּדֵי שֶׁלֹּא יִקְרַשׁ עַד שֶׁיִּזְרְקוּ דַם הַתָּמִיד וְאַחַר כָּךְ יִזְרְקוּ דַם הַפֶּסַח זְרִיקָה אַחַת כְּנֶגֶד הַיְסוֹד וְכֵיצַד עוֹשִׂין שָׁחַט הַשּׁוֹחֵט וְקִבֵּל הַכֹּהֵן הָרִאשׁוֹן שֶׁבְּרֹאשׁ הַשּׁוּרָה וְנָתַן לַחֲבֵירוֹ וַחֲבֵירוֹ לַחֲבֵירוֹ וְהַכֹּהֵן הַקָּרוֹב אֵצֶל הַמִּזְבֵּחַ זוֹרְקוֹ זְרִיקָה אַחַת כְּנֶגֶד הַיְסוֹד וְחוֹזֵר הַכְּלִי רֵיקָן לַחֲבֵירוֹ וַחֲבֵירוֹ לַחֲבֵירוֹ וּמְקַבֵּל כְּלִי הַמָּלֵא תְּחִלָּה וְאַחַר כָּךְ מַחֲזִיר הָרֵיקָן וְהָיוּ שׁוּרוֹת שֶׁל בָּזִיכֵי כֶסֶף וְשׁוּרוֹת שֶׁל בָּזִיכֵי זָהָב וְלֹא הָיוּ לַבָּזִיכִין שׁוּלַיִם שֶׁמָּא יַנִּיחֵם וְיִקְרַשׁ הַדָּם

The ten pieces of *chameitz* hidden before the search should be burnt.
While burning them, the following *Kabbalistic* prayer should be said:

יהי **May it be Your will,** *Adonai*, **our God, and God of our fathers, that just as I removed** *chameitz* **from my home and possession, so too shall You remove all the** *chitzonim** **and cause the spirit of impurity to depart from the earth. Remove the evil inclination from us and grant us a heart of flesh to serve You with truth. Abolish all the** *sitra achara*,* **all** *kelipot*,* **and consume all wickedness in smoke, and remove the dominion of defiance from the earth. And all those that distress the** *Shechinah* **remove with a spirit of destruction and a spirit of judgment, just as You destroyed Egypt and its gods in those days at this time.** *Amein. Selah.*

---

* A *Kabbalistic* term for the forces of evil.

THE ORDER OF THE *PESACH*-OFFERING

In the spirit of the verse, "May the words of our lips take the place of [the sacrifice of] bulls (Hosea 14:3)," the *Minchah* prayer is instead of the daily afternoon offering. In the time of the *Beit Hamikdash*, the *Pesach*-offering would be offered after the afternoon sacrifice. Thus, it is proper to study the laws of the *Pesach*-offering after the afternoon service, saying the following:

קרבן **The** *Pesach*-offering would be brought from male lambs or goats that were one year old. It would be slaughtered anywhere in the Courtyard of the *Beit Hamikdash* after midday on the fourteenth [of *Nissan*], after the daily afternoon offering and after the afternoon cleaning the cups [of the *menorah*]. We may not slaughter the *Pesach*-offering while we still possess *chameitz*. If one slaughters [the *Pesach*-offering] before the [afternoon] sacrifice, it is acceptable, provided one stirs its blood so that it does not coagulate until after the blood of the [afternoon] sacrifice is sprinkled. Afterwards, the blood of the *Pesach*-offering would be thrown against the altar's base with one pouring. What procedure would be followed? The slaughterer would slaughter and the *Kohen* who was first in line would receive the blood and pass it to his colleague, and his colleague would pass it to another colleague, and the *Kohen* standing next to the altar would throw it against the base [of the altar], [emptying the vessel] with one pouring. He would then pass the empty vessel to his colleague, and his colleague to his colleague. First, he would take the full vessel and then return the empty one. [There were several lines of *Kohanim* leading to the altar, among them] lines [where the *Kohanim* passed] silver containers [to each other], and [other] lines where gold containers [were passed]. The containers did not have [flat] bottoms, lest they be placed down and the blood coagulate.

KI YISHALCHA BINCHA

אַחַר כָּךְ תּוֹלִין אֶת הַפֶּסַח וּמַפְשִׁיטִין אוֹתוֹ כּוּלוֹ וְקוֹרְעִין אוֹתוֹ וּמְמַחִין אֶת קְרָבָיו עַד שֶׁיֵּצֵא הַפֶּרֶשׁ וּמוֹצִיאִין אֶת הָאֵמוּרִים וְהֵם הַחֵלֶב שֶׁעַל הַקֶּרֶב וְיוֹתֶרֶת הַכָּבֵד וּשְׁתֵּי כְּלָיוֹת וְהַחֵלֶב שֶׁעֲלֵיהֶן וְהָאַלְיָה לְעוּמַת הֶעָצֶה וְנוֹתְנָם בִּכְלֵי שָׁרֵת וּמוֹלְחָם וּמַקְטִירָם הַכֹּהֵן עַל גַּבֵּי הַמִּזְבֵּחַ כָּל אֶחָד לְבַדּוֹ וְהַשְּׁחִיטָה וְהַזְּרִיקָה וּמִחוּי קְרָבָיו וְהֶקְטֵר חֲלָבָיו דּוֹחִין אֶת הַשַּׁבָּת וּשְׁאָר עִנְיָנָיו אֵינָם דּוֹחִין אֶת הַשַּׁבָּת וְכֵן אֵין מוֹלִיכִין אֶת הַפֶּסַח לַבַּיִת כְּשֶׁחָל בְּשַׁבָּת אֶלָּא כַּת הָאַחַת הֵם מִתְעַכְּבִים עִם פִּסְחֵיהֶם בְּהַר הַבַּיִת וְהַכַּת הַשְּׁנִיָּה יוֹשֶׁבֶת לָהּ בַּחֵיל וְהַשְּׁלִישִׁית בִּמְקוֹמָהּ עוֹמֶדֶת חֲשֵׁכָה יָצְאוּ וְצָלוּ פִּסְחֵיהֶם. בִּשְׁלֹשָׁה* כִּתּוֹת הַפֶּסַח נִשְׁחָט וְאֵין כַּת פְּחוּתָה מִשְּׁלֹשִׁים אֲנָשִׁים נִכְנְסָה כַּת הָרִאשׁוֹנָה נִתְמַלְּאָה הָעֲזָרָה נוֹעֲלִין אוֹתָהּ וּבְעוֹד שֶׁהֵם שׁוֹחֲטִין וּמַקְרִיבִין אֶת הָאֵמוּרִים קוֹרְאִין אֶת הַהַלֵּל אִם גָּמְרוּ אוֹתוֹ קוֹדֶם שֶׁיַּקְרִיבוּ כּוּלָם שׁוֹנִים אוֹתוֹ וְאִם שָׁנוּ יְשַׁלְּשׁוּ עַל כָּל קְרִיאָה תּוֹקְעִין שָׁלֹשׁ תְּקִיעוֹת תְּקִיעָה תְּרוּעָה תְּקִיעָה גָּמְרוּ לְהַקְרִיב פּוֹתְחִין הָעֲזָרָה יָצְאָה כַּת רִאשׁוֹנָה נִכְנְסָה כַּת שְׁנִיָּה נוֹעֲלִין דַּלְתוֹת הָעֲזָרָה גָּמְרוּ פּוֹתְחִין יָצְאָה כַּת שְׁנִיָּה נִכְנְסָה כַּת שְׁלִישִׁית וּמַעֲשֵׂה כּוּלָן שָׁוִין וְאַחַר שֶׁיָּצְאוּ כּוּלָן רוֹחֲצִין הָעֲזָרָה וַאֲפִילוּ בְּשַׁבָּת מִפְּנֵי לִכְלוּךְ הַדָּם שֶׁהָיָה בָּהּ וְכֵיצַד הָיְתָה הָרְחִיצָה אַמַּת הַמַּיִם הָיְתָה עוֹבֶרֶת בָּעֲזָרָה וְהָיָה לָהּ מָקוֹם לָצֵאת מִמֶּנָּה וּכְשֶׁרוֹצִין לְהָדִיחַ אֶת הָרִצְפָּה סוֹתְמִין מְקוֹם יְצִיאָתָהּ וְהִיא מִתְמַלֵּאת עַל כָּל גְּדוֹתֶיהָ מִפֹּה וּמִפֹּה עַד שֶׁהַמַּיִם עוֹלִים וְצָפִים מִכָּאן וּמִכָּאן וּמְקַבֵּץ אֵלֶיהָ כָּל דָּם וְכָל לִכְלוּךְ שֶׁהָיָה בָּעֲזָרָה וְאַחַר כָּךְ פּוֹתְחִין מְקוֹם יְצִיאָתָהּ וְהַכֹּל יוֹצֵא עַד שֶׁנִּשְׁאָר הָרִצְפָּה מְנוּקָה וּמְשׁוּפָה זֶהוּ כְּבוֹד הַבַּיִת וְאִם הַפֶּסַח נִמְצָא טְרֵיפָה לֹא עָלָה לוֹ עַד שֶׁמֵּבִיא אַחֵר:

זהו הענין בקיצור גדול. וצריך האדם הירא וחרד על דבר ה' לקרות אותו בזמנו שתעלה קריאתו במקום הקרבתו וידאג על חורבן הבית ויתחנן לפני ה' בורא עולם שיבנה אותו במהרה בימינו אמן:

_____

* לכאורה צ"ל בשלש, וכן הוא במשנה פסחים ס"ד ע"א (המו"ל)

Afterwards, the *Pesach*-offering would be hung and skinned. Its belly would be ripped open and its intestines pressed until the wastes were removed. The portions to be offered on the altar would then be separated. These included the fat on the entrails, the lobe of the liver, the two kidneys and the fat which is on them, and the fat tail up to the backbone. These would be placed in a sacred vessel. A *Kohen* then salted them and offered them on the altar, each one individually. The slaughtering, dashing [the blood against the altar], the pressing of the intestines, and the offering of the fats supersede the *Shabbat* prohibitions, but other things pertaining to it do not supersede the *Shabbat*. Similarly, when [*Pesach* eve] falls on the *Shabbat*, [the people] would not bring the sacrifice to their homes [immediately], but the first [of the three] group[s mentioned below] would remain with their *Pesach*-offerings on the Mount of the *Beit Hamikdash*. The second group would wait in the *cheil* [an area outside the Temple court], and the third group would wait in the Courtyard of the *Beit Hamikdash*. At nightfall, they would go home and roast their *Pesach*-offerings. The *Pesach*-offerings would be slaughtered in three groups, each group containing no less than 30 people. The first group entered, and when the courtyard filled, it would be locked. While they were slaughtering their sacrifices and offering the portions on the altar, [the Levites] would recite the *Hallel*. If they completed it before all had offered [their sacrifices], they would repeat it. And if they completed its repetition, they would recite it a third time. For each recitation, the *Kohanim* would sound three [trumpet] blasts: a *tekiah*, a *teruah*, and a *tekiah*. After this group completed its sacrifice, the Temple court would be opened. The first group would depart and the second group would enter. The gates of the courtyard would be locked, and when it was completed, [the gates] would be opened. The second group would depart and the third group would enter. The same procedure would be carried out for all three groups. After they all departed, the courtyard would be washed. This applies even on the *Shabbat*, because of the refuse from the blood [that would collect]. How would it be washed? There was a water conduit passing through the courtyard, which had a drain. When they desired to wash the floor, they would block the drain and cause the conduit to overflow on either side. The water would rise, lifting all the blood and refuse with it. Afterwards, they would unplug the drain and everything would flow out, leaving the floor clean and bright. This is the honor of the *Beit Hamikdash*. If a *Pesach*-offering is discovered to be *treifah* [unfit to be eaten because of ritual law], one does not fulfill his obligation until he brings another one.

This is a brief summary of the matter: A person who fears Hashem and who is zealous for His word should read this passage at the appropriate time so that his recital will be considered equivalent to the sacrifice. He should grieve over the destruction of the *Beit Hamikdash* and beg Hashem, the Creator of the world, to rebuild it speedily in our days, *Amein*.

סדר הגדה

יסדר על שולחנו קערה בג' מצות מונחים זה על זה. הישראל ועליו הלוי ועליו הכהן ועליו לימין הזרוע וכנגדו לשמאל הביצה תחתיהם באמצע המרור ותחת הזרוע החרוסת וכנגדו תחת הביצה הכרפס ותחת המרור החזרת שעושין כורך:

ג' מצות — Three *Matzot*

QUESTION: Why is it customary to take *three matzot* for the *Seder*?

ANSWER: The community of Kairuwan enquired of Rav Sherira Gaon why we take three *matzot* on the evening of *Pesach*, no less and no more. He replied that there is an allusion to this in the Torah: The three measures of flour which Avraham asked Sarah to use for baking cakes (*Bereishit* 18:6), for according to our tradition this happened on *Pesach*. Others say that they are a reminder of the three "mountains of the world," i.e., Avraham, Yitzchak, and Yaakov.

(הגש"פ עם לקוטי טעמים ומנהגים מכ"ק אדמו"ר)

Alternatively, the reason for three *matzot* is that the Jews ate *matzah* for three different reasons:

1) While slaving in Egypt they were constantly rushed to work and were forced to eat *matzah*, due to lack of time to let the dough rise, as stated in the *Haggadah*, "This is the bread of affliction that our fathers ate in the land of Egypt."

2) Prior to leaving they were instructed concerning the *Pesach*-offering and commanded to eat it together with *matzot* on the night of the 15th of *Nissan*.

3) In the morning, upon leaving Egypt, "They baked *matzot* from the dough that they had brought out of Egypt, for they were driven from Egypt and they could not delay" (*Shemot* 12:39).

(הגש"פ מוצל מאש – בית אהרן – בפי' פאר אהרן מר' אברהם אהרן ז"ל פריעדמאן, טשאפ, רוסיא, תש"ב)

מצות: כהן, לוי, ישראל
Matzot: Kohen, Levi, Yisrael

QUESTION: The three *matzot* are referred to as *Kohen*, *Levi*, and *Yisrael*. According to *Chabad*, first the bottom *matzah* — *Yisrael* — is placed then the *Levi* in the middle, and finally the *Kohen* on top.

Why this order and not the reverse?

THE ITEMS ON
THE *SEDER* PLATE

It is the prevailing Lubavitch custom to begin the first *Seder* directly after the evening service and not to dwell on the text at great length, so that the *afikoman* will be eaten before midnight. The second *Seder*, by contrast, begins later in the evening. The discussion is prolonged — the participants expound the *Haggadah*, share Torah insights, and encourage each other in their divine service.

Women are obligated to fulfill all the practices of the *Seder* night including eating *matzah* and *maror*, drinking the four cups of wine, and reciting the *Haggadah*. Children should also be trained in the observance of these *mitzvos*. It is not the prevailing Lubavitch custom to wear a *kittel* at the *Seder* or to arrange one's chair so that it faces any specific direction.

It is the prevailing Lubavitch custom to arrange the *Seder* plate before *Kiddush*. One should arrange the *matzot* and the plate in the following manner: Three whole *matzot* are placed in a cloth *matzah* cover; preferably, a plastic cover should be placed over the cloth. In the notes to *Sefer Haminhagim*, the Rebbe is quoted as stating that the *matzot* in their cover should be placed on a plate. At the Rebbe's *Seder* table, however, all those other than the Rebbe would put their *matzot* in their covering on the table itself. Many *chassidim* feel that despite their geographic distance they are always "at the Rebbe's table," and they do not use a plate. The bottom one is referred to as *Yisrael*, the middle one as *Levi*, and the upper one as *Kohen*. A napkin should be placed between each *matzah* and the one above it. It is customary to choose concave *matzot*, suggesting that the *matzot* serve as a receptacle for the downward flow of Divine energy.

ANSWER: The three *matzot* in this order (כהן, לוי, ישראל) are an acronym of the word *"keli"* (כלי) — "vessel." This indicates that one is a vessel for receiving the *kedushah* — holy revelations — of the *Seder*.

When one places the bottom *matzah* first and then the others on top (ישראל, לוי, כהן), the acronym formed is *"yeilech"* (ילך) — which means to go and proceed. This indicates that the *Seder* is not only intended to make a Jew a vessel to receive *kedushah*, but also that it prepares him to propel himself to greater heights of *kedushah*, till he ultimately reaches the level of complete spiritual redemption.

(הגש״פ עם לקוטי טעמים ומנהגים וביאורים)

The items for the *Seder* plate are placed on the cloth covering the *matzot*. On the upper right is placed the *zero'a*, the shankbone. The prevailing Lubavitch custom is to use the neckbone of a fowl and to make a point of removing as much of its meat as possible to avoid any resemblance to the *Pesach*-offering.

On the upper left is the *beitzah*, an unpeeled hard-boiled egg. Although it commemorates the *Chagigah*-Festival-offering — which was not offered on the fourteenth of *Nissan* when it fell on *Shabbat* — it should nevertheless be placed on the *Seder* plate, even when the *Seder* is held on Saturday night.

In the center — lower than the *zero'a* but above the *charoset* — the *maror*, bitter herbs is placed. It is customary to use romaine lettuce and horseradish together for both the *maror* and the *chazeret*. Before the *Seder* begins, and preferably before the holiday, one should check the romaine lettuce to make sure that it contains no bugs or insects.

On the lower right the *charoset* is placed — a mixture of ground apples, pears, and nuts, to which red wine is added during the *Seder*. Although it is customary in many communities to include cinnamon and ginger, this is not the Lubavitch practice, for fear that *chameitz* might have been added to these spices during their processing.

On the lower left the *karpas* is placed. It is customary to use raw onion or boiled potato.

In the center at the bottom the *chazeret* is placed. Both romaine lettuce and horseradish are used, as mentioned above.

סימן סדר של פסח

קַדֵּשׁ • וּרְחַץ • כַּרְפַּס • יַחַץ • מַגִּיד • רָחְצָה •
מוֹצִיא • מַצָּה • מָרוֹר • כּוֹרֵךְ • שֻׁלְחָן עוֹרֵךְ •
צָפוּן • בֵּרַךְ • הַלֵּל • נִרְצָה

THE ORDER OF
THE *PESACH SEDER*

Kadeish—Reciting *Kiddush* • *Urechatz*—Washing the hands • *Karpas*—Eating a vegetable dipped in salt-water • *Yachatz*—Breaking the middle *matzah* **Maggid**—Reciting the *Haggadah* • *Rachtzah*—Washing the hands a second time • *Motzi*—Reciting the blessing *"Hamotzi"* • *Matzah*—Reciting the blessing *"al achilat matzah"* and eating the *matzah* • *Maror*—Eating the bitter herbs • *Koreich*—Eating a sandwich of *matzah* and bitter herbs • *Shulchan Oreich*—Eating the festive meal • *Tzafun*—Eating the *afikoman* • *Beirach*—Reciting grace • *Hallel*—Reciting *Hallel*, psalms of praise • *Nirtzah*—The *Seder* is favorably accepted by G-d

---

"ליל הסדר"
"Night of the *Seder*."

QUESTION: Why is tonight's ritual called "the *Seder*"?

ANSWER: *"Seder"* means "order." Every detail of tonight's ritual represents an aspect of the redemption from Egyptian bondage and is meant to help us relive the experience of the Exodus. There are many profound lessons and esoteric explanations to every detail done tonight, which everyone should, of course, endeavor to understand to the best of their ability.

By properly and carefully observing the *Seder* — order — we will merit to be recipients of the Divine revelations which were manifest this night, years ago, and are repeated tonight. Moreover, we will be prepared for the ultimate illumination — the redemption by *Mashiach*.

(מהר״ל)

* * *

In the Torah (*Shemot* 12:42) it says that tonight is *"shimurim"* — "protection [for the Children of Israel for their generations]." The word *"shimurim"* — "protection" — is written in plural to

emphasize that it has the potential to grant us protection throughout *all* the nights of the year, and for all generations — it depends on the way we conduct ourselves tonight.

(תפארת שלמה)

סימן סדר של פסח

Order of the *Pesach Seder*

QUESTION: There are 15 words in the "Order of the *Pesach Seder.*" (Excluding the word *"nirtzah,"* which is a promise that Hashem will accept our *Seder* favorably, and not an action which we perform.)

What is the significance of the number 15?

ANSWER: The number 15 is the numerical value of the letters *"yud"* and *"hei,"* the first two letters of Hashem's name. *"Yud"* represents *chachmah* — wisdom — and *"hei"* is *binah* — understanding — the elaboration and expansion of the original spark of wisdom. These two make up the faculty of *"mochin"* — "intellect."

The 15 words in the "Order of the *Pesach Seder"* teach us that though the essence of *Pesach* is faith and *kabalat ol* (submission to Hashem), we must still use our intellect and try to understand the meaning and significance of everything being done.

(הגש"פ עם לקוטי טעמים ומנהגים, וביאורים)

QUESTION: In the widely accepted version of the Order of the *Pesach Seder*, which is ascribed to Rashi or one of the authors of *Tosafot,* Rabbi Shmuel of Falaise, there are fourteen items listed. (See Avudraham for other versions.)

Why necessarily fourteen?

ANSWER: The number fourteen is the numerical value of the word *"yad"* — "hand" (יד). The fourteen stages of the *Seder* correspond to the *yad hachazakah* — strong hand — with which Hashem took us out of Egypt. It concludes with *"nirtzah"* — that the *Seder* is favorably accepted by Hashem — to indicate that in merit of doing our part, Hashem will reciprocate by doing His part — revealing His *yad chazakah* — strong hand — to take us out of exile through *Mashiach.*

(מהר"ל)

הגדה של פסח

56

Meat Bone and Egg on *Seder* plate

QUESTION: What is the significance of the meat bone and egg placed on the *Seder* plate?

ANSWER: On *Erev Pesach*, in the times of the *Beit Hamikdash*, the Jews would bring a *Pesach*-offering and a *Chagigah* — Festival-offering. As a reminder of these two offerings, we place a bone with little meat on it, which is referred to as *"zero'a,"* on our *Seder* plate and also an egg, which is *"beitzah"* in Hebrew.

"Zero'a" literally means "arm," and an egg in Aramaic is called *"bei'ah,"* which means "wanting." The placing of these two together indicates that the All Merciful desired at the time of the Exodus to redeem us with an out-stretched arm. It also suggests that it should please Him to quickly redeem us with His outstretched arm — the coming of *Mashiach*.

(ט"ז סי' תע"ג סק"ד)

Alternatively, the egg symbolizes the character of the Jewish people. Unlike other foods which soften in cooking, the more the egg is cooked the harder it becomes. Likewise, in Egypt the more the Jewish people were tortured, the stronger they became, as the Torah says, "As much as they would afflict it so would it increase and so it would spread out" (*Shemot* 1:12). Throughout history, when the Jews were oppressed, they became stronger and more steadfast in their dedication to Hashem.

(חתם סופר)

Alternatively, when a creature comes into this world through live birth, it is complete at that time. An egg, in contrast, appears as a complete entity when it is layed. In reality, however, it is incomplete, and it only completes its development when the chick is hatched. The egg is analogous to our redemption from Egyptian bondage. Though it appeared complete, it was only fully realized when the Jews received the Torah fifty days later. This transformed them from an ordinary people to a holy nation — the people beloved by Hashem.

(תורת אמת מר' ליבלי זצ"ל איגר)

קַדֵּשׁ

קידוש

אַתְקִינוּ סְעוּדָתָא דְּמַלְכָּא עִלָּאָה דָּא הִיא סְעוּדָתָא דְּקוּדְשָׁא בְּרִיךְ הוּא וּשְׁכִינְתֵּיהּ:

כשחל יו"ט בשבת אומרים תחלה יום השישי:

יוֹם הַשִּׁשִּׁי: וַיְכֻלּוּ הַשָּׁמַיִם וְהָאָרֶץ וְכָל־צְבָאָם: וַיְכַל אֱלֹהִים בַּיּוֹם הַשְּׁבִיעִי מְלַאכְתּוֹ אֲשֶׁר עָשָׂה וַיִּשְׁבֹּת בַּיּוֹם הַשְּׁבִיעִי מִכָּל־מְלַאכְתּוֹ אֲשֶׁר עָשָׂה: וַיְבָרֶךְ אֱלֹהִים אֶת־יוֹם הַשְּׁבִיעִי וַיְקַדֵּשׁ אֹתוֹ כִּי בוֹ שָׁבַת מִכָּל־מְלַאכְתּוֹ אֲשֶׁר־בָּרָא אֱלֹהִים לַעֲשׂוֹת:

Recite the *Kiddush* — קדש

QUESTION: The traditional announcement for "*Kadeish*" is "When the father comes home from *shul*, he should make *Kiddush* straight away so that the children will not fall asleep, and ask the *Mah Nishtanah*?"

Why such an elaborate statement?

ANSWER: In the city of Shpola, the *melamed* — teacher — felt that this declaration was too lengthy and taught his students to simply announce, "Now it is time to make *Kiddush*." When the *Shpola Zeida* heard of this, he called the *melamed* and admonished him. "What right do you have to change the traditional declaration? Everything connected with the *Seder* has a deep mystical meaning. It is known," the *Shpola Zeida* continued, "that Hashem himself also fulfills all the *mitzvot* that He commands" (*Midrash Rabbah Shemot* 30:9).

Hence, in reality we are saying to our Father in heaven, Hashem, "When you, Father, come home from *shul*, you must quickly make *Kiddush*" i.e. renew Your *kiddushin* — betrothal — of the Jewish people and redeem us from our exile. Lest the children not fall asleep in the exile and despair of ever being redeemed. He must act quickly so that they will ask the *Mah Nishtanah* — "Why is the long dread night of this exile being prolonged more than all the dark exiles which we have already endured?"

(סיפורי חסידים)

* * *

KADEISH
RECITING KIDDUSH

Each individual should have a cup of wine or grape juice. The cup must contain a minimum of a *revi'it*, approximately 3.5 fluid ounces. The *Kiddush* is recited while standing. We fill our cups while they are resting on the table. They are then lifted with the right hand, transferred to the left hand, and then lowered into the palm of the right hand. The right hand should be slightly cupped to simulate a vessel, with the four fingers raised, and the thumb held to the side. Preferably, the cup should be held at least three handbreadths (approximately 10 inches) above the table. It is not necessary to have another person fill one's cup.

Women and girls are obligated to drink four cups of wine or grape juice. If there is an adult male leading the *Seder*, it is customary for them to fulfill their obligation to hear *Kiddush* by listening to his recitation of the prayer and reciting *Amein*. Afterwards, they drink the wine or the grape juice from their own cup.

אתקינו **Prepare the meal of the supernal King. This is the meal of the Holy One, blessed be He, and His *Shechinah*.**

On *Shabbat*, the *Kiddush* begins as follows:

יום **The sixth day. And the heavens and the earth and all their hosts were completed. And on the seventh day God completed the work which He had made, and He rested on the seventh day from all His work which He had made. And God blessed the seventh day and made it holy, for on it God rested from all His work, which God created to make.**

QUESTION: *Kiddush* is recited *every* Shabbat and *Yom Tov*. What is unique about the *Kiddush* of the *Seder*?

ANSWER: 1) This *Kiddush* must be made over wine; it cannot be on *matzah* as on other *Shabbatot* and *Yamim Tovim*.

2) Everyone is obligated to drink a cup of wine; one cannot rely on the drinking of the one who recited the *Kiddush*.

3) On *Pesach*, *Kiddush* must be made after nightfall.

(הגש״פ עם לקוטי טעמים ומנהגים)

"And G-d blessed the seventh day." — "ויברך אלקים את יום השביעי"

QUESTION: What special blessing did *Shabbat* receive?

ANSWER: *Shabbat* is a day when it is forbidden to work, yet one spends more money for *Shabbat* than for any other day of the

סַבְרִי מָרָנָן בָּרוּךְ אַתָּה יְהֹוָה אֱלֹהֵינוּ מֶלֶךְ הָעוֹלָם בּוֹרֵא פְּרִי הַגָּפֶן:

בָּרוּךְ אַתָּה יְהֹוָה אֱלֹהֵינוּ מֶלֶךְ הָעוֹלָם אֲשֶׁר בָּחַר־בָּנוּ מִכָּל־עָם וְרוֹמְמָנוּ מִכָּל־לָשׁוֹן וְקִדְּשָׁנוּ בְּמִצְוֹתָיו, וַתִּתֶּן־לָנוּ יְהֹוָה אֱלֹהֵינוּ בְּאַהֲבָה (לשבת שַׁבָּתוֹת לִמְנוּחָה וּ) מוֹעֲדִים לְשִׂמְחָה, חַגִּים וּזְמַנִּים לְשָׂשׂוֹן אֶת־יוֹם (לשבת הַשַּׁבָּת הַזֶּה וְאֶת־יוֹם) חַג הַמַּצּוֹת הַזֶּה, וְאֶת־יוֹם טוֹב מִקְרָא קֹדֶשׁ הַזֶּה זְמַן חֵרוּתֵנוּ (בְּאַהֲבָה) מִקְרָא קֹדֶשׁ זֵכֶר לִיצִיאַת מִצְרָיִם, כִּי בָנוּ בָחַרְתָּ וְאוֹתָנוּ קִדַּשְׁתָּ מִכָּל־הָעַמִּים, (וְשַׁבָּת) וּמוֹעֲדֵי קָדְשֶׁךָ (לשבת בְּאַהֲבָה וּבְרָצוֹן) בְּשִׂמְחָה וּבְשָׂשׂוֹן הִנְחַלְתָּנוּ: בָּרוּךְ אַתָּה יְהֹוָה מְקַדֵּשׁ (הַשַּׁבָּת וְ) יִשְׂרָאֵל וְהַזְּמַנִּים:

בָּרוּךְ אַתָּה יְהֹוָה אֱלֹהֵינוּ מֶלֶךְ הָעוֹלָם שֶׁהֶחֱיָנוּ וְקִיְּמָנוּ וְהִגִּיעָנוּ לַזְּמַן הַזֶּה:

בְּמוֹצָאֵי שַׁבָּת מְקַדְּשִׁין יקנה"ז-יַיִן, קִידוּשׁ, נֵר הַבְדָּלָה, זְמַן:

בָּרוּךְ אַתָּה יְהֹוָה אֱלֹהֵינוּ מֶלֶךְ הָעוֹלָם בּוֹרֵא מְאוֹרֵי הָאֵשׁ:

week. A person may think that celebrating *Shabbat* properly will run him into poverty. Hashem, however, gave a special blessing to the *Shabbat* day: the more one spends for the sake of *Shabbat*, the more he will earn during the week.

The *Gemara* (*Beitzah* 16a) says that the money a person will have for his expenses throughout the entire year is decided upon on *Rosh Hashanah*. Exempted from this are his expenses for *Shabbat* and *Yom Tov*. If a person spends freely for *Shabbat* and *Yom Tov*, Hashem will provide him with additional sources of income to cover his expenditures.

(בְּרִית שָׁלוֹם)

When *Pesach* falls on a weekday, the *Kiddush* begins here:

סברי Attention, gentlemen:

ברוך Blessed are You, *Adonai,* **our God, King of the universe, Who created the fruit of the vine.***

ברוך Blessed are You, *Adonai,* **our God, King of the universe, Who has chosen us from among all nations, and raised us above all tongues, and sanctified us by His commandments. And You,** *Adonai,* **our God, have given us lovingly** {on the *Shabbat:* **Shabbats for rest and**}, **festivals for rejoicing, holidays and seasons for gladness** {on the *Shabbat:* **this Shabbat day and**}, **this day of the Festival of** *Matzot,* **and this day of holy convocation, the season of our freedom** {on the *Shabbat:* **in love**}, **a holy convocation commemorating the Exodus from Egypt. For You have chosen us and sanctified us from among all the nations** {on the *Shabbat:* **and the** *Shabbat*}, **and Your holy festivals** {on the *Shabbat:* **in love and in favor**}, **in gladness and in joy, You have granted us as a heritage. Blessed are You,** *Adonai,* **Who sanctified** {on the *Shabbat:* **the Shabbat, and**} **Israel and the festive seasons.**

When *Pesach* falls on Saturday night, the following blessings are added to fulfill the *mitzvah* of *Havdalah.* When reciting the blessing for fire, the prevailing Lubavitch custom is not to place the candles next to each other, nor to join them at their wicks as is usually done for *Havdalah.* Similarly, it is not customary to look at one's fingernails at this time. Instead, one merely looks at the candles when reciting the following blessing:

ברוך Blessed are You, *Adonai,* **our God, King of the universe, Who created the lights of fire.**

---

* All *Berachot* are translated in past tense, (see *Shulchan Aruch Harav* 167:5).

"This Festival of *matzot*." — "חג המצות הזה"

QUESTION: In the Torah *(Shemot* 23:15), this *Yom Tov* is called *"Chag Hamatzot."* Why do we call it *"Pesach"*?

ANSWER: The word *"Pesach"* refers to what Hashem did for the Jewish people: He skipped over our houses when He plagued the Egyptians. *Matzah* shows the praise-worthiness of the Jewish people. Thanks to their absolute faith in Hashem, they left Egypt in a hurry without waiting for the dough to rise, and they were satisfied with simple *matzot.*

Thus, in the Torah, Hashem refers to the *Yom Tov* as *"Chag Hamatzot"* to emphasize His praise of the Jewish people. We call the *Yom Tov "Pesach"* to accentuate our praise of Hashem for saving our lives and redeeming us from Egypt.

(קדושת לוי)

בָּרוּךְ אַתָּה יְהֹוָה אֱלֹהֵינוּ מֶלֶךְ הָעוֹלָם הַמַּבְדִּיל בֵּין קֹדֶשׁ לְחוֹל, בֵּין אוֹר לְחֹשֶׁךְ, בֵּין יִשְׂרָאֵל לָעַמִּים, בֵּין יוֹם הַשְּׁבִיעִי לְשֵׁשֶׁת יְמֵי הַמַּעֲשֶׂה, בֵּין קְדֻשַּׁת שַׁבָּת לִקְדֻשַּׁת יוֹם טוֹב הִבְדַּלְתָּ, וְאֶת־יוֹם הַשְּׁבִיעִי מִשֵּׁשֶׁת יְמֵי הַמַּעֲשֶׂה קִדַּשְׁתָּ, הִבְדַּלְתָּ וְקִדַּשְׁתָּ אֶת־עַמְּךָ יִשְׂרָאֵל בִּקְדֻשָּׁתֶךָ: בָּרוּךְ אַתָּה יְהֹוָה הַמַּבְדִּיל בֵּין קֹדֶשׁ לְקֹדֶשׁ: שהחיינו

שותה הכוס בישיבה בהסיבת שמאל דרך חירות:

וּרְחַץ

ונוטל ידיו ואינו מברך:

כַּרְפַּס

נוטל פחות מכזית כרפס ויטבול במי מלח או חומץ ויברך:

בָּרוּךְ אַתָּה יְהֹוָה אֱלֹהֵינוּ מֶלֶךְ הָעוֹלָם בּוֹרֵא פְּרִי הָאֲדָמָה:

יכוין להוציא גם המרור בברכה זו:

"המבדיל בין קדש לחול"
"Who made a distinction between sacred and profane."

QUESTION: In the *Gemara* (*Pesachim* 113a) Rabbi Yochanan says that there are three who are among those who will inherit the World to Come. One of them is one who recites *Havdalah* over a cup of wine at the end of *Shabbat*. The *Gemara* explains that this means he leaves over wine [in his cup] from *Kiddush* for *Havdalah*. (See *Shulchan Aruch Harav* 271:22.)

Why is this rewarded so greatly?

ANSWER: In addition to the literal meaning, this can be explained as an allegory. *Kiddush* introduces the holiness of *Shabbat*, when one leaves his daily mundane activities and ascends into a day of spiritual exaltation. *Havdalah*, on the other hand, brings one back to mundane, day-to-day life. Thus, *Kiddush* is a synonym for moments of spiritual elevation, and *Havdalah* for ordinary day-to-day activities. Hence, the Sages are telling us that one who brings some of the spirit of holiness into his daily mundane activities will live so as to earn *Olam Haba* — the World to Come.

(הדרש והעיון - בראשית)

ברוך Blessed are You, *Adonai*, our God, King of the universe, Who made a distinction between sacred and profane, between light and darkness, between Israel and the nations, between the seventh day and the six days of work — between the holiness of the *Shabbat* and the holiness of a festival You have made a distinction, and have sanctified the seventh day above the six days of work. You have set apart and made holy Your people Israel with Your holiness. Blessed are You, *Adonai*, Who made a distinction between the holy and the holy.

Regardless of the night on which *Pesach* falls, we continue:

ברוך Blessed are You, *Adonai*, our God, King of the universe, Who has granted us life, sustained us, and enabled us to reach this occasion.

We drink the wine while seated, reclining on the left side. It is the prevailing Lubavitch custom to finish the entire cup without interruption or pause.

URECHATZ
WASHING THE HANDS

Before eating the *karpas* dipped in salt-water, we wash our hands as we do before partaking of bread. **No blessing is recited for this washing.**

KARPAS
EATING A VEGETABLE DIPPED IN SALT-WATER

We take the *karpas* and dip it in salt-water. One should have in mind that the blessing about to be made applies also to the bitter herbs [of *maror* and *koreich*] that will be eaten later.

The *karpas* is eaten **without** reclining; less than a *kezayit* (the size of an olive) should be eaten. Afterwards, the prevailing Lubavitch custom is not to return the *karpas* to the *Seder* plate. Thus, from this point on, there are only five items on the plate.

The following blessing is recited before partaking of the *karpas*:

ברוך Blessed are You, *Adonai*, our God, King of the universe, Who created the fruit of the earth.

In the event one eats more than a *kezayit* of the *karpas*, the blessing *borei nefashot*, which is usually recited after eating such foods, is not recited (see *Shulchan Aruch Harav* 473:18).

"ורחץ"
"Wash the hands without reciting the *berachah* of *al netilat yadayim*."

QUESTION: Why are the hands washed without a *berachah*?

ANSWER: According to *halachah* (*Shulchan Aruch Harav* 168:3) before one eats something dipped in liquid, the hands must be washed. Some hold that this applies only to former times when people were mindful in observing purity. Thus, since there is a doubt about this requirement nowadays, a *berachah* is not recited.

The washing is done tonight even by those who do not practice it throughout the year since the washing of hands without a *berachah* and eating vegetables before the meal will stimulate the child's asking questions.

(שו"ע הרב סי' תע"ג:י"ד)

יַחַץ

ויקח מצה האמצעית ופורסה לשנים חלק אחד גדול מחבירו וחלק
הגדול יניח לאפיקומן והקטן מניח בין הב' מצות:

"יחץ"
"Breaking the *matzah*."

QUESTION: What is the reason for breaking the middle *matzah*?

ANSWER: The *matzah* is broken before reciting the *Haggadah* because the recital is to be over *lechem oni* — bread of poverty — (the poor can afford only a broken piece — *Pesachim* 115b).

The broken piece is between the two whole *matzot* because the blessing of *Hamotzi* is to be recited over a whole *matzah,* and since there is a rule that "one must not by-pass *mitzvot*." The upper [thus first accessible] *matzah* must therefore be whole, and afterwards the second *berachah* of *"al achilat matzah,"* will be made over the middle-broken *matzah*.

(הגש"פ עם לקוטי טעמים ומנהגים)

* * *

Alternatively, Hashem told Avraham of the Egyptian bondage at the *Brit bein Habetarim* — the Covenant Between the Portions. At that time He instructed him to take three heifers, three goats and three rams and split them in half (*Bereishit* 15:9). The three *matzot* commemorate the three animals, and the breaking of the middle *matzah* commemorates splitting them in half.

(הגש"פ מוצל מאש - בית אהרן בפי' פאר אהרן)

* * *

At the *Seder* table, Rabbi Menachem Mendel of Lubavitch, the Tzemach Tzedek, once observed someone measuring which piece of the middle *matzah* is bigger. The Tzemach Tzedek remarked, *"A gadol vas men darf em mestin, iz kein gadol nit"* — "One whose greatness has to be measured is not really great." True greatness is readily apparent and immediately recognized.

YACHATZ
BREAKING THE MIDDLE MATZAH

We break the middle *matzah* while it is still covered by its napkin. The larger portion is set aside to be used as the *afikoman*. The smaller portion is left between the two remaining *matzot*, over which the blessing *Hamotzi* will be recited.

It is customary to break the *afikoman* into five pieces. If it breaks into six, the sixth piece is put aside. It is not the prevailing Lubavitch custom for children to "steal" the *afikoman*.

"יחץ"
"Breaking the middle *matzah*."

QUESTION: What is the significance of hiding the larger piece of the broken *matzah* for later?

ANSWER: The *matzah* represents redemption, since it commemorates the Jews' exodus from Egypt when they ate *matzah*. Though we were redeemed from Egypt, we are still in exile anticipating the ultimate redemption through *Mashiach*.

Putting the larger piece away for later indicates our belief that *Mashiach* will come to redeem us and we will then witness even greater miracles than at the time of the redemption from Egypt.

Hiding it, alludes that exactly when this will happen is concealed from us, but nevertheless we are able to endure the exile because we live with the faith that this hidden moment will be revealed speedily in our times.

(שפת אמת)

מגיד
Reciting the *Haggadah*

QUESTION: The *Arizal* writes that the *Haggadah* should be recited with a loud voice and great joy. Why?

ANSWER: The *Gemara (Pesachim* 36a) explains that the reason the Torah *(Devarim* 16:3) refers to *matzah* as *"lechem oni"* — "bread of affliction" — is that it is *"lechem she'onim alav devarim harbeh"* — "bread upon which we declare many things." Rashi explains this to mean that one recites the *Haggadah* and the *Hallel* while the *matzot* are on the table.

מַגִּיד

ומגביה הקערה שיש בה המצות ויאמר:

הֵא לַחְמָא עַנְיָא דִי אֲכָלוּ אַבְהָתָנָא בְּאַרְעָא דְמִצְרָיִם

The word "oni" (עני) has the numerical value of 136, as does the word "kol" (קול) — "voice." The name of the festival is "Pesach" — which can be read as two words "peh sach" (פה-סח) — "the mouth that talks and relates." As slaves the Jews were unable to open their mouths to pray to Hashem, and when they were freed they were able to speak freely. Thus, tonight when the *matzah* is on the table, we demonstrate our freedom by opening our mouths to speak loudly and joyously about the miraculous Exodus that Hashem brought about.

Through *sach* (סח) — talking — about the Exodus, we will merit *chas* (חס) — mercy: Hashem with His great mercy will send the redeemer — *Mashiach*.

(של"ה, פרי עץ חיים)

"הא לחמא עניא"
"This is the bread of affliction."

QUESTION: Why is the opening statement of the *Haggadah* said in Aramaic?

ANSWER: When a Jew prays, there are angels in heaven who become his representatives to bring his prayers before Hashem. The *Gemara* (*Shabbat* 12b) says that angels do not understand Aramaic, and therefore a person should not use it to request his needs. However, when he is sick, he may pray in Aramaic because the *Shechinah* — Divine Presence — is over his bed. Thus, he can talk directly to Hashem without the angels' assistance.

The *Zohar* (*Shemot* 40b) says that Hashem comes personally on *Pesach* night to listen to His children relating the story of the Exodus. Thus, by making our opening statement in Aramaic, we are proclaiming that tonight Hashem is personally with us, and we will speak directly to Him and not through any angels.

(הגש"פ חזון עובדיה בשם אמת ליעקב)

הגדה של פסח   66

MAGGID
RECITING THE HAGGADAH

It is not the prevailing Lubavitch custom to lift up the *Seder* plate at this time. It is, however, customary to partially uncover the *matzot*. The *Haggadah* should be recited loudly and clearly, and with joy.

הא This is the bread of affliction that our fathers ate in the land of Egypt.

Alternatively, this paragraph was composed when the Jews sojourned in Babylon and at that time all spoke Aramaic. In order that everybody, including the common folk, should understand, it was said in Aramaic.

The phrase, "Next year we will be free" is in Hebrew, so that the Babylonians would not understand it and suspect the Jews of plotting against the government. This is not inconsistent with the fact that the rest of the *Haggadah* — even the *Mah Nishtanah*, the questions asked by the children — is in Hebrew; for those other parts of the *Haggadah* had been in use already in the time of the *Beit Hamikdash* (when everybody spoke Hebrew), as mentioned in the *Mishnah*.

(כל בו, הגש״פ עם לקוטי טעמים ומנהגים)

"לחמא עניא"
"Bread of affliction."

QUESTION: In the Torah (*Devarim* 16:3) *matzah* is called *"lechem oni"* — "bread of affliction." Why?

ANSWER: According to the *Gemara* (*Pesachim* 36a) the word *"oni"* is phonetically related to the word *"oneh"* (עונה), which means to answer or declare. Thus, it is *"lechem she'onin alav devarim harbeh"* — "bread upon which we declare many things." Rashi explains this to mean that one recites the *Haggadah* and the *Hallel* while the *matzot* are on the table.

כֹּל דִּכְפִין יֵיתֵי וְיֵיכוֹל. כֹּל דִּצְרִיךְ יֵיתֵי וְיִפְסַח.

Another interpretation for *"onin alav devarim harbeh"* — is the following: the *Haggadah* expounds on the Biblical passages (*Devarim* 26:5-8) which start with the words, *"Arami oveid avi"* — "An Aramean tried to destroy my father." These passages are a part of the declaration one makes when bringing *Bikkurim* — first fruits — to the *Beit Hamikdash*. As an introduction to this declaration, the Torah says, *"Ve'anita"* — "You shall proclaim loudly."

Hence, the *matzah* is a bread over which *"onin devarim harbeh"* — "much is said" — namely elaborating over the declaration in the *parshah* of *Bikkurim*, which is preceded with the word *"ve'anita,"* which is related to the word *"onin"* — "declare, proclaim."

(אור שמח חמץ ומצה פ"ז הל' ד')

Alternatively, *matzah* is bread of affliction because as slaves the Jews were constantly rushed by their supervisors to slave labor. Thus, during the years of slavery they did not have time to let their dough rise, and consequently were forced to survive on *matzot*.

Also, the Egyptian masters preferred that their slaves eat *matzah* because it is inexpensive to produce, and very filling.

(ספורנו, אבודרהם)

According to Rabbi Akiva (*Pesachim* 36a) the word *"oni"* (עני) is written in the Torah without a *"vav,"* and thus can also be read as *"ani"* — "poor." A poor man makes his bread in the least expensive way. *Matzah* is made only of flour and water with nothing else added to it. Thus, we are stating, "This is *lachma anya* — bread of poverty" i.e. poor man's bread — which was eaten by the Jews as they slaved in Egypt and could not aspire to tastier food.

* * *

Incidentally, the words *"lachma anya"* (לחמא עניא) have the numerical value of two hundred and ten, which represents the years the Jewish people spent in Egypt.

(הגר"א)

Whoever is hungry, let him come and eat. Whoever is in need, let him come and join in celebrating the *Pesach* Festival.

"כל דכפין ייתי וייכול כל דצריך ייתי ויפסח"

"Whoever is hungry, let him come and eat. Whoever is in need let him come and join in celebrating the *Pesach* Festival."

QUESTION: This announcement should have been made when inviting guests to the home, not when they are all seated at the table?

ANSWER: According to *halachah* (*Pesachim* 70a), the *Pesach*-offering had to be eaten *al hasova* — to reach satiation, i.e. like dessert, at the end of the meal. One should not be completely sated nor should he be very hungry before eating the *Pesach*-offering. This *halachah* also applies to the *afikoman,* which is eaten nowadays in lieu of the *Pesach*-offering.

The head of the household is addressing the members of his family, as well as all the guests. He tells them "Tonight we will have to eat the *afikoman,* which is in place of the *Pesach*-offering. Therefore, *kol dichfin* — whoever is hungry — *yeitei veyeichol* — let him come and eat — in order not to eat the *afikoman* on an empty stomach." To those present who are not hungry the host proclaims, *"kol ditzrich* — whoever is in need — i.e. who only needs a little bit of food to conclude the meal and be fully sated — *yeitei veyifsach* — let him join us in the eating of the *afikoman.*"

(הגש"פ חסד לאברהם לר' אברהם דוב בעריש ז"ל פלאהם)

There was once a very wealthy man who was quite a miser. Very rarely did he give any charity or allow a poor man into his house. On *Pesach* night his son heard him proclaim, *"Kol dichfin"* — "Whoever is hungry let him come and eat." In amazement he asked his father, *Mah Nishtanah?* — "Why is this night different than all other nights? — I never see you ask a poor man into the house. Why are you making such a generous invitation now?" The father responded, "Do not worry, my son, *'Avadim hayinu leParo beMitzrayim'* — 'We were slaves to Pharaoh in Egypt' — and just as Pharaoh made promises but did not carry them out (see *Bereishit* 44:18, Rashi), I also do the same."

(קול אומר קרא)

הַשַׁתָּא הָכָא. לְשָׁנָה הַבָּאָה בְּאַרְעָא דְיִשְׂרָאֵל. הַשַׁתָּא עַבְדִּין לְשָׁנָה הַבָּאָה בְּנֵי חוֹרִין:

"כל דכפין ייתי וייכול...לשנה הבאה בני חורין"

**"Whoever is hungry, let him come and eat...
next year free men."**

QUESTION: What is the connection between the meal and the redemption?

ANSWER: According to the *Gemara* (*Gittin* 55b) the destruction of Jerusalem came about through a meal, as detailed in the incident of Kamtza and Bar Kamtza.

A certain man had a friend named Kamtza and an enemy named Bar Kamtza. He once threw a party and said to his servant, "Go and bring Kamtza." The man went and brought Bar Kamtza. When the host saw him he said, "What are you doing here? Get out." Trying to avoid the humiliation of being told to leave, Bar Kamtza said, "Since I am here, let me stay, and I will pay you for whatever I eat and drink." The host would not allow this. "Then let me give you half the cost of the party" he asked. "No" said the host. "Then let me pay for the whole party," he pleaded. The man still said, "No," and he took him by the hand and put him out. Bar Kamtza then said, "Since the Rabbis were sitting there and did not stop him, this shows that they agreed with him. I will go and inform against them to the government." The ultimate outcome was the destruction of the *Beit Hamikdash* and exile.

Thus, we are saying, "Unlike that meal which brought about the exile, tonight everybody is graciously invited, and hopefully in merit of our brotherly love, we will be redeemed."

"הא לחמא עניא די אכלו אבהתנא בארעא דמצרים כל דכפין ייתי
וייכול...השתא הכא לשנה הבאה בארעא דישראל"

**"This is the bread of affliction that our fathers ate in the
land of Egypt. Whoever is hungry, let him come and eat...
This year [we are] here; next year, in the land of Israel."**

QUESTION: What is the connection between the three passages; *"Hei lachma..."* — "This is the bread..." — *"kol dichfin..."* — "whoever is hungry..." and *"hashata hacha..."* — "this year here..."?

This year [we are] here; next year, in *Eretz Yisrael*. This year we are slaves; next year free men.

---

* The phrase *"Leshanah haba'ah"* ("next year"), which appears here twice, literally means "the coming year." The first time this phrase appears, Rabbi Sholom DovBer Schneerson, the fifth Lubavitcher Rebbe used to stress the second syllable *(haba'ah):* the second time, he used to stress the third syllable *(haba'ah)*. The latter more clearly implies the *present* tense (cf. *Rashi* on *Bereishit* 29:6) — i.e., the year that is coming *now*.

ANSWER: One can well imagine the despair of the poor man who is not with his family at his own *Seder* table. The host who graciously invites him reads the downhearted expressions on the face of his guest. To relieve his distraught state and make him feel at ease, the host proclaims, "This is the bread of affliction our fathers ate in the land of Egypt. Do not feel uncomfortable; our parents experienced deprivation and had to rely on this meager food. In the end they were redeemed and left with great wealth. Eat to your hearts content, and hopefully next year we will merit to be in the land of Israel, where each person will be in his own castle, celebrating together with his family."

(הגש״פ אשל ברמה מר׳ אברהם ז״ל ליכטשטיין)

"לשנה הבאה בני חורין"
"Next year free men."

QUESTION: *"B'nei chorin"* literally means "Children of *Chorin*"; who are the *"Chorin"*?

ANSWER: In addition to being enslaved in Egypt, the Jewish people suffered persecution and subjugation under four kingdoms: Babylon, Media-Persia, Greece, and Rome. They were redeemed from Egypt through Moshe, from Babylon through Ezra the Scribe, from Media-Persia through Mordechai, from Greece through Matityahu the *Kohen*, and we will speedily be redeemed from Rome through *Mashiach*. The last letters of the names of the redeemers <div dir="rtl">(משיח, משה רבינו, עזרא הסופר, מרדכי, מתתיהו כהן)</div> spell the word <div dir="rtl">חורין</div> — "free." We are expressing the wish that by next year we will be *"b'nei chorin"* — a people reclaimed by our redeemers — i.e. entirely free from all exiles.

(הגש״פ מוצל מאש - בית אהרן - בפי׳ פאר אהרן)

מְסַלְּקִין הַקְּעָרָה עִם הַמַּצּוֹת לְצַד אַחֵר וּמוֹזְגִין לוֹ כּוֹס ב'
וְכָאן הַבֵּן שׁוֹאֵל מַה נִּשְׁתַּנָּה:

מַה נִּשְׁתַּנָּה הַלַּיְלָה הַזֶּה מִכָּל הַלֵּילוֹת:

שֶׁבְּכָל הַלֵּילוֹת אֵין אָנוּ מַטְבִּילִין אֲפִלוּ פַּעַם אֶחָת, הַלַּיְלָה הַזֶּה שְׁתֵּי פְעָמִים:

"Why is this night different?" — "מה נשתנה"

QUESTION: In what order should the four questions be asked?

ANSWER: In many communities the first question focuses on the *matzah*, which is a Biblical requirement. The second is about the *maror*, which is a Rabbinical requirement, and then the questions about dipping and reclining follow. In the *Nusach Ari Haggadah* the order starts with the question concerning dipping. This is in accordance with the Rambam's *Haggadah* (*Chameitz U'matzah*, ch. 8), Rabbi Sa'adya Ga'on, *Rabbeinu* Yitzchak Alfasi, *Rabbeinu* Asher, and also the Jerusalem Talmud (*Pesachim* 10:4).

Seemingly, the order should be *matzah* first, then *maror*, for in the present era eating *matzah* has the status of a Biblical command, and eating *maror* is only a Rabbinic injunction. Dipping, by contrast, is merely a custom. Nevertheless, the dipping is given primacy because it is the careful adherence to Jewish custom which makes the most powerful impression on a child. When he sees that his parents observe matters of obvious importance, the impact is not as great — what alternative do they have? However, when he sees them paying close attention to details which are seemingly minor, he realizes how all-encompassing a Jew's commitment to *Yiddishkeit* must be.

(לקוטי שיחות ח"א ע' 244)

"מה נשתנה"
"Why is this night different?"

QUESTION: On *Shabbat* and on *Yom Tov* we usually only drink one cup of wine (i.e. for *Kiddush*). On *Pesach* we drink four. Why doesn't the child ask about this as well during the *Mah Nishtanah*?

The *Seder* plate is moved slightly to the side (with the *matzah* remaining uncovered — *Hamelech Bimesibo*, p. 201), and the second cup of wine is filled in order to motivate the children to ask questions.

The youngest child capable of doing so asks the Four Questions. Our custom is to preface these questions with the following *Yiddish* phrase: *"Tatte, ich vel bei dir fregen fir kashaos"* — "Father, I will to ask you four questions." For mystical reasons, this phrase is recited even if the child's father is no longer living.

In many families, it is customary that all the children recite the Four Questions. After the last child finishes reciting the questions, the prevailing Lubavitch custom is that the person leading the *Seder* repeats the Four Questions in an undertone, complete with their introduction and *Yiddish* translation.

מה נשתנה Why is this night different from all other nights?

On all other nights, we do not dip even once, but on this night we dip twice.

ANSWER: The child asks about the unusual things that he sees. On the table he sees *matzah*, *maror*, salt water, *charoset*, and on the chairs he sees pillows for reclining. His inquisitive mind, thus, immediately prompts him to ask about those items. On the other hand, though he sees wine on the table initially, he only sees the drinking of *four* cups over the course of the *Seder*.

(ברכת חיים על מועדים מר' חיים יעקב ז"ל צוקרמן)

"On this night we dip twice." — "הלילה הזה שתי פעמים"

QUESTION: Why necessarily *two* times?

ANSWER: The descent of the Jewish people to Egypt began with Yosef's visit to his brothers when they were in the fields. At that time, they stripped him of his shirt and sold him to the Ishmalites, who ultimately brought him to Egypt. To convince Yaakov that he was devoured by a wild beast, they slaughtered a kid goat and *dipped* the shirt in the blood (*Bereishit* 37:31).

At the conclusion of the Egyptian bondage, Hashem gave the laws of the *Pesach*-offering and instructed, "You shall take a bundle of hyssop and *dip* it into the blood and touch the lintel and the two doorposts with some of the blood" (*Shemot* 12:22). Since the Egyptian bondage started and concluded with dipping, tonight we dip twice.

(הגש"פ עם פי' ילקוט שמעוני, ועי' דעת זקנים מבעלי התוס', שמות י"ב:ח)

שֶׁבְּכָל הַלֵּילוֹת אָנוּ אוֹכְלִין חָמֵץ אוֹ מַצָּה,
הַלַּיְלָה הַזֶּה כֻּלּוֹ מַצָּה:
שֶׁבְּכָל הַלֵּילוֹת אָנוּ אוֹכְלִין שְׁאָר יְרָקוֹת,
הַלַּיְלָה הַזֶּה מָרוֹר:
שֶׁבְּכָל הַלֵּילוֹת אָנוּ אוֹכְלִין בֵּין יוֹשְׁבִין וּבֵין
מְסֻבִּין, הַלַּיְלָה הַזֶּה כֻּלָּנוּ מְסֻבִּין:

"בכל הלילות אין אנו מטבילין אפילו פעם אחת הלילה הזה שתי פעמים"
"On all nights we do not dip even once, but tonight we dip twice."

QUESTION: Tonight we actually dip three times, not twice: *Karpas* in salt water, *maror* in *charoset*, and *chazeret* (for *koreich*) in *charoset*?

ANSWER: The reason for having *maror* and *chazeret* on the *Seder* plate is that there is a question if *maror* should be eaten plain or in a *matzah* sandwich (*koreich*). Hence, since it is an unresolved matter, we eat it both ways in order to be sure that we have fulfilled the *mitzvah* of eating *maror*. Therefore, the dipping of the *maror* and *koreich* are counted as one, and together with *karpas* dipped in salt water, tonight we dip two times. (ט"ז סי' תע"ה סק"ו)

We say, "all nights we do not dip even once," although at the beginning of any meal where bread is eaten it is dipped in salt? (See *Shulchan Aruch HaRav* 167:8).

The reason for dipping tonight is to express that we are free people and conduct ourselves in the manner of the affluent. Only dipping into sauces and liquids is a sign of comfort and indulgence, and not dipping into salt.

"Chameitz or matzah." — "חמץ או מצה"

QUESTION: What lesson do the words *"chameitz"* and *"matzah"* impart?

ANSWER: The words *"chameitz"* (חמץ) and *"matzah"* (מצה) are spelled with similar letters: Each has a *"mem"* and a *"tzaddik."* The only difference is that one has a *"hei"* and the other has a *"chet,"* which only differs slightly in appearance from a *"hei."* (The *"hei"*

On all other nights, we eat *chameitz* or *matzah*, but on this night, only *matzah*.

On all other nights, we eat any type of vegetables, but on this night we eat *maror*.

On all other nights, we eat either sitting upright or reclining, but on this night we all recline.

---

has a small opening between the left "foot" and the "roof," and the *"chet"* is closed on all three sides.) This alludes to the *halachah* that *"chameitz bemashehu,"* even the minutest amount of *chameitz* mixed in food makes it forbidden to be eaten on *Pesach*.

* * *

The minutest amount of *chameitz* is forbidden because *matzah* represents redemption, and the Jews baked *matzah* upon leaving Egypt because *"lo yachlu lehitmahemei'ha"* — "they were unable to delay" — their departure from Egypt even by the smallest interval of time.

(הגש״פ מוצל מאש – בית אהרן – בפי׳ פאר אהרן מר׳ אברהם אהרן ז״ל פריעדמאן, טשאפ, רוסיא, תש״ב)

"מה נשתנה הלילה הזה"
"Why is this night different?"

QUESTION: Where is there an allusion in the Torah to specifically these four questions?

ANSWER: The words *"Tevilah, umatzah, umaror, vehaseivah"* (טבילה ומצה, ומרור, והסיבה) — "Dipping, and *matzah*, and bitter herbs, and reclining" — have the numerical value of seven hundred and thirty seven, which is exactly the numerical value of the words *"Vehayah ki yishalcha bincha machor"* (והיה כי ישאלך בנך מחר) — "When your son will ask you tomorrow" (*Shemot* 13:14).

(הגש״פ מוצל מאש, בית אהרן, בפי׳ פאר אהרן)

עֲבָדִים הָיִינוּ לְפַרְעֹה בְּמִצְרָיִם וַיּוֹצִיאֵנוּ יְהֹוָה אֱלֹהֵינוּ מִשָּׁם בְּיָד חֲזָקָה וּבִזְרוֹעַ נְטוּיָה. וְאִלּוּ לֹא הוֹצִיא

עבדים היינו לפרעה במצרים ויוציאנו ה' אלקינו משם ביד חזקה ובזרוע נטויה"
"We were slaves to Pharoah in Egypt, and G-d took us out from there with a strong hand and an outstretched arm"

QUESTION: After the child asks the four questions, the *Haggadah* is recited starting with *"Avadim hayinu."* Where in the *Haggadah* is the answer to the four questions?

ANSWER: An answer to a young child's question has to be concise and clear. Otherwise, he will remain with his query and become more perplexed. The opening statement "We were slaves to Pharaoh in Egypt and Hashem took us out from there with a strong hand and an outstretched arm" briefly answers *all* the four questions. The father is telling his child that the four things he is asking about are done to remind us: 1) We were slaves. 2) Hashem freed us.

Consequently, the dipping of the food exemplifies comfort and indulgence, and it is thus a symbol of freedom. On the other hand, it can be viewed as a symbol of bondage, since the word *karpas,* when reversed, can be read ס' פרך (the letter *samach* has the numerical value of 60) and alludes to the sixty myriads of Jews (600,000), who were enslaved in *perach* — hard labor. The salt water recalls the bitter tears of bondage while the *charoset* resembles the mixture that was used to make the bricks.

We eat *matzah* because it was the food eaten in Egypt through-out the years of slavery and also because it commemorates the fact that when we were freed, we did not have enough time to let the dough rise and instead quickly baked *matzah*. *Maror* reminds us of the embitterment of our lives through the slavery, and we sit reclining like free people. The purpose of the remainder of the *Haggadah* is to relate the narrative of the Exodus of Egypt.

(אברבנאל)

After the questions are concluded, the *Seder* plate is returned to its place, the *matzot* are partially uncovered, and the recitation of the *Haggadah* continues:

עבדים We were slaves to Pharaoh in Egypt, and *Adonai*, our God, took us out from there with a strong hand and an outstretched arm. Had the Holy One,

---

"עבדים היינו...ואלו לא הוציא הקדוש ברוך הוא
את אבותינו ממצרים הרי אנו ובנינו..."

"We were slaves to Pharaoh in Egypt...If the Holy One blessed be He had not taken our fathers out of Egypt, then we and our children..."

QUESTION: Since it starts *"Avadim hayinu"* — "We were slaves" — it should have concluded, "If *we* were not redeemed, we and our children and grandchildren would have remained in Egypt." Why the mention of *"avoteinu"* — "our fathers"?

ANSWER: The Jews were originally supposed to be in Egypt 400 years. In actuality, they were there only 210 years. To make up the additional 190 years, Hashem counted the Egyptian Exile as though it started at the birth of Yitzchak, and according to some opinions it is predated to the *Brit bein Habitarim* — Covenant Between the Portions — which He made with our father Avraham (*Shemot* 12:40, Rashi).

In this proclamation, *"avoteinu"* — "our fathers" — refers to Avraham, Yitzchak, and Yaakov. Were it not for the fact that Hashem dated the *galut* back to them, we would have been short many years, and thus, we, our children, and grandchildren would have remained in Egypt to complete the 400 years.

(שי לחגים ומועדים מר' שלמה יהלומי בשם קרן ישועה מר' יהושע זצ"ל שאפירא מריבטיץ)

This answers the question concerning why it says *"avoteinu"* — "our fathers" — though the *Gemara* (*Berachot* 16b) says, *"Ein korin avot ela leshelosha"* — "The title of *'avot'* — 'fathers' — is only used in reference to three [Avraham, Yitzchak, and Yaakov]." Since *"avoteinu"* here refers to the period during the lifetime of Avraham, Yitzchak, and Yaakov, which was counted into the four hundred years of Egyptian bondage, the term *"avoteinu"* — "our fathers" — is appropriate.

(בשיחת ליל פסח תשכ"ג הקשה כ"ק אדמו"ר הקושיא ועי"ש תירוצו,
ובספר פה אחד על הגש"פ מהחיד"א, כתב, "דהיינו דוקא לומר אבות סתם
אמנם לומר אבינו או אבותינו לית לן בה.")

הַקָּדוֹשׁ בָּרוּךְ הוּא אֶת־אֲבוֹתֵינוּ מִמִּצְרַיִם הֲרֵי אָנוּ וּבָנֵינוּ וּבְנֵי בָנֵינוּ מְשֻׁעְבָּדִים הָיִינוּ לְפַרְעֹה בְּמִצְרָיִם.

"וְאִלּוּ לֹא הוֹצִיא הקדוש ברוך הוא את אבותינו ממצרים הרי אנו ובנינו ובני בנינו משעבדים היינו לפרעה במצרים"

"If the Holy One blessed be He had not taken our fathers out of Egypt, then we, our children and our children's children would have remained enslaved to Pharaoh in Egypt."

QUESTION: Since it starts with *"Avadim hayinu"* — "We were slaves" — it should have concluded *"avadim hayinu"* — "we would have remained enslaved" — instead of varying the expression and saying *"meshubadim hayinu."* Why the inconsistency?

ANSWER: The word *"meshubadim"* can also mean "indebted" or "obligated." If the Jews would have remained in Egypt the entire 400 year period and then Pharaoh would have set them free, many Jews might have felt an everlasting indebtedness to Pharaoh. Regardless of the difficult enslavement they experienced, they would have thanked him for being "generous" and freeing them. Now that it was Hashem who took us out, *against* Pharaoh's will, we only owe praise to Him, and we have absolutely no indebtedness or obligations to Pharaoh.

(אמרי שפר עה"ת - ר' שלמה ז"ל קלוגער)

"הרי אנו ובנינו ובני בנינו משעבדים היינו לפרעה במצרים"

"Then we, our children and our children's children would have remained enslaved to Pharaoh in Egypt."

QUESTION: Why does it list specifically three generations instead of saying, *"kulanu"* — "all of us"?

ANSWER: According to the original decree, the Jews were to be in Egypt for four hundred years. However, they were there only two hundred and ten years. King David says that the average human lifespan is seventy years (see Psalms 90:10). The people of the generation that left Egypt were twenty years old. Thus, had the redemption not taken place, they would have been in Egypt for another fifty years plus the seventy-year lifespan of their children and the seventy-year of their grandchildren, which totals one hundred and ninety.

(אונזער אלטען אוצר בשם ר' שאול ז"ל מאמסטרדם)

blessed be He, not taken our fathers out of Egypt, then we, our children, and our grandchildren, would still be enslaved to Pharaoh in Egypt.

"מצוה עלינו לספר ביציאת מצרים"

"We would still be obligated to discuss the Exodus from Egypt."

QUESTION: What is the uniqueness of this *mitzvah* on *Pesach*? Isn't there a daily *mitzvah* to remember the Exodus from Egypt throughout the year?

ANSWER: 1) The daily obligation can be fulfilled by mental remembrance and meditation, while that of the night of *Pesach* must be verbalized, as it is said, "You shall *tell* your child." 2) Every day it is sufficient to just *mention* the Exodus, while on *Pesach* there must be an elaborate recounting of the Exodus. 3) Tonight it is done in the form of responding to the child or someone else.

(הגש"פ עם לקוטי טעמים ומנהגים)

"וכל המרבה לספר ביציאת מצרים הרי זה משבח"

"Everyone who discusses the Exodus from Egypt at length is praiseworthy."

QUESTION: What is the benefit of going into great length in retelling the story of the Exodus?

ANSWER: Hashem said to Moshe, "You will then be able to tell your children and grandchildren My miraculous signs that I have performed among them, *vidatem* — and you will know — that I am G-d" (*Shemot* 10:2). Since the Torah is telling us to relate to our children and grandchildren what happened in Egypt, should it not have said "*veyeide'u*" — "and thus *they* will know"?

Parents are obligated to teach their children about Hashem and enhance and strengthen their children's faith in Him. Their efforts carry a two-fold reward: 1) Ultimately, their work will bear fruit, and they will merit to have children who will be attached to Hashem. 2) Through teaching and talking to the children, *vidatem* — you (the parents) will know — you, too, will experience an enhancement and strengthening of your faith.

וַאֲפִילוּ כֻּלָּנוּ חֲכָמִים כֻּלָּנוּ נְבוֹנִים כֻּלָּנוּ יוֹדְעִים אֶת־
הַתּוֹרָה מִצְוָה עָלֵינוּ לְסַפֵּר בִּיצִיאַת מִצְרַיִם. וְכָל
הַמַּרְבֶּה לְסַפֵּר בִּיצִיאַת מִצְרַיִם הֲרֵי זֶה מְשֻׁבָּח:

Thus, the one who elaborates about the Exodus becomes a *"meshubach"* — a person with enhanced spirituality — because of his increased insight into G-dliness.

(שפת אמת)

"וכל המרבה לספר ביציאת מצרים הרי זה משבח"
"Everyone who discusses the Exodus from Egypt at length is praiseworthy."

QUESTION: The Torah (*Shemot* 13:8) commands *"vehegadeta lebincha"* — "and you shall tell to your son" — and the liturgical work that relates the Exodus is called the *"Haggadah."* Why doesn't it say *"vechol hamarbeh lehagid"*?

ANSWER: The word *"lesapeir"* — "to tell" — resembles the word for "sapphire" — *"sapir."* The *Haggadah* is telling us that just as the sapphire is a brilliant stone, by retelling the story of the Exodus we "brighten up" the darkness of the *galut* — exile.

To support the theory that it is necessary for all to elaborate concerning the redemption from Egyptian bondage, the *Haggadah* relates about the Rabbis who were *"mesaperim"* — "relating" — the story of the Exodus all that night [of *Pesach*]." In view of the above, it can be explained that *"mesaperim"* — they illuminated — the darkness (night) of the *galut*, and for them the time of exile shone like the brightness of the sapphire.

(הגדה של פסח צוף אמרים מר' משה חיים ז"ל קליינמאן)

"וכל המרבה לספר ביציאת מצרים"
"And everyone who discusses the Exodus from Egypt at length is praiseworthy."

QUESTION: The word *"vechol"* — "and everyone" — is superfluous. It could have said *"vehamarbeh"* — "and he who elaborates"?

[Therefore,] even if we were all wise, all men of understanding, all well-versed in Torah, we would still be commanded to tell about the Exodus from Egypt; and whoever discusses the Exodus from Egypt at length is praiseworthy.

ANSWER: The word *"chol"* (כל) is an acronym for *Kohanim* (כהנים) and *Levi'im* (לוים). The *Haggadah* is teaching that even the *Kohanim* and *Levi'im* who were not enslaved — and for that matter, even converts — should engage in elaborate discussion of the redemption from Egypt. The *Haggadah* supports this with the fact that Rabbi Akiva, who was the son of a convert; Rabbi Elazar ben Azariah and Rabbi Tarphon, who were *Kohanim*; and Rabbi Yehoshua and Rabbi Eliezer, who were *Levi'im*, spent the entire night discussing the Exodus.

(שמחת הרגל להחיד"א)

"וכל המרבה לספר ביציאת מצרים הרי זה משבח"
"And everyone who discusses the Exodus from Egypt
at length is praiseworthy."

QUESTION: Instead of saying that the person is *"meshubach"* — "praiseworthy" — it should have said he performed the *mitzvah "behidur"* — in a splendid manner?

ANSWER: When one witnesses an unusual event, he often recounts it to his friends. As time passes on, there is a decline in his enthusiasm, until he finally no longer repeats what he saw. However, when a person or his family experiences a miracle, he talks about it his entire life. In addition, he conveys it to his children and his descendents continue to relate the episode which occurred to their ancestor.

The *Haggadah* is teaching that if in contemporary times one still discusses the Exodus at length, *he is meshubach* — of prime quality and pedigree. It is an indication that *he* is a descendant from those who were in Egypt and not a member of a family who converted to Judaism at a later date.

(מעשה ידי יוצר לר"ש ז"ל קלוגער)

מַעֲשֶׂה בְּרַבִּי אֱלִיעֶזֶר וְרַבִּי יְהוֹשֻׁעַ וְרַבִּי אֶלְעָזָר בֶּן
עֲזַרְיָה וְרַבִּי עֲקִיבָא וְרַבִּי טַרְפוֹן שֶׁהָיוּ מְסֻבִּין בִּבְנֵי
בְרַק. וְהָיוּ מְסַפְּרִים בִּיצִיאַת מִצְרַיִם כָּל אוֹתוֹ הַלַּיְלָה
עַד שֶׁבָּאוּ תַלְמִידֵיהֶם וְאָמְרוּ לָהֶם רַבּוֹתֵינוּ הִגִּיעַ זְמַן
קְרִיאַת שְׁמַע שֶׁל שַׁחֲרִית:

"מעשה ברבי אליעזר ורבי יהושע ורבי אלעזר בן עזריה ורבי עקיבא ורבי טרפון"
"It happened that Rabbi Eliezer, Rabbi Yehoshua, Rabbi Elazar ben Azaryah, Rabbi Akiva and Rabbi Tarphon were reclining [at a Seder] in B'nei Berak."

QUESTION: Why are the names of the Rabbis mentioned in this order?

ANSWER: Rabbi Eliezer and Rabbi Yehoshua were the teachers of Rabbi Akiva. Rabbi Elazar ben Azaryah is mentioned before Rabbi Akiva because he came from a prominent family and was a *nasi* — leader of the generation. Rabbi Akiva is mentioned before Rabbi Tarphon because the occurrence took place in B'nei Berak, where Rabbi Akiva was the Chief Rabbi (*Sanhedrin* 32:2). Even though Rabbi Tarphon was also Rabbi Akiva's teacher, Rabbi Akiva later became his colleague (*Ketubot* 84:2), and he is therefore mentioned last. (הגש"פ עם לקוטי טעמים ומנהגים)

Alternatively, according to the *Gemara (Berachot* 46b) when there are three persons reclining, the custom is that the senior person occupies the middle position. The one next to him in rank reclines above him (or on his right), and the third one below him (or on his left). Hence, Rabbi Elazar ben Azaryah, the head of the Jewish community, was considered the most venerable and was in the middle. To his right were Rabbi Eliezer and Rabbi Yehoshua, the teachers of Rabbi Akiva. To his left were Rabbi Akiva and Rabbi Tarphon, who were younger. Thus, the *Haggadah* is relating the order of their reclining around Rabbi Elazar ben Azaryah. (הגש"פ עם לקוטי טעמים ומנהגים בשם מאיר עין)

"They were reclining in B'nei Berak." — "שהיו מסובים בבני ברק"

QUESTION: Why is it important to know in which city they gathered?

ANSWER: In the *Gemara (Pesachim* 120b) Rabbi Elazar ben Azaryah rules that the *Pesach*-offering must be eaten before midnight. Hence, the *mitzvah* of elaborating on the redemption from Egyptian

מעשה It happened that Rabbi Eliezer, Rabbi Yehoshua, Rabbi Elazar ben Azaryah, Rabbi Akiva, and Rabbi Tarphon were reclining [at the *Seder*] in B'nei Berak. They discussed the Exodus from Egypt all that night, until their students came and told them: "Our teachers, the time for reciting the morning *Shema* has arrived."

---

bondage would not apply after midnight, since it is obligatory only at the time "when [*Pesach*] *matzah* and *maror* actually lie before you." If so, why was he "discussing the Exodus from Egypt all that night"?

According to the *Gemara* (*Sanhedrin* 32b) Rabbi Akiva was the chief Rabbi of B'nei Berak. His opinion is that the *Pesach*-offering may be eaten the entire night and, thus, discussing the Exodus should be the entire night. Therefore, since he was in Rabbi Akiva's city, Rabbi Elazar discussed the redemption from Egyptian bondage the entire night in deference to him.

(שם משמואל - סאכאטשאב)

Perhaps this explains the seemingly extra words, *"kol oto halaylah"* — "all of *that* entire night." The emphasis is that only on *that* entire night did they all discuss the Exodus since they were in B'nei Berak where Rabbi Akiva's authority prevailed. In other years, however, when they celebrated elsewhere, not all discussed the Exodus the entire night.

"עד שבאו תלמידיהם ואמרו להם רבותינו הגיע זמן קריאת שמע של שחרית"
"Until their students came and told them: 'Our Masters! The time has come for reciting the morning *Shema*!'"

QUESTION: It would have sufficed to state, "The time of reciting the *Shema* has arrived." The words *"shel shacharit"* — "of the morning" — appear to be superfluous?

ANSWER: According to *halachah*, the *Shema* must be read in the evening and again in the morning. The time for reciting the evening *Shema* is between *tzeit hakochavim* — nightfall — and *alot hashachar* — the rising of the morning star. The time to recite the morning *Shema* starts at *neitz hachamah* — sunrise. In case of emergency, one can read the evening *Shema* up to sunrise, and the morning *Shema* from the rise of the morning star and on (see Rambam, *Keriat Shema* 1:10, 12).

The students emphasized that the time for reciting the *morning Shema* had arrived to indicate that it was already after sunrise. It was the time of day when evening *Shema* can no longer be said under any circumstances and only the morning *Shema* may be recited.

(מקראי קודש מהגר״ח ז״ל אבולעפײא)

אָמַר רַבִּי אֶלְעָזָר בֶּן עֲזַרְיָה הֲרֵי אֲנִי כְּבֶן שִׁבְעִים שָׁנָה וְלֹא זָכִיתִי שֶׁתֵּאָמֵר יְצִיאַת מִצְרַיִם בַּלֵּילוֹת עַד

"אמר רבי אלעזר בן עזריה הרי אני כבן שבעים שנה"

"Rabbi Elazar ben Azaryah said: 'I am like a 70 year-old man.'"

QUESTION: Why did Rabbi Elazar ben Azaryah say, "I am *like* a 70 year-old man"?

ANSWER: Once there was a dispute over a *halachic* issue between Rabbi Yehoshua and the *nasi*, Rabban Gamliel. The Rabbis were upset with the way Rabban Gamliel handled matters and decided to demote him and appoint Rabbi Elazar ben Azaryah as *nasi*. Rabbi Elazar ben Azaryah was hesitant to accept the position because he was only 18 years old and his beard was black. Overnight, a miracle occurred and his beard became filled with 18 streaks of white hair. Thus, he said, "I am *like* a 70 year-old man."

* * *

(מסכת ברכות כ"ז ע"ב)

Alternatively, his *neshamah* was a reincarnation of the *neshamah* of the prophet Shmuel. Since Shmuel lived only 52 years (*Mo'eid Kattan* 28a), and Rabbi Elazar ben Azaryah was now 18 years old, he said, "I am like a man of 70 years old."

(אר"י ז"ל)

"הרי אני כבן שבעים שנה ולא זכיתי שתאמר יציאת מצרים בלילות"

"I am like a seventy-year old man, yet I did not succeed in proving that the Exodus from Egypt must be mentioned at night."

QUESTION: What did being like a man of 70 years old have to do with his wanting to prove that the redemption from Egypt should be mentioned in the evening prayers?

ANSWER: There are two types of miracles. One is clearly supernatural while the other is something highly unlikely in the normal course of events, but not contrary to the laws of nature. In the *Gemara* (*Shabbat* 53b) there is a dispute: when Hashem performs a supernatural miracle (for instance, a poor widower is made able to nurse his son), does it indicate the greatness of the recipient of the miracle or some defect, since the natural order instituted at the time of creation was distorted on his behalf? (He did not merit that the gates of income be opened for him to earn a livelihood in a normal way — Rashi).

אמר **Rabbi Elazar ben Azaryah said: I am like a seventy-year-old man. Nevertheless, I did not succeed in proving that the Exodus from Egypt must be mentioned at night**

The miracles the Jews witnessed in Egypt on the first day of *Pesach* were of both categories. The slaying of *all* the firstborns during the night and melting the idols were supernatural miracles. The Jews' march to freedom in the morning was not supernatural because after being smitten with so many plagues, the Egyptians were anxious for them to leave. In fact, the Egyptians' stubbornness till then was only due to Hashem's making them stubborn, but once He returned them to their normal state of mind, it is only natural that they should want to be rid of the Jews as soon as possible.

The opinion that the redemption should be mentioned in the evening prayers holds that a supernatural miracle proves the praiseworthiness of the person benefited. Thus, the Exodus should be mentioned to recall the supernatural miracle which occurred during the night that led to the redemption. The Sages, however, hold that it proves the opposite, and therefore the Exodus should be recalled only during the day, when the redemption actually took place.

The occurrence of the eighteen streaks of white hair in the beard of Rabbi Elazar ben Azaria, who was only eighteen years old, is supernatural. Consequently, he personally preferred that the Exodus be mentioned at night, since otherwise it might indicate that a supernatural miracle demonstrates some shortcoming of the person benefited. (יריעות שלמה – ר' שלמה ז"ל קלוגער)

"ולא זכיתי שתאמר יציאת מצרים בלילות"
"Yet I did not succeed in proving that the Exodus from Egypt must be mentioned at night."

QUESTION: Why was he so interested in proving that the Exodus of Egypt should be mentioned at night?

ANSWER: The issue in dispute between Rabbi Elazar ben Azaryah and the Rabbis was whether the portion in the Torah which discusses the *mitzvah* of *tzitzit*, and which also mentions the

שֶׁדְּרָשָׁהּ בֶּן זוֹמָא. שֶׁנֶּאֱמַר לְמַעַן תִּזְכֹּר אֶת־יוֹם צֵאתְךָ מֵאֶרֶץ מִצְרַיִם כֹּל יְמֵי חַיֶּיךָ. יְמֵי חַיֶּיךָ הַיָּמִים. כֹּל יְמֵי חַיֶּיךָ לְהָבִיא הַלֵּילוֹת. וַחֲכָמִים אוֹמְרִים יְמֵי חַיֶּיךָ הָעוֹלָם הַזֶּה. כֹּל יְמֵי חַיֶּיךָ לְהָבִיא לִימוֹת הַמָּשִׁיחַ:

Exodus of Egypt (*Bamidbar* 15:37-41), should be recited together with the evening *Shema*. In the Torah this portion is followed by Korach's insurrection against Moshe. According to the *Midrash*, the juxtaposition of these two is because during his dispute, Korach also mocked the *mitzvah* of *tzitzit* with the derisive question, "Does an all *techeilet* — blue wool — garment require a single *techeilet* thread in its *tzitzit*?" Through this challenge, he sought to prove that there were illogical laws in the Torah which were the product of Moshe's imagination.

When Korach led his insurgence against Moshe, he relied upon the fact that the prophet Shmuel would be among his descendants and assumed that he would be spared in his merit (see *Bamidbar* 16;7 Rashi). Since Rabbi Elazar ben Azaryah was a reincarnation of the prophet Shmuel, Korach was thus also his ancestor. In order to rectify Korach's offence concerning the *mitzvah* of *tzitzit*, he made an extra effort that the Exodus of Egypt, which is mentioned in the *parshah* of *tzitzit*, should be mentioned at night.

(הגש״פ מוצל מאש - בית אהרן בפי׳ חכמת אהרן)

"Until Ben Zoma explained it." — "עד שדרשה בן זומא"

QUESTION: What assistance did Rabbi Elazar ben Azaryah receive from Ben Zoma's explanation?

ANSWER: At this time, though he appeared to be 70, Rabbi Elazar ben Azaryah was actually only eighteen years old. For quite some time, he endeavored to obtain the approval of the Rabbis to mention the Exodus from Egypt at night and was unsuccessful. Rabbi Elazar ben Azaryah attributed his lack of success to the fact that he was very young.

until Ben Zoma explained it: as it is said:[1] "So that you may remember the day you left Egypt *all* the days of your life." [The phrase] "the days of your life" refers to the days; [adding the word] "all" includes the nights as well. The Sages interpreted [the phrase] "the days of your life" as referring to the present-day world, and "*all* the days of your life" as including the Days of *Mashiach*.

1. *Devarim* 16:3.

Ben Zoma says, "Who is wise? He who learns from every person." (*Pirkei Avot* 1:4) When Ben Zoma's teachings became popular and accepted, the Sages changed their attitude towards Rabbi Elazar ben Azaryah, and regardless of his age, they listened attentively to what he had to say.

(שער בת רבים פ׳ האזינו בשם נחלת עזריאל)

"כל ימי חייך להביא לימות המשיח"
"'All the days of your life' indicates the inclusion [literally — to bring] of the days of *Mashiach*."

QUESTION: When something is learned from an extra word in a *pasuk*, the expression is usually *"lerabot"* — "to add." Why, is the term *"lehavi"* — "to bring" — used here?

ANSWER: The *Haggadah* intentionally uses this expression to convey a very important lesson: The goal of every Jew *"kol yemei chayecha"* — "all the days of your life" — [should be] *"lehavi limot haMashiach"* — "to bring about the days of *Mashiach*." This is accomplished through learning Torah and doing *mitzvot*.

(ספר השיחות תש״ג)

"The days of *Mashiach*" — "לימות המשיח"

QUESTION: Who is the *Mashiach*?

ANSWER: In the *Gemara* (*Sanhedrin* 98b) there are four opinions regarding the identity of *Mashiach*. Some say his name is Shiloh (שילה), others say Yinon (ינון), a third opinion is Chaninah (חנינה), and a fourth view is Menachem (מנחם). The first letter of each one of these four names spells "*Mashiach*" (משיח).

Jewry eagerly awaits the revelation of the redeemer who will lead us out of *galut*. Not knowing definitely what his name will be, we call him "*Mashiach*," an acronym of the four possible names for the redeemer.

(הגש״פ צוף אמרים)

בָּרוּךְ הַמָּקוֹם. בָּרוּךְ הוּא. בָּרוּךְ שֶׁנָּתַן תּוֹרָה לְעַמּוֹ יִשְׂרָאֵל. בָּרוּךְ הוּא.

"ברוך המקום"
"Blessed is the Omnipresent."

QUESTION: Why is Hashem referred to as *"HaMakom"* — "the Place"?

ANSWER: To dispel the myth that the world is an entity in itself, Hashem is referred to as *"HaMakom"* — "the Place" — to emphasize that the world is contained in Him and not He in the world. He is not limited by space and therefore present everywhere.

(מדרש רבה בראשית ס״ח:ט)

Alternatively, according to *Kabbalists*, Hashem is referred to as *"Makom"* — "Place" — because His Holy four letter Name, the Tetragrammaton (י-ה-ו-ה) has the numerical value of one hundred and eighty-six, the same as *"makom"* (מקום), according to *gematria beribu'a* – numerology involving "squares."

The numerical value of *"yud"* when squared (10 x 10) is one hundred. The square of *"hei"* is twenty-five (5 x 5). The square of *"vav"* is thirty-six (6 x 6), and the square of the final *"hei"* is twenty-five (5 x 5). Thus, 100 + 25 + 36 + 25 = 186.

(לקוטי שיחות חכ״א ע׳ 301)

"ברוך המקום ברוך הוא ברוך שנתן תורה לעמו ישראל ברוך הוא כנגד ארבעה בנים"
"Blessed is the Omnipresent, blessed be He! Blessed is He who gave the Torah to His people Israel, blessed be He! The Torah speaks of four children."

QUESTION: What is the connection between the four *"Baruchs"* and the four sons?

ANSWER: Each of the four sons has his unique understanding and way of seeing Hashem's influence in the world:

1) The *Chacham*, with his great wisdom, sees Hashem as *"Baruch HaMakom"* — the One Who causes the existence of the world.

ברוך Blessed is the Omnipresent, blessed be He. Blessed be He who gave the Torah to His people, Israel; blessed be He.

2) The *Rasha* knows about Hashem, but views Him as a G-d Who is removed from the world, and therefore he blatantly violates Hashem's will and thinks that he can get away from Him. He uses the term *"Hu,"* in the third person (which is usually used to refer to someone not present), to indicate his disbelief in individual Divine providence and to assert that Hashem is not personally involved with the world.

3) The *Tam* is a sincere person who studies Torah and is growing up to become a *Chacham* (see *Avudraham*) just as Yaakov is referred to as *"Ish tam yosheiv ohalim"* — "a plain man of integrity dwelling in tents [of Torah]" (*Bereishit* 25:27). He sees Hashem's greatness through his study of Torah and therefore proclaims, *"Baruch shenatan Torah le'amo Yisrael"* — "Blessed is He who gave the Torah to His people, Israel."

4) The *She'eino Yodei'a Lishol* views Hashem as something abstract and therefore speaks of Him as *"Baruch Hu"* in the third person. Since he is illiterate in Torah knowledge and does not comprehend the greatness and glory of Hashem, Divinity is something totally alien and foreign to him.

(הגש"פ אשל ברמה מר' אברהם ז"ל ליכטשטיין)

* * *

Some explain that these four *"Baruchs"* are not said by the same person, but the leader of the *Seder* would proclaim *"Baruch HaMakom"* — "Blessed is the Omnipresent" — and the participants in the *Seder* would respond, *"baruch Hu"* — "blessed be He." Then the leader would continue, *"baruch shenatan Torah le'amo Yisrael"* — "blessed is He Who gave the Torah to His people, Israel" — and again the participants would respond *"baruch Hu"* — "blessed be He."

Accordingly, later on (p. 106) when the *Haggadah* says, *"Baruch shomer havtachato LeYisrael baruch Hu"* — "Blessed is He Who keeps His promise to Israel, blessed be He" — it was a declaration made by the leader of the *Seder* and a response from the participants.

(מלבי"ם)

כְּנֶגֶד אַרְבָּעָה בָנִים דִּבְּרָה תוֹרָה. אֶחָד חָכָם. וְאֶחָד רָשָׁע. וְאֶחָד תָּם. וְאֶחָד שֶׁאֵינוֹ יוֹדֵעַ לִשְׁאוֹל:

"The Torah speaks of four sons." — "כנגד ארבעה בנים דברה תורה"

QUESTION: What is the common denominator among the four sons?

ANSWER: They are all present at the *Pesach Seder* table and their attendance expresses some interest and concern. Unfortunately, today we often encounter a *fifth* son, one to whom *"Pesach"* is a meaningless word and the *Seder* an unknown event. We must reach out with dedication and warmth to such sons long before *Pesach* and make every effort to bring about their presence at the *Seder* table.

(לקוטי שיחות ח"א ע' 252)

"אחד חכם ואחד רשע ואחד תם ואחד שאינו יודע לשאול"
"One wise, and one wicked, and one simple and one does not know how to ask."

QUESTION: Why is the word *"echad"* — "one" — repeated before each of the four sons?

ANSWER: Generally, the term *"echad"* expresses the oneness of Hashem. The *Haggadah* is teaching that every Jew, regardless of what he openly declares about Hashem or the Torah, still has a "spark" of *"echad"* — Hashem — in him. Therefore, it is proper and necessary to spend time with him and bring him closer to Hashem.

(ספר השיחות תש"ג)

Alternatively, in a certain Yeshivah there was once a teacher who had a very difficult child in his class. Exasperated and disillusioned, he went into the principal's office and told him, "You must take this child out of my class immediately. I can no longer deal with him." After asking the teacher to sit down and relax, the principal said to him, "Did you realize that if this child is out of your class, you no longer have a job?" The teacher, somewhat puzzled, asked, "Why? There are still another fifteen children in the class besides him." To this the principal responded, "What I meant is the following: Think of him as the only student in your class. If expelling him would also mean the end of your position in our school due to the lack of students, would you still want him taken out?" The teacher reconsidered and decided to give the child another chance.

כנגד The Torah speaks of four sons: one wise, and one wicked, and one simple, and one who does not know how to ask.

The *Haggadah* is teaching parents and educators to treat every child as if he were *"echad"* — their only one. The undivided attention and extra care usually given to an only child is something which every child deserves and which accomplishes wonders.

"אחד חכם ואחד רשע"
"One wise, and one wicked."

QUESTION: The Torah does not categorize the children. How does the *Haggadah* know which portion refers to the *Chacham* and which to the *Rasha*?

ANSWER: A very important ingredient in observing Torah and *mitzvot* is *Kabbalat Ol* — submitting to the yoke of Hashem. A Jew must fulfill the *mitzvot* of the Torah whether he understands their significance or not. The wise person fulfills Hashem's commandments and afterwards studies and tries to understand as much as possible. The wicked refuse to accept what Hashem says as long as they themselves cannot find a rationale for it.

When the Torah talks of the sons, concerning two it says, *"Ki yishalcha bincha machar"* — "When your son asks you tomorrow" *(Shemot* 13:14 and *Devarim* 6:20). Concerning another one the Torah says, "And it shall be when your children say to you, 'What is this service to you' " *(Shemot* 12:26), without mentioning the word *"machar"* — "tomorrow." A son who listens to his father and fulfills his instructions promptly and only *machar* — afterwards — seeks an explanation is either a wise son — *Chacham* — or a *Tam* — simple, but sincere. The one who, when instructed, obstinately refuses to act unless he comprehends the significance and who will not wait until tomorrow is a *Rasha* — a wicked person.

(פון אונזער אלטען אוצר בשם אמרי יעקב)

חָכָם מַה הוּא אוֹמֵר מָה הָעֵדֹת וְהַחֻקִּים
וְהַמִּשְׁפָּטִים אֲשֶׁר צִוָּה יְהוָה אֱלֹהֵינוּ אֶתְכֶם
וְאַף אַתָּה אֱמָר לוֹ כְּהִלְכוֹת הַפֶּסַח אֵין
מַפְטִירִין אַחַר הַפֶּסַח אֲפִיקוֹמָן:

"אחד חכם ואחד רשע"
"One wise, and one wicked."

QUESTION: 1) Why is the *Chacham* placed next to the *Rasha?* 2) Why *"ve'echad"* with a *"vav"*?

ANSWER: The *Gemara* (*Sanhedrin* 44a) says that even a Jew who sinned is still a Jew. This is due to the spark of G-dliness in every Jewish person's innermost being. In some it is obvious and revealed, while in others it is concealed, but regardless of the situation, it always remains intact. Putting the *Rasha* next to the *Chacham* is a message that the *Chacham* must do everything in his power to bring to surface the *"pintele Yid"* — "spark of G-dliness" — that is concealed in the *Rasha*.

The added *"vav"* teaches that the *Chacham* should encourage the *Rasha* to become "attached" to him. While doing this he should be careful that the relationship should provide an opportunity for him to influence the *Rasha* and not, G-d forbid, the reverse.
(הגש"פ לקוטי טעמים, מנהגים וביאורים)

Alternatively, placing the *Chacham* — wise son — next to the *Rasha* — wicked son — conveys an encouraging message to the *Rasha*. It is meant to teach him that he, too, has the potential to be a *Chacham*.

Simultaneously, it is also a word of caution to the wise son to not be overly proud of his accomplishments, for there is only a slight distance between himself and his brother. If he does not continue to advance in Torah and *Yiddishkeit*, he may, G-d forbid, slip back and that difference may disappear.

(לקוטי שיחות ח"א ע' 250, וח"ג ע' 1016)

חכם The wise son, what does he say? "What are the testimonies, statutes and laws that *Adonai*, our God, has commanded you?"[1] You should reply to him, [teaching him] the laws of *Pesach* [until their conclusion]: One may not eat any dessert after the *Pesach*-offering.

1. *Devarim* 6:20.

"חכם מה הוא אומר..."
"The wise son, what does he say..."

QUESTION: Instead of *"mah hu omeir"* — "what does he say" — it should have said *"mah hu sho'eil"* — "What does he ask"?

ANSWER: The *Haggadah* is teaching us that the character of a person and his intelligence can often be recognized by the style and tone of his speech. Hence, a *Chacham* — a wise person — *mah hu* — what he is — *omeir* — he says — i.e. from a person's way of talking it can be seen what he is. Likewise, a *Rasha* — a wicked person — *mah hu* — what he is — *omeir* — he says — i.e. from what he says and how he says it one can see that he is a *Rasha*.

(הגש"פ עם ליקוט טעמים ומנהגים בשם אדמו"ר מהריי"ץ)

"אמור לו כהלכות הפסח אין מפטירין אחר הפסח אפיקומן"
"You should reply to him the laws of *Pesach*, [up to] 'one may not eat any dessert after the *Pesach*-offering.'"

QUESTION: 1) *"Kehilchot hapesach"* literally means "like the *halachot* of *Pesach*." It should have said [reply to him] *"kol hilchot hapesach"* — "all the laws of *Pesach*"? 2) It should have written *"ad ein maftirin"* — "up to 'one is not to eat'"?

ANSWER: It was forbidden to eat any food after eating the *Pesach* lamb so that the taste of the meat would remain distinct. The same applies today to the *afikoman* which is in lieu of the *Pesach*-offering. The *Haggadah* is instructing the father that when his son the *Chacham* asks about the testimonies, statutes and laws, *"af atah emor lo"* — his answer should be *"kehilchot hapesach"* — just like the laws of *Pesach*. Just as there is a law that *"ein maftirin"* — nothing is eaten after the *pesach* lamb/*afikoman* in order that the taste remain clear — likewise, your answer should be clear and succinct so that afterwards the *Chacham* should be left with a clear understanding and no doubts or ambiguities.

(הגש"פ מוצל מאש - בית אהרן בפי' אגודת אזוב בשם ר' שלום זצ"ל מבעלז)

רָשָׁע מַה הוּא אוֹמֵר מָה הָעֲבוֹדָה הַזֹּאת לָכֶם. לָכֶם וְלֹא לוֹ. וּלְפִי שֶׁהוֹצִיא אֶת־עַצְמוֹ מִן הַכְּלָל כָּפַר

רשע מה הוא אומר
"The wicked son, what does he say?"

QUESTION: The reference to the *Rasha* in the Torah is the *pasuk* "And it shall come to pass when your children will say to you, 'What is this service to you?' " (*Shemot* 12:26) What in the *pasuk* indicates that the son is wicked?

ANSWER: Children must respect and honor their parents. They should seek their guidance and follow their instruction. A good child does not tell his parents *his* decision and expect them to listen to him.

Since the Torah mentions a child who "will say to you," i.e. one who *tells* the parent *his* opinion, the *Haggadah* deduces that we are not dealing with a good child, but unfortunately the opposite.

(הדרש והעיון)

"מה העבודה הזאת לכם"
"What is this service to you?"

QUESTION: Why is the *Chacham* so highly praised over the *Rasha*? He also says, "What are the testimonies, etc., that G-d, our G-d commanded *"etchem"* — "you" — and not *"otanu"* — "us"?

ANSWER: A major difference is that the *Chacham* says, "G-d our G-d," which shows that he recognizes that there is a Supreme Authority which also governs him. On the other hand, the *Rasha* makes no mention of Hashem, which indicates that he does not recognize Him and wants nothing to do with Him.

* * *

Perhaps, King Shlomo alludes to this explanation when he says, "I perceived that wisdom excels foolishness as light excels darkness" (Ecclesiastes 2:13). With this analogy he means the following: Concerning the first day of creation the Torah says, "And G-d called to the light day and to the darkness He called night" (*Bereishit* 1:5). The *Midrash* (*Rabbah* 1:6) asks why doesn't it say, "And to the darkness *G-d* called night" the same as it says about the light? The *Midrash* answers, Hashem does not link His Name with evil, but only with good.

רשע The wicked son, what does he say? "What is this service to you?"[1] [By saying] "to you," [he implies] "but not to himself." Since he excludes himself from our people at large, he denies the foundation of our faith.

1. *Shemot* 12:26.

Hence, King Shlomo is saying that the wisdom of the *Chacham* of the *Haggadah* excels over the foolishness of the wicked in the *Haggadah* (and there is no greater fool than a *Rasha* — wicked person), the same way that light excels over darkness. Light is associated with Hashem and darkness is not, similarly, the *Chacham* associates himself with Hashem and the *Rasha* does not.

(הגש״פ עם פי׳ ילקוט שמעוני)

"ולפי שהוציא את עצמו מן הכלל כפר בעקר"
"By excluding himself from the community he has denied that which is fundamental."

QUESTION: How does excluding *"et atzmo"* — "himself" — prove that he is a *Rasha*? Perhaps he is modest and reluctant to talk about himself.

ANSWER: The *Gemara* (*Gittin* 56b) relates that the wicked Titus was one of the generals assigned to lead the Roman armies to conquer Jerusalem and destroy the *Beit Hamikdash*. When he entered the Sanctuary, he stuck a sword into the *Parochet* — curtain, in front of the Holy of Holies — and miraculously, blood began to flow from it. The *Gemara* says *"kesavar harag et Atzmo"* — "He imagined that he had killed '*et Atzmo*' — 'Hashem.'"

Consequently, in this passage too, the words *"et Atzmo"* refer to Hashem. Since he excludes Hashem from his statement, the *Haggadah* places him in the relevant category.

(פון אונזער אלטען אוצר בשם ר׳ יוסף בער ז״ל סאלאווייטשיק מבריסק)

"You too, blunt his teeth." — "ואף אתה הקהה את שניו"

QUESTION: Why does the *Haggadah* instruct us to do something to his teeth particularly?

ANSWER: The word *"Rasha"* (רשע) has the numerical value of 570. The word *"Tzaddik"* (צדיק) has the numerical value of 204. The numerical difference between *"Rasha"* and *"Tzaddik"* is 366. The word *"shinav"* (שניו) adds up to 366. The *Haggadah* teaches us to work diligently to remove every part of *"shinav"* (366) from the *Rasha* and convert him into a *Tzaddik*.

(ברכת חיים על מועדים מר׳ חיים יעקב ז״ל צוקרמן)

בְּעִקָּר. וְאַף אַתָּה הַקְהֵה אֶת־שִׁנָּיו וֶאֱמָר לוֹ בַּעֲבוּר זֶה עָשָׂה יְהֹוָה לִי בְּצֵאתִי מִמִּצְרָיִם. לִי וְלֹא לוֹ אִלּוּ הָיָה שָׁם לֹא הָיָה נִגְאָל:

"You, too, blunt his teeth." — "ואף אתה הקהה את שניו"

QUESTION: The words *"Ve'af atah"* — "You too [blunt his teeth]" — are extra. It should have just said, "blunt his teeth"?

ANSWER: The *Midrash* says, that in Egypt when the Jews were told to prepare a *Pesach*-offering and that everyone should register with a group in order to be able to eat of it, there were some wicked people who ridiculed the whole idea and mocked the ones who were planning to make a *Pesach*-offering. On the night of *Pesach* Hashem performed a miracle and an aroma emanated from *Gan Eden* which permeated the *Pesach*-offering as it was being roasted. The scornful attitude of the wicked instantly melted away and their teeth became blunt, and they begged for an opportunity to partake of the aromatic and delicious *Pesach*-offering.

Tonight, when the wicked son comes with his attitude and makes a mockery of all the *avodah* — work — connected with the *Pesach*-offering and the *Yom Tov* in general, the *Haggadah* instructs, *"Ve'af atah"* — "You too" — give him the same treatment his predecessors were given in Egypt when they thought that they were smarter than everyone else. Just as their teeth became blunt while everyone else enjoyed eating the luscious *Pesach*-offering, do the same again tonight: give him an answer which will "blunt his teeth."

(הגש"פ מרבה לספר לספר מר' ידידי' טיאה וייל ז"ל, קארלסרוא, תקנ"א, ועי' מד"ר שיר השירים א:י"ב)

"ואמר לו בעבור זה עשה ה' לי בצאתי ממצרים. לי ולא לו אלו היה שם לא היה נגאל"
"And say to him: 'It is because of this that G-d did for me when I went out of Egypt.' 'For me'—but not for him. Had he been there, he would not have been redeemed.'"

QUESTION: In Hebrew third person is used to address a venerable person. To the wicked *Rasha* one should say *"li velo lecha"* — "to me and not to *you*" — *"ilu hayita sham"* — "had *you* been there" — *"lo hayita nig'al"* — "*you* would not have been redeemed"?

Therefore you should blunt his teeth, and tell him: "It is because of this that _Adonai_ did for me when I went out of Egypt,"[1] "for me" — but not for him! Had he been there, he would not have been redeemed.

1. _Shemot_ 13:8.

ANSWER: Among the children at the father's table there is a _Chacham_ — wise son — and a _Rasha_ — wicked son. The father and the _Chacham_ are enjoying a conversation regarding many facets of Torah. The wicked son, uninterested and impatient, barges in with his audacious comment, "Of what purpose is this work to you?" The _Haggadah_ is instructing the father not to pay attention to his rude son and his comments, but _"ve'emor lo"_ — to continue talking to _him_, i.e. the _Chacham_, and to tell him that he too should not respond. Rather, he should know that this is what Hashem did for "me and not for him" (the wicked son) — had he been in Egypt, he would not have been redeemed.

To answer, argue, or reason with the wicked is to no avail. King Shlomo says, "Do not answer a fool according to his foolishness" (Proverbs 26:4).

(הגר"א)

"אלו היה שם לא היה נגאל"
"Had he been there, he would not have been redeemed."

QUESTION: With such a harsh response the father will lose his son entirely. Why not attempt to bring him closer to the Torah through a friendly approach?

ANSWER: The Jews received the Torah only after they left Egypt. The father is, in fact, telling his son the following: "In Egypt where we did not yet have the Torah, for people like you who were _there_, there was no hope. Today, however, we do have the Torah. Study Torah and you will see the beauty of _Yiddishkeit_ and definitely resolve to change your ways."

Incidentally, as an introduction to the four sons, we bless Hashem for giving the Torah to the Jewish people, and then mention that the Torah speaks of four sons. The fact that Torah discusses four sons indicates that through Torah there is hope for _every_ person, regardless of his status.

(לקוטי שיחות ח"א ע' 252)

תָּם מַה הוּא אוֹמֵר מַה זֹּאת. וְאָמַרְתָּ אֵלָיו בְּחֹזֶק יָד הוֹצִיאָנוּ יְהוָה מִמִּצְרַיִם מִבֵּית עֲבָדִים:

"The simple son." — "תם"

QUESTION: Who is the *Tam*?

ANSWER: A *Chassid* of the Mezeritcher Maggid once traveled to be with his Rebbe for *Pesach*. The winter had been severe, and the roads were bad. When he reached a small village near Mezeritch, the sun was setting and it was impossible to go on before *Yom Tov*.

The local innkeeper invited the distressed *Chassid* for *Pesach* and promised him a beautiful kosher *Seder*. The innkeeper and his sons said the *Haggadah* with tremendous *hislahavut* — enthusiasm. The sons asked the questions, and their father answered with great joy.

When they got to the "Four Sons" they said, "*Chacham*, what does he say?; *Rasha*, what does he say?" — all with a special emphasis unlike that of the rest of the *Haggadah*. When they came to "*Tam*, what does he say?" they became very sad, saying it with choked voices and with tears. And when they came to the answer, "With a strong hand Hashem took us out of Egypt," they read it with great happiness.

The *Chassid* could not understand their strange *Haggadah* reading, which made it seem that they did not know where to be sad and where to be happy. The same thing happened on the second night, with the same tears, and the same joy.

When he came to the Maggid, he told how sad he was not to be at the Maggid's *Seder*, and his great wonder at the innkeeper's *Seder*. The Maggid calmed him and said it was worth being away for *Pesach* to sit with the innkeeper and his sons, "They are great *tzaddikim* and know the true intentions of the *Haggadah*." The Maggid continued:

The *Haggadah* complains bitterly about the foolishness of man's ways. People pay attention to the *Chacham* — what does he say? They pay attention to the *Rasha* — what does he say? But they pay no attention to hear: "*Tam*" — "there" [in Aramaic *Tam* means "there" (see *Beitzah* 4b)] — i.e. in Heaven, what does He say? And if He will ask, "What you have accomplished, what have you done about your actions that have pushed off your redemption," what will *you* say?

תם The simple son, what does he say? "What is this?" You should tell him: "With a strong hand, *Adonai* brought us out from Egypt, from the house of bondage."[1]

1. *Shemot* 13:14.

As depressing as this may be, immediately we are comforted and gladdened by the answer: "Hashem took us out of Egypt with a strong hand." Hashem took the Jews out by force whether they were ready or deserving to be redeemed or not. He simply showed tremendous mercy and redeemed them forcefully. And thus, we too can hope that Hashem will have mercy on us and redeem us.

(התורה והעולם - ויקרא - מהרב ניסן ז״ל טעלושקין)

"תם מה הוא אומר מה זאת"
The simple son, what does he say? "What is this?"

QUESTION: Regarding the *Tam*, the Torah says, "When your child asks you *'machar'* — 'tomorrow' — what is this?" (*Shemot* 13:4) The word *"machar"* — "tomorrow" — seems superfluous?

ANSWER: Rashi explains, "Sometimes the word *'machar'* (tomorrow) means *'achshav'* — 'now' — and sometimes it means *'le'achar zeman'* — 'in a time to come.'"

Rashi is not just offering an explanation of the term *"machar,"* but also teaching an important lesson about rearing children. The term *"machar"* is not just a relative period of time, but a description of two types of *"bincha"* (children).

There is a child who is *"achshav"* — "now." He lives in the same spirit that you do and is a Torah observing Jew as yourself. There is also another child, who is *"achar zeman"* — "of a later time." He considers his Torah-observant father an "old timer" and considers himself a progressive denizen of a different spiritual era.

The Torah is instructing every father, "Even if you have a child who presently does not agree with your Torah way of thinking, you must bear in mind that he is *'bincha'* — 'your child.' Moreover, you as a father have to help him and give him the answers which will make him *'achshav'* — a Torah observant Jew like yourself."

(לקוטי שיחות ח״ו ע׳ 268)

וְשֶׁאֵינוֹ יוֹדֵעַ לִשְׁאוֹל אַתְּ פְּתַח לוֹ שֶׁנֶּאֱמַר וְהִגַּדְתָּ לְבִנְךָ בַּיּוֹם הַהוּא לֵאמֹר בַּעֲבוּר זֶה עָשָׂה יְהוָֹה לִי בְּצֵאתִי מִמִּצְרָיִם:

"וְשֶׁאֵינוֹ יוֹדֵעַ לִשְׁאוֹל"
"The son who does not know how to ask."

QUESTION: Is "the one who does not know how to ask" really an absolute illiterate?

ANSWER: The popular portrayal of him as a young immature child is inaccurate. Were it true, he would not have been placed at the end to be spoken to after all other children since he would have definitely fallen asleep by this time. Moreover, how could he be expected to understand the balance of the *Haggadah*, which is, after all, directed to him?

Obviously, "the one who does not know how to ask" is an intelligent person who unfortunately, knows very little about Torah and *Yiddishkeit*. Afraid that his question may be totally out of place, he sits quietly throughout the *Seder* and does not ask anything. Therefore, the *Haggadah* instructs: First deal with your children, and then spend the evening teaching the highly intelligent and secularly learned guest at your table who is currently a *"She'eino Yodei'a Lishol"* — one who does not know how to formulate questions in Torah matters although he is eager to hear and learn.

"אַתְּ פְּתַח לוֹ"
"You must initiate him."

QUESTION: Since the *Haggadah* instructs the *father* to teach his son, it should have said *"atah"* in the masculine instead of *"at"* which is feminine?

ANSWER: "The one who does not know how to ask" is actually a very intelligent person who unfortunately knows very

ושאינו The son who does not know how to ask, you must initiate him, as it is said: "You shall tell your son on that day: 'It is because of this that *Adonai* did for me when I went out of Egypt.'"[1]

1. *Shemot* 13:8.

---

little about *Yiddishkeit*. The *Haggadah* instructs us not to give him a watered-down version of the Torah, but instead *"at* (את) *petach lo"* — tell him everything from א to ת (beginning to end) about Torah and *Yiddishkeit*.

(ברוך שאמר לר' ברוך הלוי ז"ל עפשטיין)

Alternatively, in *Yeshivot* the older students are taught by Rebbes. The kindergarten is commonly taught by female teachers, and the *Rosh Yeshivah* is not expected to lower himself to teach the small children. Similarly, many may claim that it is below their dignity to deal directly with someone who knows nothing about *Yiddishkeit* and teach him the rudiments. Hence, the *Haggadah* instructs that it is incumbent upon each of us become like the kindergarten teacher who warmly and enthusiastically teaches and deals with the beginners.

"שנאמר והגדת לבנך ביום ההוא לאמר
בעבור זה עשה ה' לי בצאתי ממצרים"

"You must initiate him, as it is said: 'You shall tell your son on that day, saying, 'It is because of this that G-d did for me when I went out of Egypt.' "

QUESTION: The word *"leimor"* — "saying" — is superfluous?

ANSWER: The *"She'eino Yodei'ah Lishol"* is sitting at the *Seder* and does not know what he should say, so the *Haggadah* instructs that *"at petach lo"* — "you must initiate him." However, it is not sufficient that you just tell him, but it must reach the point of *"leimor"* — "saying" — i.e. he, too, will become an active participant in the *Pesach* celebration, and *he* will say to others, "I am celebrating tonight because of what Hashem did for *me* when I went out of Egypt."

(פנים יפות פ' בא)

יָכוֹל מֵרֹאשׁ חֹדֶשׁ תַּלְמוּד לוֹמַר בַּיּוֹם הַהוּא
אִי בַּיּוֹם הַהוּא יָכוֹל מִבְּעוֹד יוֹם תַּלְמוּד לוֹמַר
בַּעֲבוּר זֶה. בַּעֲבוּר זֶה לֹא אָמַרְתִּי אֶלָּא בְּשָׁעָה
שֶׁיֵּשׁ מַצָּה וּמָרוֹר מֻנָּחִים לְפָנֶיךָ:

**"One may think [that the obligation to discuss
the Exodus begins] from the first day of the month."**

QUESTION: Why would we think that the discussion of the
Exodus should be from the first of the month or on *Erev Pesach*?

ANSWER: Since it was on *Rosh Chodesh* that Moshe told the
Jews in Egypt about the *mitzvah* of the *Pesach*-offering, one would
think that the discussion of the Exodus should always commence
on *Rosh Chodesh*, and since the actual offering took place on *Erev
Pesach*, one would think that the discussion of the Exodus should
at least commence at that time. However, the phrase *"ba'avur zeh"*
— "because of this" — rejects these two initial considerations and
instructs that it should be done "when the *matzah* and *maror* are
placed before you," i.e. at the *Seder*.

* * *

QUESTION: Since the teaching of the phrase *"ba'avur zeh"* —
"because of this" — supersedes the teaching of *"bayom hahu"* —
"on that day" — why does it say *"bayom hahu"* altogether?

ANSWER: The words *"ba'avur zeh"* can also be explained to
refer to the *Pesach*-offering, and infers that the discussion of the
Exodis starts while it is still day. Hence, one of the two
expressions is superfluous. Consequently, since the Torah does
write both expressions [*bayom hahu* and *ba'avur zeh*], we must say
that *"ba'avur zeh"* does not mean the same thing as *"bayom hahu,"*
but refers to the night.

(הגש"פ עם לקוטי טעמים ומנהגים)

**"One may think [that the obligation to discuss
the Exodus begins] from the first day of the month."**

QUESTION: What is the connection between this verse and
the *She'eino Yodei'a Lishol*?

יכול One may think [that the obligation to discuss the Exodus begins] from the first day of the month [of *Nissan*]. The Torah therefore says,[1] "[You shall tell your son] on that day," [i.e., on the day of the Exodus]. From the phrase "on that day," one might infer "while it is still day." [Hence,] the Torah adds "it is because of this." The expression 'because of *this*' implies that [the obligation only begins] when *matzah* and *maror* are placed before you.

1. *Shemot* 13:8.

ANSWER: This verse is not a part of the response to the *She'eino Yodei'a Lishol*. Rather, since the *pasuk*, "*Vehigadeta lebincha*" was quoted in regard to the *She'eino Yodei'a Lishol*, the *Haggadah* proceeds to offer a Rabbinic interpretation of it. Thus, it is in the *Haggadah* parenthetically.

(אבודרהם)

"יכול מראש חדש...בעבור זה לא אמרתי אלא בשעה שיש מצה ומרור מנחים לפניך"

"One may think [that the obligation to discuss the Exodus begins] from the first day of the month... The expression 'because of *this*' implies that [the obligation only begins] when *matzah* and *maror* are placed before you."

QUESTION: What is wrong with starting the discussion of the Exodus even without *matzah* and *maror* on the table?

ANSWER: The *Haggadah* imparts an extremely important lesson about the education of children. It is not sufficient to merely instruct your child about Torah and *mitzvot*. You must first show your own commitment, and then you can endeavor to convince them. You cannot just say to your child, "Go to *shul* or take a *sefer* and learn." You must be a living example for the child to emulate. Thus, the appropriate way to discuss the Exodus is not academically, but when he sees that *matzah* and *maror* are placed in front of *you*.

* * *

A non-observant father once sent his child to a Hebrew school. As the child's *Bar-Mitzvah* was approaching, he took his son to the Hebrew book store and asked the salesman for a *Bar-Mitzvah* set. The salesman opened the box and the boy saw in it a pair of *tefillin* and a *tallit*. Having no knowledge of these strange items, he asked his father with a puzzled expression on his face, "What are these?" The father told him, "My son, this is what every Jew must have once he becomes *Bar-Mitzvah*." The young boy looked up to his father inquisitively and asked, "So Father, when are you becoming *Bar-Mitzvah*?"

מִתְּחִלָּה עוֹבְדֵי עֲבוֹדָה זָרָה הָיוּ אֲבוֹתֵינוּ וְעַכְשָׁו
קֵרְבָנוּ הַמָּקוֹם לַעֲבֹדָתוֹ. שֶׁנֶּאֱמַר וַיֹּאמֶר יְהוֹשֻׁעַ
אֶל־כָּל־הָעָם כֹּה־אָמַר יְהֹוָה אֱלֹהֵי יִשְׂרָאֵל בְּעֵבֶר
הַנָּהָר יָשְׁבוּ אֲבוֹתֵיכֶם מֵעוֹלָם תֶּרַח אֲבִי אַבְרָהָם
וַאֲבִי נָחוֹר וַיַּעַבְדוּ אֱלֹהִים אֲחֵרִים:

"מתחלה עובדי עבודה זרה היו אבותינו
ועכשיו קרבנו המקום לעבודתו"

**"In the beginning our fathers worshipped idols but now
the Omnipresent has brought us close to His service"**

QUESTION: The words *"mitechilah"* — "in the beginning" —
and *"ve'achshav"* — "but now" — are superfluous. It should have
just said our parents served idols and Hashem has brought us
close to His service?

ANSWER: In the early 1930's an non-observant Jew traveling
on a train was informed by the conductor that a famous Rabbi
known as the *"Chafeitz Chaim"* was in the last car. Eager to see
him, the gentleman hastened to this car. The *Chafeitz Chaim* was
engrossed in a *sefer* and did not pay any attention to his observer.
Upon lifting his eyes, he noticed the man and asked if there was
any way he could help him. The gentleman apologetically said, "I
only came to see what you look like." With a pleasant smile, the
Chafeitz Chaim questioned, "And what did you see?" The man
responded, "Frankly, I am very disappointed. I expected to see a
well groomed person, dressed in the most modern style, and you
are garbed in the old style. You do not meet my expectations in
any way."

The *Chafeitz Chaim* looked up at him and replied, "If anything,
it is I who is in accordance with the latest style and you are the
one who is not with the times." The gentlemen arrogantly said,
"Rabbi, on what grounds do you make your statement? *My*
wardrobe is of the latest style — *yours* is antiquated!" The *Chafeitz
Chaim* responded, "In the *Haggadah* we read, *'mitechilah'* — 'In the
beginning our fathers served idols.' This was the ancient style.

מתחילה In the beginning, our fathers worshipped idols, but now the Omnipresent has brought us close to His service, as it is said:[1] "And Yehoshua said to all the people: So says *Adonai*, the God of Israel: 'Your fathers always dwelt beyond the [Euphrates] River — Terach, the father of Avraham and the father of Nachor, and they served other gods.'

1. *Joshua* 24:2-4.

However, *'ve'achshav'* — the present style — is being close to Hashem's service. The religious Jew who is serving Hashem with all his heart and soul is the one who is truly in accordance with the latest style."

"מתחלה עובדי עבודה זרה היו אבותינו
ועכשו קרבנו המקום לעבדתו"
"In the beginning our fathers worshipped idols; but now the Omnipresent has brought us close to His service."

QUESTION: Why do we begin by mentioning negative aspects of Jewish history?

ANSWER: As explained before (p. 100), the *She'eino Yodei'a Lishol* is a highly intelligent person who unfortunately lacks a Torah background and, thus, is not in the position to formulate a question intellectually. The *Seder* is one of his first exposures to the Torah way of life. He is told that it is never too late to embrace Torah and *mitzvot*, and regardless of his past, he can always start anew. He should not feel uncomfortable because our ancestors, too, originally had no connection to Torah and *mitzvot*, but ultimately accepted it and reached great heights.

In addition, many people have difficulty returning to *Yiddishkeit* because it means leaving their friends and society. The *Haggadah's* message is that Avraham was brought up in a home of one of the major idol merchants and in an environment steeped in paganism. Nevertheless, he detached himself from everyone and conducted his life in the path which he considered right and just.

(ברכת חיים בשם אוהב ישראל)

וָאֶקַּח אֶת־אֲבִיכֶם אֶת־אַבְרָהָם מֵעֵבֶר הַנָּהָר וָאוֹלֵךְ אוֹתוֹ בְּכָל־אֶרֶץ כְּנָעַן וָאַרְבֶּה אֶת־זַרְעוֹ וָאֶתֶּן לוֹ אֶת־יִצְחָק: וָאֶתֵּן לְיִצְחָק אֶת־יַעֲקֹב וְאֶת־עֵשָׂו וָאֶתֵּן לְעֵשָׂו אֶת־הַר שֵׂעִיר לָרֶשֶׁת אוֹתוֹ וְיַעֲקֹב וּבָנָיו יָרְדוּ מִצְרָיִם: בָּרוּךְ שׁוֹמֵר הַבְטָחָתוֹ לְיִשְׂרָאֵל. בָּרוּךְ הוּא

"וארבה את זרעו ואתן לו את יצחק"
"I multiplied his seed and I gave him Yitzchak."

QUESTION: Why does it say *"va'arbeh"* — "I multiplied" — when Yitzchak was his only child?

ANSWER: The word *"arbeh"* (ארבה) has the numerical value of 208, which is the same numerical value as the name "Yitzchak" (יצחק). Although Yitzchak was an only son, he gave his father Avraham as much *"nachas"* as another parent would have had from many children.

(לקוטי שיחות ח"א ע' 110)

"ואתן לו את יצחק"
"And I gave him Yitzchak."

QUESTION: Hashem instructed Avraham to call his son "Yitzchak" "because of the laughter" (*Bereishit* 17:19, Rashi). Why was the future tense ("he will laugh") used for his name?

ANSWER: Avraham and Sarah had undertaken the difficult task of changing the course of the world by educating people about Torah and G-dliness, and they were very successful at it. However, they had also encountered great difficulties, and Avraham was even cast into the burning furnace by King Nimrod.

As Avraham and Sarah aged and remained childless, those who previously feared them began to laugh and rejoice. "Soon Avraham and Sarah will die," they thought to themselves, "and without a child to continue their work, they will be gone and forgotten, and so will the ideas and ideals they propagated."

ואקח 'And I took your father Avraham from beyond the river and led him throughout the land of Canaan. I multiplied his seed and I gave him Yitzchak. To Yitzchak I gave Yaakov and Esau. I gave Mount Seir to Esau as an inheritance, and Yaakov and his children went down to Egypt.'"

ברוך Blessed is He Who keeps His promise to Israel,

Avraham was concerned about this and prayed to Hashem for a child who would continue his work. Hashem promised him, "Your wife will bear you a son. Name him 'Yitzchak' because he will follow in your footsteps, and *'he will laugh'* at all those who think that the teachings of Avraham and Sarah will be forgotten."

"ברוך שומר הבטחתו"
"Blessed is He Who keeps His promise."

QUESTION: Why bless the Divine for keeping His promise? Even mortal man must do so!

ANSWER: Hashem told Avraham, "I will give all the land that you see to you and to your descendants forever" (*Bereishit* 13:15). He also told him, "Your offspring shall be aliens in a land which does not belong to them. They will serve them and they shall oppress them...and afterwards they shall leave with great wealth" (ibid. 15:13,14). At the time of these promises Avraham had no children. Afterwards Yishmael and Yitzchak were born. We thank Hashem for fulfilling His promise through Yitzchak and not through Yishmael. Thanks to this, we became the recipients of Torah and *Eretz Yisrael*.

(ברוך שאמר)

"שהקדוש ברוך הוא חשב את הקץ לעשות"
"For the Holy One, blessed be He, calculated the end [of the bondage], in order to do."

QUESTION: What calculation did Hashem make?

שֶׁהַקָּדוֹשׁ בָּרוּךְ הוּא חָשַׁב אֶת־הַקֵּץ לַעֲשׂוֹת כְּמָה
שֶׁאָמַר לְאַבְרָהָם אָבִינוּ בִּבְרִית בֵּין הַבְּתָרִים. שֶׁנֶּאֱמַר
וַיֹּאמֶר לְאַבְרָם יָדֹעַ תֵּדַע כִּי גֵר יִהְיֶה זַרְעֲךָ בְּאֶרֶץ לֹא

ANSWER: The Jews were destined to be enslaved for 400 years. In actuality, however, they left Egypt after being there only 210 years. The reason for the reduction of years was that Hashem took into consideration the *avodat perech* — extra hard labor — which the Egyptians forced the Jews to perform which was equivalent to 400 years of normal slavery. The word *"keitz"* (קץ) has the numerical value of 190. We praise Hashem for calculating the *"keitz"* — 190 years as *"la'asot"* — actual work.

The *Haggadah* then continues to tell us that the 400 years originated from, *"Kemah she'amar le'Avraham"* — "As He told Avraham" — that "Your children will be strangers in a land which does not belong to them and they shall serve them and be treated harshly for 400 years, and afterwards they shall come out with great wealth."

(סי' קול יעקב)

* * *

Alternatively, though in actuality the Jews were in Egypt for only 210 years, the 400 years Hashem refers to are counted from the birth of Yitzchak. Yitzchak was born on *Pesach* (see *Bereshit* 18:10, Rashi) and exactly 400 years later to the day, Hashem took the Jews out of Egypt. We thank Him for *"chisheiv et hakeitz"* — calculating the destined time of 400 years to the exact day — *"la'asot"* — in order to do *"kemah she'amar l'Avraham"* — "as He promised Avraham" — that afterwards they would come out with great wealth.

Unlike the former explanation, here the word *"la'asot"* — "to do" — is not the conclusion of the initial phrase *"chisheiv et hakeitz,"* but the start of the succeeding one.

(שמחת הרגל להחיד"א)

* * *

blessed be He. The Holy One, blessed be He, calculated the end [of the bondage] in order to do as He had said to Avraham our father at the 'Covenant Between the Portions,' as it is said:[1] "And He said to Avram: 'Know with certainty that your descendants will be strangers in a land which does not belong to them,
1. *Bereishit* 15:13-14.

That the 400 years of the Egyptian exile started with the birth of Yitzchak is alluded to in the *pasuk*, "He remembered His covenant forever... that He made with Avraham and His vow to Yitzchak" (Psalms 105:8-9). The name "Yitzchak" which is normally spelled with a *"tzaddik"* (יצחק), is spelled here with a *"sin"* (ישחק). The numerical difference between *"tzaddik"* (90) and *"sin"* (300) equals 210. In merit of reducing the numerical value of his name by 210, the Jews were in Egypt only for 210 years and the other 190 will be made up by dating back the promise, "Your children will be strangers," to the birth of Yitzchak.

(עיון יעקב, בכורות ה' ע"ב בשם מדרש דברי הימים, ועי' פני דוד להחיד"א ס"פ וישב
דמתרץ מדוע לפי"ז היו במצרים רד"ו שנה ולא ק"צ שנה)

"ויאמר לאברם ידע תדע כי גר יהיה זרעך בארץ לא להם"
"He said to Avram, 'Your children will be strangers in a land which does not belong to them.' "

QUESTION: The words *"be'eretz lo lahem"* — "in a land which does not belong to them" — seem extra. Obviously, a stranger is not in his own land?

ANSWER: When Yosef came before Pharaoh, he predicted that there would be seven years of abundance and seven years of famine. He advised Pharaoh to save up food for the seven years of famine. When the famine came as predicted, the people of Egypt came to Yosef to buy food, and when they ran out of money, Yosef took their cattle in lieu of money. When they ran out of cattle, he took their land.

Afterwards, Yosef relocated the people to different cities from one end of Egypt to the other. He did this so that the Egyptians would be strangers in the places where they lived and be unable to embarrass his brothers by calling them strangers or refugees (see *Bereishit* 47:21 Rashi).

לָהֶם וַעֲבָדוּם וְעִנּוּ אֹתָם אַרְבַּע מֵאוֹת שָׁנָה: וְגַם אֶת־
הַגּוֹי אֲשֶׁר יַעֲבֹדוּ דָּן אָנֹכִי וְאַחֲרֵי כֵן יֵצְאוּ בִּרְכֻשׁ גָּדוֹל:

Hashem told Avraham, "Your children will be in the exile of Egypt for 400 years and be strangers in the land. However, it will be tolerable, because it will be *eretz lo lahem* — a land which does not belong to *them* — to the *Egyptians*. Thus, they will not feel less comfortable than their Egyptian neighbors."

(מדרש שמואל על אבות פ"ב: ט"ו, ר"ט אומר היום קצר וכו')

* * *

Alternatively, Hashem was telling Avraham that the reason "your children will be strangers in a land" is *"lo lahem"* — "not for their own sake" — i.e. to cleanse them of their sins. Rather, the purpose was to elevate the *nitzotzot* — sparks of G-dliness — in Egypt.

(אדמו"ר מוהריי"ץ בסה"ש תרצ"ז ע' 220)

"ועבדום וענו אתם"
"They will enslave them, and oppress them."

QUESTION: Why was it decreed that *"ve'enu otam"* — "they will oppress them" — in addition to being enslaved?

ANSWER: The words *"ve'enu otam"* literally mean, "they will impoverish them." Hashem is telling Avraham that when the Jews leave Egypt they would make them, i.e. the Egyptians, poor.

The primary purpose of the Egyptian exile was to enable the Jews to elevate the *nitzotzot* — sparks of G-dliness — enclothed in the material substance of the Egyptians. At the departure, the Jews "took out" (elevated) all these spiritual sparks. On the *pasuk* *"Vayenatzlu et Mitzraim"* — "they emptied Egypt" (*Shemot* 12:36), the *Gemara* (*Berachot* 9b) says that they transformed Egypt into the equivalent of a [bird] trap containing no grain and the depth of the sea without any fish.

(אדמו"ר מוהריי"ץ בסה"ש תרצ"ז ע' 220, ועי' תורת מנחם ליל ב' דחה"פ תשח"י)

"ועבדום וענו אתם ארבע מאות שנה"
"They will enslave them, and oppress them for four hundred years."

QUESTION: When Hashem promised Avraham that he would inherit *Eretz Yisrael*, he asked, *"bamah eida"* — "Whereby shall I know [that I am to inherit it]. (*Bereishit* 15:8) For questioning this his children were enslaved by Pharoah for 210 years, which due to the extremely difficult labor were equivalent to 400 years of normal slavery (see *Nedarim* 32a). What is the significance of the number 400?

הגדה של פסח

and they will enslave them and oppress them for four hundred years. Ultimately, I will judge the nation which they shall serve, and afterwards they shall leave with great wealth.'"

ANSWER: There is a system of letter-substitution, known as *"At-bash"* (א-ת, ב-ש"י). In *At-bash* the "א" interchanges with the "ת", the "ב" with the "ש", etc. According to this system, the "ה" interchanges with the "צ" and the "מ" interchanges with the "י". Thus, the letters of the word *"bamah"* — "whereby" (במה) — which Avraham used to inquire about the worthiness of his children to inherit *Eretz Yisrael*, interchange with the letters "ש-י-צ." The total numerical value of the letters "ש - י - צ" is exactly 400.

(שפתי כהן עה"ת)

"ועבדום וענו אתם ארבע מאות שנה"

"They will enslave them, and oppress them for four hundred years."

QUESTION: When the famine was felt in the land of Canaan, Yaakov asked his children to go down to Egypt and purchase food. Seeing their reluctance, he said to them, *"Lamah titra'u"* (למה תתראו) — "Why are you afraid [to go down to Egypt]" (see *Targum Yonatan ben Uziel*). Behold, I have heard, *"Ki yeish shever bemitzraim"* (כי יש שבר במצרים) — "There are provisions in Egypt." *"Redu shamah"* (רדו שמה) — "Go down there" (*Bereishit* 42:1-2).

Why were they reluctant, and how did Yaakov persuade them?

ANSWER: They were well aware that Hashem told Avraham that his children would be enslaved in a strange land for four hundred years. Thus, they did not want to leave Canaan, out of fear that with their departure the exile of four hundred years would commence.

Therefore, Yaakov said to them, *"Lamah titra'u"* — "Why are you afraid?" Grammatically he should have said, *"Lamah tire'u"* (למה תראו). Through adding the extra "תי", which has the numerical value of four hundred, he meant to say to them, *"Lamah* — Why — *taf tire'u* (תי תראו) — are you afraid of the four hundred years? I saw prophetically, *ki yeish* — there will be — *shever* — a break — i.e. a reduction in the amount of years to be — *bemitzraim* — in Egypt. *Redu shamah* — the exile there will be only a total of two hundred and ten years (which is the numerical value of the word רדו)."

(קרבן פסח על הגש"פ מהרב גדלי' ז"ל סילווערסטאן)

"I will judge." — "דן אנכי"

QUESTION: Since it was willed and decreed by Hashem that they be enslaved for 400 years, why were the Egyptians punished?

ANSWER: True, Hashem said that the Jews would be enslaved and oppressed, but never did He ordain that they be subjected to *avodat perach* — extremely hard labor. Nor did He say that the Jewish male babies should be killed. For exceeding their prerogatives and making the Jews suffer much more than was destined, they deserved punishment.

(רמב״ן, בראשית ט״ו:י״ד. ועי׳ ראב״ד הל׳ תשובה פ״ו:ב)

"וגם את הגוי אשר יעבדו דן אנכי ואחרי כן יצאו ברכוש גדול"
"And also the nation, that they shall serve, I will judge; and afterwards they shall leave with great wealth."

QUESTION: In *halachah* there is a rule: "*Kam leih bederabah mineih*" — When one is due two punishments (e.g. death and a fine), we do not inflict both, but mete out the severest penalty. Why were the Egyptians punished by losing their lives as well as their money?

ANSWER: The rule of "*Kam leih bederabah mineih*" applies only in cases which are ruled by our courts *(Beit Din)*. If one commits a crime for which one is liable to the death penalty when done intentionally, he is exempt from monetary payments even in an instance where he does it *beshogeig* — unintentionally (Rambam, *Geneivah* 3:1-2). However, this does not apply when the entire matter is being ruled by Heavenly court. Hashem, reserves the right to punish individuals as He sees fit. Therefore, Hashem emphasized *"Dan Anochi"* — "I personally will judge and punish them." Hence, the Egyptians justly pay money and suffer for their iniquity.

(פרשת דרכים, דרך מצרים דרוש חמישי)

Alternatively, this rule applies only when the two punishments are for the same act, e.g. stabbing someone to death on *Shabbat* and damaging his clothes in the process. In such a case, the murderer is put to death but does not have to pay for the damaged clothing.

However, the Egyptians received punishments for separate acts. They deserved the ten plagues as punishment for torturing the Jews *(avodat perech)*, and they deserved to drown as punishment for drowning the Jewish children. They lost their wealth due to their

failure to compensate the enslaved Jewish people for their work. Thus, it is not considered a case of double punishment.

(שארית מנחם מר' מ"מ זצ"ל, וישווא ויזניץ)

"ואחרי כן יצאו ברכש גדול"
"And afterwards they shall leave with great wealth."

QUESTION: Why didn't Avraham say to Hashem, "No thank you, keep the wealth and do not make my children suffer *galut* — exile"?

ANSWER: In addition to their simple meaning, the words *"ve'acharei chein yeitze'u birechush gadol"* also refer to 1) Torah, 2) redemption and 3) the Messianic era.

1) The words *"yeitze'u birechush"* (יצאו ברכש) — "leave with wealth" — have the numerical value of 629, which is the same numerical value as *"zehu Torah"* — "This is Torah" (זהו תורה).

2) The *"וי"* in *"v'acharei chein"* — *"and* afterwards" — seems extra. It would be sufficient to say *"acharei chein"* — "afterwards."

Our father Yaakov was very concerned about the Jewish people being in *galut*. Therefore, he took the letter *vav* from Eliyahu's name as a pledge that he will come and announce the redemption of his children (Rashi, *Vayikra*, 26:42).

During the *"B'rit Bein Habetarim"* — "Covenant Between the Portions" — that Hashem made with Avraham, Avraham was informed of all the different exiles the Jewish people would experience (*Bereishit Rabbah* 44:17). At that time, Hashem promised him that, in addition to being redeemed from Egypt, *"v'acharei chein"* — *"and* afterwards" — there will be an ultimate redemption heralded by Eliyahu thanks to the *"וי"* Yaakov will take from his name as a pledge.

3) The words *"birechush gadol"* (ברכש גדול) add up to 565 (עם הכולל — counting the statement itself as a total of one), which is also the same numerical value as *"zeh bizeman Melech Hamashiach"* (זה בזמן מלך המשיח) — "This — great wealth — will be in the era of King *Mashiach*."

Avraham did not argue with Hashem because Torah, redemption, and *Mashiach* are worth much more than all the difficult trials and tribulations of *galut*.

(שפתי כהן, עה"ת)

וְהִיא שֶׁעָמְדָה לַאֲבוֹתֵינוּ וְלָנוּ שֶׁלֹּא אֶחָד בִּלְבַד עָמַד עָלֵינוּ לְכַלּוֹתֵנוּ

"והיא שעמדה"
"This is what has stood."

QUESTION: Why do we raise the cup of wine when reciting this passage?

ANSWER: Throughout history many have endeavored to cause us to assimilate in order to detach us from Hashem and Torah and thus destroy us spiritually.

In order to avoid intermarriage and assimilation our Sages instituted certain ordinances. Since wine drinking brings people together and promotes intimacy, sharing wine with non-Jews is prohibited, and we are not to drink any wine which was handled by a non-Jew (*Shabbat* 17b). Thus, with the lifting of the cup of wine we are proclaiming that thanks to adhering to the law concerning "this" — wine — i.e. the command not to mingle with non-Jews by drinking wine — we have maintained our identity and averted their every effort to destroy us.

(הגש״פ עם פי׳ קרבן פסח מהרב גדלי׳ ז״ל סילווערסטאן)

"והיא שעמדה לאבותינו"
"And this is what has stood by our fathers and us."

QUESTION: What does the word *"Vehi"* — "And *this"* — refer to?

ANSWER: The word *"vehi"* (והיא) is an acronym for:
ו = The six sections of *Mishnah*
ה = The five *Chumashim*
י = The ten commandments
א = Hashem, the only One, Blessed be He

והיא And this is what has stood by our fathers and us, for not only one has risen up against us to annihilate us, but in every

---

In the merit of learning Torah, observing *mitzvot,* and believing in Hashem, we have outlived all nations who have tried to destroy us.

(אברבנאל)

Alternatively, *"Vehi"* refers to the *"havtachah"* — "assurance" — that Hashem gave to Avraham that He will ultimately redeem the Jewish people. Our absolute faith and reliance that Hashem will fulfill His promise speedily in our time and take us out of exile has helped us survive throughout the millennia.

(מחזור ויטרי)

Alternatively, the words *"Vehi she'amdah"* — "And this is what stood" — is a continuation to the last words of the previous phrase, "[And afterwards they shall leave] *with great wealth."* The *Haggadah* is saying that throughout the years we have lived among many peoples who wanted to annihilate us, and what has stood for us has been *our great wealth.* Through it we have been able to bribe money-hungry oppressors and assure our existence. If this did not work, then instead of afflicting us bodily they would suffice with confiscating our wealth and expelling us from their lands. So at least we went unharmed and the future of our people was preserved.

(פון אונזער אלטען אוצר)

"שלא אחד בלבד עמד עלינו לכלתנו"
"For not only one has risen against us to annihilate us."

QUESTION: Instead of "not only one," it should have said *"harbeih amdu aleinu lechaloteinu"* — "many have risen against us to annihilate us"?

אֶלָּא שֶׁבְּכָל־דּוֹר וָדוֹר עוֹמְדִים עָלֵינוּ לְכַלּוֹתֵנוּ. וְהַקָּדוֹשׁ בָּרוּךְ הוּא מַצִּילֵנוּ מִיָּדָם:

יעמיד הכוס ויגלה הפת:

ANSWER: As long as Hashem keeps a watchful eye over the Jewish people, we will remain in existence regardless of the efforts of alien nations to annihilate us. What stood by our fathers was that fortunately *"shelo echad bilvad"* — the One and Only was not the one who sought our annihilation, G-d forbid. For this we are grateful and rejoice. (צוף אמרים בשם מהר"א זצ"ל מקודינאב)

Alternatively, the phrase "not only one" can also be explained as a message to *Klal Yisrael:* the greatest threat is not our external enemies, but primarily *"shelo echad bilvad"* — the fact that we are not united as one. Lack of unity and rampant internal discord *"amad aleinu lechaloteinu"* — pose the greatest danger of annihilation. (ליקוטי יהודה בשם שפת אמת)

"שלא אחד בלבד עמד עלינו לכלותנו
אלא שבכל דור ודור עומדים עלינו לכלותינו"
"For not only one has risen up against us to annihilate us, but in every generation they rise up against us to annihilate us."

QUESTION: What misconception does the *Haggadah* seek to dispel by stating "not only one." It could have omitted this, simply stating, "In every generation they rise up...and Hashem saves us"?

ANSWER: There are many Jews who imagine that the nations of the world are our friends. They think that the only problem in Persia, for instance, was that there lived a wicked man called Haman and that the only problem during the holocaust was that there was a wicked man called Hitler ימ"ש.

Therefore the *Haggadah* says, "Strike this erroneous thought from your mind. Be aware that it is *not* that only one [wicked person] who is permeated with hatred for the Jews rises up

generation they rise up against us to annihilate us, and the Holy One, blessed is He, saves us from their hand.

We put down our cups and uncover the matzah.

---

against us, and then induces the innocent masses to follow him. Rather, in every generation "they" — *the entire people* — rise up against us to annihilate us. Anti-Semitism exists everywhere, but people generally lack the courage to display it openly until a brazen individual stands at the forefront and brings this concealed hatred to the surface."

"והקדוש ברוך הוא מצילנו מידם"
"And the Holy One, blessed be He, saves us from their hand."

QUESTION: The word *"miyadam"* — "from their hand" — seems superfluous. "And G-d saves us" would be sufficient?

ANSWER: Not only does Hashem perform miracles which rescue us from annihilation, but He causes our oppressors to assist in our salvation.

In Egypt, Pharaoh ordered the drowning of the Jewish children and the enslavement of the Jewish people, anticipating that the Jews would remain there forever. Little did he know that *his own* daughter had saved Moshe (who would ultimately redeem the Jews) and had raised him in *his* palace. In the days of Achashveirosh, when Haman planned the destruction of the Jewish people, it was *he* who advised the killing of Vashti, thus making it possible for Esther to become Queen. Hence, Hashem's method of saving us is *"miyadam"* — through the work of *their* hands.

(הגש"פ מגדל עדר החדש בפי' גבול בנימין)

Alternatively, Hashem's salvation is extremely great. Not only does He save us when our enemies plot against us, but even if we are already in their hands and it seems as though our doom is sealed, miraculously He releases us from their grasp.

(שי לחגים ולמועדים בשם ר' קלונימוס-קלמן האדמו"ר מפיאסצנא, ה.י.ד., בגיטו ורשה, תש"א)

צֵא וּלְמַד מַה־בִּקֵּשׁ לָבָן הָאֲרַמִי לַעֲשׂוֹת
לְיַעֲקֹב אָבִינוּ. שֶׁפַּרְעֹה לֹא גָזַר אֶלָּא עַל הַזְּכָרִים

"Go out and learn." — "צא ולמד"

QUESTION: Why does the piece following *"Vehi she'amdah"* —
"This is what has stood" — start with the words *"Tzei ulemad"* —
"Go out and learn"?

ANSWER: As previously stated (p. 114), *"Vehi she'amdah"* —
"This is what has stood" — refers to the cup of wine — the fact that
we did not mix with the gentile world. The *Haggadah* illustrates this
principle by citing the relationship of Lavan and Yaakov, as if to say
"From this *'tzai ulemad'* — go out and learn how true it is." Yaakov
lived with Lavan and married into his family, yet Lavan, being a
gentile, hated Yaakov the Jew to the extent that he wanted to
destroy everything he possessed. This is a proof to the sad truth that
joining with the nations of the world will not change their attitude
towards the Jew nor benefit him.

(הגש"פ עם פי' חגיגת הפסח מהרב גדלי' ז"ל סילווערסטאן)

Alternatively, Pinchas was assigned by Moshe to head the war
against Midyan. When Bilaam noticed him, he performed sorcery
and flew up into the skies. Immediately Pinchas uttered His Holy
name and flew after him. When he caught him, he held onto his
head and wanted to kill him by the sword. When Bilaam pleaded
for his life, and promised that never again would he curse the
Jews, Pinchas said to him, "You are Lavan the Aramean who
wanted to destroy our father Yaakov; then you went down to
Egypt and advised Pharoah to annihilate his children. When they
left Egypt, you invited the wicked Amalek to attack them. Later
you endeavored to curse them, and when your curses were of no
avail, you advised [Balak] to cause the Jews to commit adultery,
because of which 24,000 were killed. It is impossible to let you live
anymore," and he killed him.

(תרגום יונתן בן עוזיאל במדבר ל"א:ח)

Thus, from this we can learn that "it was not only one that
wanted to destroy us," rather in every generation there is an
attempt to destroy the Jewish people and fortunately Hashem
saves us.

(של"ה)

צא Go out and learn what Lavan the Aramean wanted to do to our father, Yaakov. Pharaoh decreed only against the males,

"Go out and learn." — "צא ולמד"

QUESTION: It should have said *"bo ulemad"* — *"come and learn"*?

ANSWER: When a student is home, there are many distractions which make it difficult for him to study properly. To really succeed in learning a prerequisite is *"tzei"* — "go out" — i.e. leave your home, leave your environment, leave the amenities to which you are accustomed, and immerse yourself in the study of Torah.

(ר׳ אהרן זצ״ל מקאארלין)

"מה בקש לבן הארמי לעשות ליעקב אבינו. שפרעה לא גזר
אלא על הזכרים ולבן בקש לעקור את הכל"

**"...what Lavan the Aramean wanted to do to our father Yaakov.
Pharaoh decreed only against the males,
but Lavan wanted to uproot everyone."**

QUESTION: Tonight we are celebrating our redemption from Egyptian bondage. Why do we minimize the evil intentions of Pharoah in contrast to Lavan?

ANSWER: On the contrary, with this we are emphasizing Hashem's unlimited love for the Jewish people and the tremendous debt we owe Him. Hashem promised that however much we would forsake the Torah and despite our being in the land of our enemies, He would not reject us nor permit our obliteration (see *Vayikra* 26:44). While this is true, it does not exclude, G-d forbid, partial elimination. Consequently, when Lavan sought to uproot everything, it was incumbent on Hashem to thwart his plans. Since Pharoah, however, decreed only against the males, and thus planned only a partial destruction of the Jewish people, Hashem's promise did not obligate Him to intervene. Nevertheless, in Egypt Hashem showed His great love for the Jewish people and prevented even a partial destruction.

(הגש״פ עם פי׳ קהלת משה מר׳ ראובן ז״ל מרגליות בשם ר׳ חיים זצ״ל מאטיניא ועי׳ הגש״פ חזון עובדיה)

וְלָבָן בִּקֵּשׁ לַעֲקֹר אֶת־הַכֹּל. שֶׁנֶּאֱמַר אֲרַמִּי אֹבֵד אָבִי וַיֵּרֶד מִצְרַיְמָה וַיָּגָר שָׁם בִּמְתֵי מְעָט וַיְהִי שָׁם לְגוֹי גָּדוֹל עָצוּם וָרָב:

"ולבן בקש לעקור את הכל"
"But Lavan wanted to uproot everyone."

QUESTION: Where do we find that this was Lavan's intention?

ANSWER: According to *halachah* (*Gittin* 64a) if one sends a *shaliach* — representative — to betroth a wife for him, and the representative dies before returning, the sender is forbidden to marry any woman out of concern that she may be a relative to the one the *shaliach* chose. Eliezer was sent as a representative to betroth a wife for Yitzchak. During the meal Lavan put poison in Eliezer's food and miraculously Betuel ended up eating it. Had his vile plan been realized, Eliezer would have died and Yitzchak would have been unable to marry anyone, making it impossible for Yaakov to be born. Thus, there would have been no Jewish nation.

(פון אונזער אלטען אוצר ועי' בהגש"פ חזון עובדיה, ע' רפ"ג)

* * *

Alternatively, when Yaakov and his family fled the house of Lavan, Lavan and his contingency chased after them intending to kill him. Fortunately, Hashem interceded and instructed him not to harm Yaakov. In their dialogue, Lavan said to Yaakov, "The daughters are my daughters, the children are my children, the flock is my flock, and all that you see is mine" (*Bereishit* 31:43). With this he was alluding that he was not happy with the way Yaakov was bringing up his family, and he told him "Regardless of the way you conduct your life, I want you to know that the children belong to me, and they should be brought up according to the standards of contemporary society." Likewise, with his claim "The flock is my flock and all that you see is mine" he meant, "the world — business — is mine and your Torah laws are incompatible with it. To succeed one must forsake Torah ethics and conduct business according to my approach."

If Lavan had had his way, he would have estranged Yaakov's family from Torah and *mitzvot*, which ultimately would have led to their complete annihilation both spiritually and physically as members of the Jewish people.

(לקוטי שיחות ח"ג)

but Lavan wanted to uproot all, as it is said:[1] **"An Aramean sought to destroy my father, and he went down to Egypt and sojourned there with a small number of people, and he became a nation there, great, powerful, and numerous."**

1. *Devarim* 26:5.

"ארמי אבד אבי וירד מצרימה"
"An Aramean [Lavan] sought to destroy my father [Yaakov]. And he went down to Egypt."

QUESTION: How did Lavan's evil intentions cause Yaakov to go down to Egypt?

ANSWER: When Yaakov came to Lavan's home, he clearly stated that he would work for him seven years so that he could marry Rachel, his younger daughter. Lavan fooled him and gave him Leah instead. After seven days of celebration for his marriage with Leah, he was given Rachel as wife and had to work an additional seven years.

Leah was the first to bear children, and afterwards Rachel gave birth to Yosef. Yaakov's preferential treatment of Yosef evoked the brothers' envy, and consequently they sold him, bringing about his slavery in Egypt. Eventually Yoseph rose to the position of viceroy to Pharoah and this set the stage for Yaakov's descent to Egypt.

Had Lavan dealt honestly with Yaakov, giving him Rachel immediately, he would not have married Leah at all. Rachel would have been the mother of all his children, and Yosef would have been the firstborn. Hence, his younger siblings would have had great respect for him, and no jealousy whatsoever would have prevailed.

(תורת משה)

* * *

"ארמי אבד אבי"
"An Aramean [Lavan] sought to destroy my father [Yaakov]."

QUESTION: Why does it say *"Arami oveid avi"* — "An Aramean [sought to] *destroys* my father" — in present tense, and not *"destroyed* my father" — in past tense?

ANSWER: The *pasuk* is in present tense to indicate that this is not a matter of history. Rather, the nations oppression of the Jewish people is ongoing and constant.

וַיֵּרֶד מִצְרַיְמָה אָנוּס עַל פִּי הַדִּבּוּר. וַיָּגָר שָׁם מְלַמֵּד
שֶׁלֹּא יָרַד יַעֲקֹב אָבִינוּ לְהִשְׁתַּקֵּעַ בְּמִצְרַיִם אֶלָּא לָגוּר
שָׁם. שֶׁנֶּאֱמַר וַיֹּאמְרוּ אֶל פַּרְעֹה לָגוּר בָּאָרֶץ בָּאנוּ כִּי
אֵין מִרְעֶה לַצֹּאן אֲשֶׁר לַעֲבָדֶיךָ כִּי כָבֵד הָרָעָב בְּאֶרֶץ
כְּנָעַן וְעַתָּה יֵשְׁבוּ נָא עֲבָדֶיךָ בְּאֶרֶץ גֹּשֶׁן:

"וירד מצרימה"
"And he went down to Egypt."

QUESTION: It should have said *"leMitzraim"*?

ANSWER: The word *"Mitzraimah"* (מצרימה) has the numerical value of three hundred and eighty-five, which is the same numerical value as the word *"Shechinah"* (שכינה) — "Divine Presence." This alludes to Hashem's promise to Yaakov *"Anochi eireid imcha Mitzraimah"* — "I shall descend with you to Egypt" (*Bereishit* 46:4).

(הגש״פ מוצל מאש - בית אהרן - בפי׳ פאר אהרן)

"אנוס על פי הדבור"
"Compelled by Divine decree."

QUESTION: The literal translation of *"dibur"* is "word." What word compelled the Egyptian bondage?

ANSWER: The *Gemara* (*Nedarim* 32a) says that when Hashem promised Avraham that he would inherit *Eretz Yisrael*, he asked, *"bamah eida"* — "whereby shall I know [that I am to inherit it]" (*Bereishit* 15:8). For questioning His promise, Avraham was punished that his children were enslaved by the Egyptians for 210 years. Thus, the *word* which compelled the Jews to go to Egypt was the word *"bamah"* (במה).

(שארית מנחם מר׳ מנחם מענדל זצ״ל האגער, וישוואָ וויזניץ)

"ויאמרו אל פרעה לגור בארץ באנו כי אין מרעה לצאן
אשר לעבדיך כי כבד הרעב בארץ כנען"
"And they said to Pharaoh: 'We have come to sojourn in the land; for there is no grazing for your servants' flocks, for the famine is severe in the land of Canaan.' "

QUESTION: Why did they not tell him that they came to Egypt because they had no food to eat *themselves?*

וירד *"And he went down to Egypt"* — compelled by Divine decree. *"And sojourned there"* — this teaches that our father Yaakov did not go down to Egypt with the intention of settling there, but merely to live there temporarily, as it is said:[1] "And they (Yaakov's sons) told Pharaoh: 'We have come to sojourn in the land, for there is no pasture for the flocks of your servants, for the famine is severe in the land of Canaan, and now, please let your servants dwell in the land of Goshen.'"

1. *Bereishit* 47:4.

ANSWER: The brothers wanted to convey to Pharaoh how severe the famine was in Canaan. They told him: "Grass is usually reserved for the flock. People consume fruits and vegetables. The situation is so critical in Canaan that people are eating grass and there is no grazing left for the animals."

(רבינו בחיי)

"ועתה ישבו נא עבדיך בארץ גשן"
"Now, please let your servants dwell in the land of Goshen."

QUESTION: Why did the brothers make a request for Goshen specifically?

ANSWER: When Avraham came to Egypt, Pharoah took Sarah not just as a concubine, but for a wife. Therefore, he gave her a *ketubah* stating that in the event she would survive him, all his possessions and everything he owned would be hers for the remainder of her life. In addition, he unconditionally gave her the land of Goshen to be hers forever. Since the land belonged to our matriarch Sarah, the brothers expressed the wish to live there.

(פרקי דרבי אליעזר פכ"ו)

* * *

Incidentally, the episode of Pharoah and Sarah took place on the night of *Pesach*. The Torah (*Bereishit* 12:17) relates that Hashem afflicted Pharoah along with his household with *"nega'im gedolim"* — "severe plagues." These plagues were ten in number, alluding that in years to come his descendants, too, would be struck with ten plagues for causing the Jewish people to suffer.

In the words *"nega'im gedolim"*(נגעים גדלים) the usual *"vav"* in the word *"gedolim"* (גדולים) is eliminated, leaving a total of ten letters and alluding to the ten plagues administered by the angel.

(ביאור הרד"ל על פרקי דר"א)

בִּמְתֵי מְעָט כְּמָה שֶׁנֶּאֱמַר בְּשִׁבְעִים נֶפֶשׁ יָרְדוּ אֲבֹתֶיךָ מִצְרָיְמָה וְעַתָּה שָׂמְךָ יְהֹוָה אֱלֹהֶיךָ כְּכוֹכְבֵי הַשָּׁמַיִם לָרֹב: וַיְהִי שָׁם לְגוֹי מְלַמֵּד שֶׁהָיוּ יִשְׂרָאֵל מְצֻיָּנִים שָׁם:

גָּדוֹל עָצוּם כְּמָה שֶׁנֶּאֱמַר וּבְנֵי יִשְׂרָאֵל פָּרוּ וַיִּשְׁרְצוּ

"בשבעים נפש ירדו אבתיך מצרימה"
"With seventy souls your fathers went down to Egypt."

QUESTION: Since *"shivim"* is plural, it should have said *"nefashot"*?

ANSWER: The *Midrash Rabbah* (*Vayikra* 4:6) relates that Rabbi Yehoshua ben Korcha once explained to a heathen the difference between the Jewish nation and the nations of the world is that "In the case of Eisav six souls are mentioned in Torah, and yet the word used of them in Torah is *'nefashot'* — 'souls' — in the plural, as it is written, 'And Eisav took his wives, and his sons, and his daughters, and all the *souls* of his house' (*Bereishit* 36:4).

In Yaakov's family, on the other hand, there were seventy souls, and yet the word used for them in Torah is *"nefesh"* — 'soul' — in the singular, as it is written, 'And all the *nefesh* who emerged from the loins of Yaakov' were seventy *Nefesh* (*Shemot* 1:5). The reason is that Eisav and his family worshipped many different deities while all in Yaakov's family worshipped only one G-d."

Based on this, it could be said that with the expression *nefesh* — soul — in singular, the *pasuk* is indicating that the source of the Jewish people's strength, which helped them endure the Egyptian bondage, was the fact that they were *"nefesh"* — united as one among themselves — and they all worshipped the One and Only — Hashem.

(ויקרא רבה ד:ו - עי' מתנת כהונה)

* * *

Alternatively, the Hebrew word *"nefesh"* (נפש) has the numerical value of 430. It alludes to the four hundred and thirty years of the Egyptian bondage and the sojourning of Avraham and his offspring, the time which elapsed after Hashem told him of the decree at the *Brit bein Habetarim*—the Covenant Between the Parts (see *Shemot* 12:41, Rashi).

במתי *"With a small number of people"* — as it is said:[1] "With seventy individuals your fathers went down to Egypt, and now *Adonai,* your God, has made you as numerous as the stars of heaven." *"And he became there a nation"* — this teaches that [the Jews] were distinctive there.

"Great, powerful" — as it is said:[2] "And the Children of Israel were fruitful and increased abundantly and multiplied,

1. *Devarim* 10:22.   2. *Shemot* 1:7.

"ועתה שמך ה' אלקיך ככוכבי השמים לרב"
"And now G-d, your G-d, has made you as numerous as the stars of heaven."

QUESTION: In what ways are the Jewish people like stars?

ANSWER: From earth, the stars appear very small. However, in heaven, the stars are actually immense. Hashem assured Avraham that although on earth the nations of the world consider the Jewish people "very small" (of minor significance), in reality, up in heaven they are of primary importance. (דברי שאול)

* * *

The stars twinkle in the high heavens. By their light, even one who walks in the darkness of night will not stumble. Every Jew, man or woman, possess enough moral and spiritual light to influence friends and acquaintances and bring them out of the darkness into the light. (היום יום, ה' חשון)

* * *

When one stands on the ground and looks up to the sky, the stars appear to be minute specks. In reality the stars are larger than the earth. As we approach them, we can begin to appreciate their size and beauty.

The same is true of a Jew. Although, he may superficially appear to be insignificant, as one becomes closer and gets to know more about him, one can perceive the great and beautiful *"Pintele Yid"* (spark of Judaism) within him. (בעש"ט)

"ובני ישראל פרו וישרצו"
"And the Children of Israel were fruitful, and increased abundantly."

QUESTION: According to the *Midrash Rabbah* (*Shemot* 1:8) they bore six children at each birth (Rashi). Why did Hashem cause such an unusual phenomenon?

וַיִּרְבּוּ וַיַּעַצְמוּ בִּמְאֹד מְאֹד וַתִּמָּלֵא הָאָרֶץ אֹתָם: וָרַב
כְּמָה שֶׁנֶּאֱמַר וָאֶעֱבֹר עָלַיִךְ וָאֶרְאֵךְ מִתְבּוֹסֶסֶת בְּדָמָיִךְ
וָאֹמַר לָךְ בְּדָמַיִךְ חֲיִי וָאֹמַר לָךְ בְּדָמַיִךְ חֲיִי: רְבָבָה
כְּצֶמַח הַשָּׂדֶה נְתַתִּיךְ וַתִּרְבִּי וַתִּגְדְּלִי וַתָּבֹאִי בַּעֲדִי
עֲדָיִים שָׁדַיִם נָכֹנוּ וּשְׂעָרֵךְ צִמֵּחַ וְאַתְּ עֵרֹם וְעֶרְיָה:

ANSWER: According to the *Yalkut*, the Jews were enslaved in Egypt for a total of *one hour*. This enigmatic statement is explained as follows:

In Psalms (90:4) it is stated, "A thousand years in your eyes are like the day that has passed and a watch of the night." According to an opinion in the *Gemara* (*Berachot* 3a), the night is divided into four watches (each consisting of three hours). Thus, one day and one watch — which equal fifteen hours — are one thousand years in Hashem's eyes. Consequently, to Hashem, 66 years and 8 months are one hour (1000 years ÷ 15 = 66 years and 8 months). Hence, the *Midrash* is saying that the entire Egyptian bondage lasted sixty six years and eight months.

Hashem had told Avraham that his descendants would be slaves in Egypt for a total of four hundred years. In order to lessen the years of slavery, He increased the birthrate by six fold. Thus, six times the normal population working for sixty six years and eight months is exactly equal to four hundred years of slavery (66 years and 8 months x 6 = 400 years).

(פרדס יוסף בשם ר' מאיר יחיאל הלוי זצ"ל מאסטראוואצא)

"וּבְנֵי יִשְׂרָאֵל פָּרוּ וַיִּשְׁרְצוּ...וַתִּמָּלֵא הָאָרֶץ אֹתָם"
**"The Children of Israel were fruitful and increased abundantly...
and the land became filled with them."**

QUESTION: The *Midrash* (*Shir Hashirim* 1.15:3) relates that Rebbi, Rabbi Yehudah *HaNasi*, once noticed while delivering a lecture that the congregation had become drowsy. In order to rouse them he said: "One woman in Egypt brought forth six hundred thousand children in one birth." A disciple named Rabbi Yishmael son of Rabbi Yose said to him: "Who can that have been?" He replied: "This was Yocheved, who bore Moshe, who was counted as equal to six hundred thousand of Israel."

Why did he use this particular unbelievable story to awaken them when they drowsed off during his lecture?

and they became very, very powerful and the land became filled with them." *"And numerous"* — as it is said:[1] "I passed over you and saw you wallowing in your blood and I said to you: 'Through your blood, you will live,' and I said to you: 'Through your blood you will live.' I made you as numerous as the plants of the field, and you increased and grew, and became very beautiful; [your] breasts developed and your hair sprouted, but you were naked and bare."

1. *Ezekiel* 16:6-7.

ANSWER: The episode related in the *Midrash* can be seen as a metaphor for a certain period of Jewish history. The destruction of the second *Beit Hamikdash* took place in the year 3828, and Rebbi was born approximately 50 years afterwards, becoming the leader of the fourth generation after the destruction. The Roman government oppressed the Jews bitterly, and the Jews were losing hope for the coming of *Mashiach* and the ultimate redemption. Rebbi noticed that while he was propagating Torah, the community was "falling asleep" in their faith, i.e. thinking that there would never, G-d forbid, be a *ge'ulah* — redemption — and that the *galut* is eternal.

In an effort to dispel this kind of thinking, Rebbi told his listeners that in Egypt a woman gave birth to 600,000 children. The message to his generation was "Do not despair! Our fathers in Egypt thought that they were doomed to be slaves forever and there was no hope to be redeemed. Suddenly, however, Yocheved gave birth to Moshe, who ultimately took out all the 600,000 enslaved Jews from Egypt and brought them to Sinai for the giving of the Torah — the greatest event in Jewish history. We, too, must never give up hope. The salvation of G-d can come in the wink of an eye — immediately and unexpectedly."

(מצאתי בכתבי אבי הרב שמואל פסח ז״ל באגאמילסקי)

"רבבה כצמח השדה נתתיך"
"I made you as numerous as the plants of the field."

QUESTION: Usually, to describe the large number of the Jewish people, the Torah compares them to dust of the earth or the stars of the heaven (see *Bereishit* 13:16 and 15:5). Why here are they compared to the grass of the field?

ANSWER: The nature of grass is that the more it is cut, the stronger it grows back. One of the miracles experienced in Egypt was that "As much as they would afflict it (the Jewish people), so it would increase and so it would spread out" (*Shemot* 1:12). In other words, Hashem instilled in the Jews the quality of grass, which grows stronger the more it is cut down.

(אבודרהם)

וַיָּרֵעוּ אֹתָנוּ הַמִּצְרִים וַיְעַנּוּנוּ וַיִּתְּנוּ עָלֵינוּ עֲבֹדָה
קָשָׁה: וַיָּרֵעוּ אֹתָנוּ הַמִּצְרִים כְּמָה שֶׁנֶּאֱמַר הָבָה
נִתְחַכְּמָה לוֹ פֶּן יִרְבֶּה וְהָיָה כִּי תִקְרֶאנָה מִלְחָמָה וְנוֹסַף
גַּם הוּא עַל־שֹׂנְאֵינוּ וְנִלְחַם בָּנוּ וְעָלָה מִן הָאָרֶץ:

"The Egyptians treated us badly."

QUESTION: Instead of *"vayarei'u otanu"* — which literally means "they made us bad" — it should have said *"vayarei'u lanu"* — "they treated us badly"?

ANSWER: The Jewish people are distinguished by their character traits. They are known to be merciful, bashful, and kind (*Yevamot* 79a). Under Egyptian bondage, the Jews were exposed to inhumane treatment, causing them to lose their refined character and ultimately transforming them into corrupt people. Thus, through affliction and hard labor — *"vayarei'u otanu hamitzrim"* — the Egyptians *made us* bad people.

(אלשיך)

Alternatively, the word *"vayarei'u"* (וירעו) is from the same root as *"rei'a"* (רֵעַ) — which means friend. The *Haggadah* is saying that first *vayarei'u otanu* — they became *friendly* with us — and with *"peh rach"* — "soft talk" — they induced us to help in the development of Egypt and in fact, even paid wages for the labor (see *Pesachim* 39a, Rashi). Afterwards they made us suffer by enslaving us *"befarech"* — "with vigor."

(הגש"פ קבוץ חכמים מהרב עבדאל סומך ז"ל מבגדאד)

Due to this, the herb that is used for *maror* is one which is soft and sweet when it begins growing, but in the end it is hard and bitter.

(פסחים ל"ט א' רש"י, ושו"ע הרב סי' תע"ג סעי' ל"א)

"Come, let us act cunningly with them."

QUESTION: Instead of *"lo"* — which literally means "to him" — in singular, it should have said *"lahem"* — "to them" — in plural?

ANSWER: The Egyptian bondage started after the death of all of Yaakov's sons. Levi outlived them all and passed away at the

וירעו "And the Egyptians treated us badly and they made us suffer, and they imposed harsh labor upon us."[1] *"And the Egyptians treated us badly"* — as it is said:[2] "Come, let us act cunningly with them lest they multiply, and, if there should be a war, they may join our enemies, and wage war against us and leave the land."

1. *Devarim* 26:6.   2. *Shemot* 1:10.

age of 137 (*Shemot* 6:16). Since Levi was 43 when the brothers arrived in Egypt (ibid. 2:2, Ibn Ezra), he lived in Egypt proper 94 years. Deducting this from the 210 years the Jews were in Egypt, it can be derived that the actual enslavement was 116 years. Since Moshe was 80 years old when he took the Jews out of Egypt, he was born 36 years after the death of Levi.

According to the *Midrash* (ibid. 1:20) from the beginning of the enslavement and up till the day Moshe was cast into the river, the Egyptians were thinking of ways to decimate the Jewish people. The word *"lo"* (לו) — "to him" — has the numerical value of 36, and thus, the Torah is saying that they plotted cunningly *"lo"* — for 36 years.

(פרדס יוסף, שמות)

"והיה כי תקראנה מלחמה ונוסף גם הוא אל שונאינו ונלחם בנו ועלה מן הארץ"
"If there be a war, they may join our enemies and wage war against us and leave the land."

QUESTION: Instead of fearing that the Jews would join the enemy, they should have worried that the Jews would multiply and eventually revolt against them and leave the land?

ANSWER: Pharaoh and his advisors knew that the Jews on their own would not wage war because fighting was against their nature. Even if they would have attempted it, they would have been easily defeated because, *"Hayadayim yedei Eisav"* — the use of physical strength is the character trait of Eisav and not that of the Children of Israel (see *Gittin* 57b).

On the other hand, they knew that the Jews are very intelligent and that any country in which they settle benefits immensely from their brain-power. Therefore, they were concerned that in the event of a war against them, the Jews would join their enemies, and the combination of "Jewish heads" and non-Jewish strength would definitely make the enemy victorious and allow the Jews to leave the land.

(עיטורי תורה, שמות)

וַיְעַנּוּנוּ כְּמָה שֶׁנֶּאֱמַר וַיָּשִׂימוּ עָלָיו שָׂרֵי מִסִּים לְמַעַן
עַנֹּתוֹ בְּסִבְלֹתָם וַיִּבֶן עָרֵי מִסְכְּנוֹת לְפַרְעֹה אֶת־פִּתֹם
וְאֶת־רַעַמְסֵס: וַיִּתְּנוּ עָלֵינוּ עֲבֹדָה קָשָׁה כְּמָה שֶׁנֶּאֱמַר
וַיַּעֲבִדוּ מִצְרַיִם אֶת־בְּנֵי יִשְׂרָאֵל בְּפָרֶךְ: וַיְמָרְרוּ אֶת־
חַיֵּיהֶם בַּעֲבֹדָה קָשָׁה בְּחֹמֶר וּבִלְבֵנִים וּבְכָל־עֲבֹדָה
בַּשָּׂדֶה אֵת כָּל־עֲבֹדָתָם אֲשֶׁר עָבְדוּ בָהֶם בְּפָרֶךְ:

"And they made us suffer." — "וַיְעַנּוּנוּ"

QUESTION: As an introduction to the enslavement of the Jewish people in Egypt, the Torah states, "A new king arose over Egypt who did not know Yosef" (*Shemot* 1:8). How could even a new ruler be ignorant of Yosef and his great services to Egypt?

ANSWER: Yosef was indeed one of the most popular figures and well known by everybody for his accomplishments on behalf of the Egyptian people. The Torah does not mean that the new king did not know of the existence of such a person as Yosef in Egyptian history, but that he did not pay attention to the lessons that can be learned from Yosef.

It was destined by Hashem that Yosef become a ruler in Egypt. The attempts of his brothers to hurt him and Potifar's endeavors to eliminate him through incarceration turned out to his good and benefit, and as a result of these events Yosef rose to glory. Had the new king carefully studied the story of Yosef, he would have realized that "Many thoughts are in man's heart, but it is the counsel of Hashem that prevails" (Proverbs 19:21). He then would not have tried to harm and annihilate the Jewish people, for Hashem promised that he would ultimately come to their rescue and redeem them.

(אמרי אש)

"They set taskmasters over him." — "וישימו עליו שרי מסים"

QUESTION: In lieu of *"alav"* — "over him" — in the singular, it should have said *"aleihem"* — "over them" — in the plural?

ANSWER: According to the *Gemara* (*Sotah* 11a) *"alav"* — "over him" — refers to Pharaoh. In the beginning, the Jews refused to permit the Egyptians to enslave them, arguing that it was beneath their dignity to do such arduous labor. In order to trick the Jews into working, Pharaoh too, began to work. The Egyptians told the Jews, "You have no excuse not to work. If it is not below King Pharaoh's dignity to do work, you can surely do so."

* * *

ויענונו *"And they made us suffer"* — as it is said:[1] "They placed taskmasters over them in order to oppress them with their burdens, and they built storage cities for Pharaoh, Pitom and Raamseis." *"And they imposed harsh labor upon us"* — as it is said:[2] "And the Egyptians made the Children of Israel to serve with rigor. They embittered their lives with harsh labor, with mortar and bricks, as well as with all kinds of labor of the field; toil which they made them serve was with rigor."

1. *Shemot* 1:11. 2. *Shemot* 1:13-14.

There is no limit to how low the nations of the world will stoop in order to oppress the Jews. For instance, it is incumbent upon a king to conduct himself majestically at all times in order to maintain the respect and reverence due to his position. Nevertheless, when it came to torturing the Jews, the people abandoned their respect for the King and put him to work. The king, too, did not care about maintaining his stature and self-esteem, and consented to engage in menial labor.

"וימררו את חייהם"
"And they embittered their lives."

QUESTION: Why in the Torah (*Shemot* 1:13) do the words *"va-yemararu et chayeihem"* have a cantillation ("trope") of *kadma ve'azla?*

ANSWER: When Hashem spoke to Avraham, He told him that the Jewish people would be in Egypt for a period of 400 years. Actually, they lived in Egypt only 210 years. One reason for the Jews' departure 190 years early is that the Egyptians made them work extremely hard. Therefore, in 210 years they had endured the equivalent of 400 years of normal suffering.

The *"trope"* of *kadma ve'azla* expresses this thought: The word *"kadma"* means to rise early, and the word *"azla"* means to leave. The Torah is telling us that they rose and left Egypt earlier than the appointed 400 years because *"vayemararu et chayeihem"* — "they made their lives extremely bitter" — to the extent that 210 years were the equivalent of 400 years.

It is interesting to note that the numerical value of the words *"kadma ve'azla"* (קדמא ואזלא) is 190, the number of years deducted from the original 400.

(קול אליהו - זכרון ישראל מר' ישראל ז"ל קעסלער)

וַנִּצְעַק אֶל־יְהֹוָה אֱלֹהֵי אֲבֹתֵינוּ וַיִּשְׁמַע יְהֹוָה
אֶת קֹלֵנוּ וַיַּרְא אֶת־עָנְיֵנוּ וְאֶת־עֲמָלֵנוּ וְאֶת־
לַחֲצֵנוּ: וַנִּצְעַק אֶל־יְהֹוָה אֱלֹהֵי אֲבֹתֵינוּ כְּמָה
שֶּׁנֶּאֱמַר וַיְהִי בַיָּמִים הָרַבִּים הָהֵם וַיָּמָת מֶלֶךְ
מִצְרַיִם וַיֵּאָנְחוּ בְנֵי יִשְׂרָאֵל מִן הָעֲבֹדָה וַיִּזְעָקוּ
וַתַּעַל שַׁוְעָתָם אֶל־הָאֱלֹהִים מִן הָעֲבֹדָה:
וַיִּשְׁמַע יְהֹוָה אֶת־קוֹלֵנוּ כְּמָה שֶׁנֶּאֱמַר וַיִּשְׁמַע
אֱלֹהִים אֶת־נַאֲקָתָם וַיִּזְכֹּר אֱלֹהִים אֶת־בְּרִיתוֹ אֶת־
אַבְרָהָם אֶת־יִצְחָק וְאֶת־יַעֲקֹב:

"ונצעק אל ה' אלקי אבותינו וישמע ה' את קולינו"
**"And we cried out to G-d, the G-d of our fathers,
and G-d heard our voice."**

QUESTION: Why in regard to our crying out does it say "G-d,
the G-d of our fathers" while in regard to His hearing it says only,
"And G-d heard," without mentioning "the G-d of our fathers"?

ANSWER: The *Gemara* (*Berachot* 10b) says, "If a person asks in his
prayers that they be answered because of his own merit, the fulfillment of his prayers is made in the merit of others. But if he prays to
be helped in the merit of others (his forbears or Hashem's mercy),
the fulfillment of his prayers is made dependent upon his merit."

When the Jews in Egypt turned to Hashem, they considered
themselves very insignificant and, thus, prayed to be helped in the
merit of their fathers. However, Hashem recognized their
greatness and responded to their plea in their own merit.

(הגש"פ עם פי' ילקוט שמעוני)

"וימת מלך מצרים ויאנחו בני ישראל מן העבדה ויזעקו
ותעל שועתם אל האלקים מן העבדה"
**"And the king of Egypt died, and the Jewish people groaned
from the work, and their cry went up to G-d from the work."**

QUESTION: Instead of *"min ha'avodah"* — "from the work" —
it should read *"al ha'avodah"* — "because of the work"? Moreover,
why didn't the Jews cry before the king died?

ונצעק "And we cried out to *Adonai*, the God of our fathers, and *Adonai* heard our voice, He saw our suffering, our difficult labor, and our oppression."[1] *"And we cried out to Adonai, the God of our fathers* — as it is said:[2] "And it came to pass after those many days, that the king of Egypt died, and the Children of Israel groaned from the work, and they cried out, and their outcry went up to God from the work."

וישמע *"And Adonai heard our voice"* — as it is said:[3] "And God heard their cries, and God remembered His covenant with Avraham, Yitzchak, and Yaakov."

1. *Devarim* 26:7. 2. *Shemot* 2:23. 3. *Shemot* 2:24.

ANSWER: The Egyptians knew very well that if the Jews would have cried to Hashem, He would have answered their prayers and free them from slavery. Therefore, they made the Jews work extremely hard, and whenever a supervisor would notice a Jew crying, he would beat him and yell, "There is no time for crying; get back to your work!"

When Pharaoh died, all of Egypt sadly attended his funeral. The Egyptians, not wanting productivity to suffer, did not let their slaves attend. During the funeral, *while working,* the Jews cried bitterly about their enslavement. The supervisors were unable to stop them because they claimed they were mourning their wonderful "dearly departed" king.

Hashem heard the cries of the "pretend-mourners," which came to Him *min ha'avodah — from* the work — and He knew that they were not lamenting the king's death, but their slavery.

(שער בת רבים)

וַיַּרְא אֶת־עָנְיֵנוּ זוֹ פְּרִישׁוּת דֶּרֶךְ אֶרֶץ כְּמָה שֶׁנֶּאֱמַר וַיַּרְא אֱלֹהִים אֶת־בְּנֵי יִשְׂרָאֵל וַיֵּדַע אֱלֹהִים:

וְאֶת־עֲמָלֵנוּ אֵלּוּ הַבָּנִים כְּמָה שֶׁנֶּאֱמַר כָּל הַבֵּן

"ואת עמלינו אלו הבנים שנאמר כל הבן הילוד היאורה תשליכוהו"
"'And our difficult labor,' this refers to the children as it is said, 'Every boy that is born you shall throw into the river.'"

QUESTION: How is it proven from this *pasuk* that they worked hard?

ANSWER: Unlike all other instances of verses introduced by the words *"kemah shene'emar"* — "as it is said" — in the *Haggadah*, this one is not a proof to the preceding statement (that *amaleinu* refers to the children). It merely wants to show that there was an agonizing problem concerning their children.

From the fact that no proof is needed that *"amaleinu"* — "difficult labor" — means children we can learn that the *Haggadah* considers it obvious that to raise or educate children properly, parents or teachers must work laboriously. It is not something that just happens by osmosis, but through sweat and toil. If parents make the requisite effort, then their parenting will be crowned with success and they will be rewarded with much *Yiddish nachas*.

(הגש"פ עם לקוטי טעמים, מנהגים וביאורים)

"כל הבן הילוד היארה תשליכוהו"
"Every boy that is born, you shall throw into the river."

QUESTION: "Every boy" includes the Egyptian male infants (*Shemot* 1:22, Rashi). What did Pharoah have against the Egyptian male infants?

וירא **"And He saw our suffering"** — this refers to the disruption of family life, as it is said:[1] "And God saw the Children of Israel and God took note."

ואת **"And our difficult labor"** — this refers to the children, as it is said:[2] "Every boy that is born

1. *Shemot* 2:25. 2. *Shemot* 1:22.

ANSWER: The Jewish midwives Shifra and Puah did not obey Pharaoh's original order to kill the Jewish children. Pharaoh summoned them and asked, "The Jews have a rule — '*dinah demalchuta dinah*' — 'the law of the government is binding' — why are you not obeying my order?" The midwives told Pharaoh that this principle applies only to a law for *all* the residents of the land. However, since "the Hebrew women are unlike the Egyptian women" — i.e. the law pertains only to the Hebrew women and not the Egyptian (ibid. 1:19) — they were not obligated to observe it (see *Choshen Mishpat* 369:8).

Pharaoh, who was eager for the death of the Jewish boys, then issued a decree that *all* newborn boys, including the Egyptian, be killed. Thus, the Jews would have to obey since "the law of the government is binding."

(פנינים יקרים על שמות בשם שב שמעתתא מקצוה"ח)

"וכל הבת תחיון"
"And every daughter you shall keep alive."

QUESTION: Pharaoh's sole concern was for all the boys to be cast into the river, while the fate of the girls did not seem to interest him. Why did he add, "Every daughter you shall keep alive"?

ANSWER: The word *"techayun"* literally means "you shall give them life — i.e. you shall be the actual source of their life." Pharaoh ordered the Egyptians to cast Jewish children into the river to cause their physical death. The same Egyptians were also told by Pharaoh that those children who would remain physically alive (i.e., the girls) were to be *given life* by them, that is, assimilated and totally raised in the Egyptian way of life in order to exterminate their Jewish souls.

הַיִּלּוֹד הַיְאֹרָה תַּשְׁלִיכֻהוּ וְכָל־הַבַּת תְּחַיּוּן: וְאֶת־
לַחֲצֵנוּ זֶה הַדְּחַק כְּמָה שֶׁנֶּאֱמַר וְגַם רָאִיתִי אֶת־
הַלַּחַץ אֲשֶׁר מִצְרַיִם לוֹחֲצִים אֹתָם:

This explains the difference in the command to the Jewish midwives and the Egyptians respectively: The Jewish midwives were simply told to leave the girls alone, "If it be a girl *vechayah* — let her live" (1:16). Pharaoh hoped that by telling them to let the girls live, it would be easier for him to persuade them to carry out his order to kill the boys. However, to the Egyptians he said "*techayun*," not just to let the Jewish girls live, but to "give them life," i.e. to make sure to assimilate them into Egyptian culture.

The Torah cites both decrees together in the same *pasuk* to indicate that "Every daughter you shall keep alive" (i.e. give them life), is a decree equivalent in its harshness and even surpassing the decree regarding the boys, "Every son that is born you shall cast into the river." To destroy the soul is equal to the killing the body, and indeed even worse — for spiritual death far surpasses physical death.

(לקוטי שיחות ח"א)

"ואת לחצנו זה הדחק כמה שנאמר וגם ראיתי את הלחץ אשר מצרים לוחצים אתם"
"'And our oppression' this refers to the pressure, as it is said, 'I have also seen the oppression with which the Egyptians oppress them.'"

QUESTION: What exactly was the pressure they had to contend with?

ANSWER: When Yaakov and his family arrived in Egypt, they asked for permission to live in Goshen. Considering the size of their family at that time, the land was spacious and comfortable. In the course of years, not only did the families enlarge, but they were giving birth to sextuplets. Though they needed more space and pleaded for it, the Egyptians denied their requests and forced them to live in their old, cramped living quarters.

(רבינו בחיי)

you shall throw into the river, and every girl you shall keep alive." *"And our oppression"* — this refers to the pressure, as it is said:[1] "I have also seen the oppression with which the Egyptians oppress them."

1. *Shemot* 3:9.

"וירא את ענינו...ואת עמלנו...ואת לחצנו"

**"And He saw our suffering...our labor...
and our oppression."**

QUESTION: *"Anyeinu"* refers to *"perishut derech eretz"* — "disruption of family life." *"Amaleinu"* refers to *"banim"* — "the children" — and *"lachatzeinu"* refers to *"dechak"* — "the pressure." Why did Hashem resolve to redeem the Jewish people from Egyptian bondage because of these three things in particular?

ANSWER: Originally Hashem had told Avraham that his children would be in Egyptian servitude for four hundred years. In reality, however, they were there for only two hundred and ten years. Since Hashem does not change His mind, the early departure must have been due to the Jews' accomplishing in only 210 years what is normally achieved in 400 years. Here are some possible explanations for this productivity: 1) They worked day and night. 2) They were blessed with very large families so that there was extra manpower. 3) The Egyptians worked them so hard that they accomplished the equivalent of four hundred years of slavery in this short period.

This passage is referring to the above-mentioned: when Hashem saw the suffering caused by *"perishut derech eretz"* — the disruption of family life because of working nights — and *"amaleinu"* — the many children that were born and slaved — and *"lachatzeinu"* — the unusual oppression they suffered — He decided the time was up for them to be in Egypt.

(של"ה, חנוכת התורה)

וַיּוֹצִאֵנוּ יְהוָֹה מִמִּצְרַיִם בְּיָד חֲזָקָה וּבִזְרֹעַ נְטוּיָה וּבְמֹרָא גָּדוֹל וּבְאֹתוֹת וּבְמֹפְתִים: וַיּוֹצִאֵנוּ יְהוָֹה מִמִּצְרַיִם לֹא עַל יְדֵי מַלְאָךְ וְלֹא עַל יְדֵי שָׂרָף וְלֹא עַל יְדֵי שָׁלִיחַ אֶלָּא הַקָּדוֹשׁ בָּרוּךְ הוּא בִּכְבוֹדוֹ וּבְעַצְמוֹ. שֶׁנֶּאֱמַר וְעָבַרְתִּי בְאֶרֶץ מִצְרַיִם בַּלַּיְלָה הַזֶּה וְהִכֵּיתִי כָל־בְּכוֹר בְּאֶרֶץ מִצְרַיִם מֵאָדָם וְעַד בְּהֵמָה וּבְכָל־אֱלֹהֵי מִצְרַיִם אֶעֱשֶׂה שְׁפָטִים אֲנִי יְהוָֹה: וְעָבַרְתִּי בְאֶרֶץ מִצְרַיִם אֲנִי וְלֹא מַלְאָךְ. וְהִכֵּיתִי כָל בְּכוֹר בְּאֶרֶץ מִצְרַיִם אֲנִי וְלֹא שָׂרָף. וּבְכָל אֱלֹהֵי מִצְרַיִם אֶעֱשֶׂה שְׁפָטִים אֲנִי וְלֹא הַשָּׁלִיחַ. אֲנִי יְהוָֹה. אֲנִי הוּא וְלֹא אַחֵר:

והכתי כל בכור בארץ מצרים אני ולא שרף
"I will slay every firstborn in the land of Egypt,
I and not a seraph."

QUESTION: Moshe told the Jewish people that "Hashem will pass through to smite Egypt...and He will not permit the destroyer to enter your homes to smite" (*Shemot* 12:23). Since Hashem Himself and not an agent carried out the plague of killing the firstborn, who is "the destroyer"?

ANSWER: A few million Jews lived in Egypt. In such a populace, it is statistically normal that some people die each day. If the *Malach Hamavet* (Angel of Death) had killed a Jew during the night of the plague of the firstborn, Pharaoh would not have agreed that a miracle had taken place. He would have claimed that there had been an epidemic which claimed Egyptians and

ויוציאנו "And *Adonai* brought us out of Egypt with a strong hand, with an outstretched arm, with great manifestations, and with signs and wonders."[1] *"And Adonai brought us out of Egypt"* — not through an angel, not through a seraph, not through a messenger, but the Holy One, blessed be He, in His glory and by Himself, as it is said:[2] "And I will pass through the land of Egypt on that night and I will slay every firstborn in the land of Egypt, from man to beast, and against all the gods of Egypt I shall execute judgments, I am *Adonai*." *"And I will pass through the land of Egypt,"* — I and not an angel; *"And I will slay every firstborn,"* — I and not a seraph; *"And against all the gods of Egypt, I shall execute judgments"* — I and not the messenger; *"I am Adonai,"* — it is *I* and no other.

1. *Devarim* 26:8. 2. *Shemot* 12:12.

Jews alike. Therefore, Moshe told them that on that night Hashem will not permit "the destroyer" *(Malach Hamavet)* to kill a single Jew.

(הגר"א)

"אני ולא מלאך...אני ולא שרף...אני ולא השליח"
"I and not an angel...I and not a seraph...
I and not the messenger."

QUESTION: Since it says *"malach"* and *"saraf,"* it should say *"shaliach"* and not *"hashaliach"*?

ANSWER: The first letters of the words *"malach"* (מלאך), *"saraf"* (שרף), and *"hashaliach"* (השליח) spell the name Moshe (משה). The *Haggadah* is emphasizing that what happened in Egypt on the night of the redemption — the smiting of the firstborn and the melting down of their idols — was all the work of Hashem Himself and not to be mistakenly regarded as the action of a human being — Moshe.

בְּיָד חֲזָקָה זֶה הַדֶּבֶר כְּמָה שֶׁנֶּאֱמַר הִנֵּה יַד יְהֹוָה הוֹיָה בְּמִקְנְךָ אֲשֶׁר בַּשָּׂדֶה בַּסּוּסִים בַּחֲמֹרִים בַּגְּמַלִּים בַּבָּקָר וּבַצֹּאן דֶּבֶר כָּבֵד מְאֹד: וּבִזְרֹעַ נְטוּיָה זוֹ הַחֶרֶב כְּמָה שֶׁנֶּאֱמַר וְחַרְבּוֹ שְׁלוּפָה בְּיָדוֹ נְטוּיָה עַל יְרוּשָׁלָיִם. וּבְמֹרָא גָדֹל זֶה גִּלּוּי שְׁכִינָה כְּמָה שֶׁנֶּאֱמַר אוֹ הֲנִסָּה אֱלֹהִים לָבֹא לָקַחַת לוֹ גוֹי מִקֶּרֶב גּוֹי בְּמַסֹּת בְּאֹתֹת וּבְמוֹפְתִים וּבְמִלְחָמָה וּבְיָד חֲזָקָה וּבִזְרֹעַ נְטוּיָה וּבְמוֹרָאִים גְּדוֹלִים כְּכֹל אֲשֶׁר עָשָׂה לָכֶם יְהֹוָה אֱלֹהֵיכֶם בְּמִצְרַיִם לְעֵינֶיךָ:

"ביד חזקה זה הדבר"
"With a strong hand — this refers to the pestilence."

QUESTION: Why does the plague of *dever* — pestilence — particularly emphasize the "strong hand"?

ANSWER: Witnessing the plagues, the magicians said to Pharaoh, "This is a *finger* of G-d" (*Shemot* 8:15). *Dever* — pestilence — was the fifth of the ten plagues. Since a hand has five fingers, the Egyptians now felt the *"Yad hachazakah"* — "strong *hand*."

(הגש״פ מעשה נסים מר׳ יעקב ז״ל מליסא)

"ככל אשר עשה לכם ה' אלקיכם במצרים לעיניך"
"Like all that G-d, your G-d, did for you in Egypt before your eyes."

QUESTION: Since it says *"lachem"* — "for you" — in plural, it should have said *"le'eineichem"* — "your eyes" — in plural?

ביד *"With a strong hand"* — this refers to the pestilence, as it is said:[1] "Behold, the hand of *Adonai* will be on your livestock that are in the field, on the horses, on the donkeys, on the camels, on the herds and on the flocks, a very severe pestilence." *"And with an outstretched arm"* — this refers to the sword, as it is said:[2] "His sword was drawn in his hand, stretched out over Jerusalem." *"And with great manifestations"* — this refers to the revelation of the Divine Presence, as it is said:[3] "Has any god ever miraculously come to take for himself a nation from amidst a nation with trials, with signs, and with wonders, and with war, and with a strong hand and with an outstretched arm, and with great manifestations, like all that *Adonai* your God did for you in Egypt before your eyes?"

1. *Shemot* 9:3. 2. *I Chronicles* 21:16. 3. *Devarim* 4:34.

ANSWER: Pharoah stubbornly refused to free the Jewish people because he claimed that they were supposed to be enslaved by him for four hundred years and that one hundred and ninety years remained. The word *"le'einecha"* (לעיניך) — "before your eyes" — has the numerical value of one hundred and ninety. The *pasuk* is thus saying "No god ever tried to take for himself a nation from the midst of another nation, like your G-d did for you in Egypt, and thereby spare you *'le'einecha'* — one hundred and ninety years of enslavement."

(הגש"פ קבוץ חכמים מרב עבדאל סומך ז"ל מבגדאד)

וּבְאֹתוֹת זֶה הַמַּטֶּה כְּמָה שֶׁנֶּאֱמַר וְאֶת־
הַמַּטֶּה הַזֶּה תִּקַּח בְּיָדֶךָ אֲשֶׁר תַּעֲשֶׂה־בּוֹ אֶת־
הָאֹתֹת: וּבְמוֹפְתִים זֶה הַדָּם כְּמָה שֶׁנֶּאֱמַר
וְנָתַתִּי מוֹפְתִים בַּשָּׁמַיִם וּבָאָרֶץ:

"ובאתות זה המטה"
"And with signs — this refers to the staff."

QUESTION: From where did Moshe get the *"mateh"* — "staff"?

ANSWER: This staff was one of the ten things which were created on *erev Shabbat* at twilight (*Pirkei Avot*, 5:6). There were Hebrew letters engraved on it which were an acronym for the ten plagues. It was given to Adam when he was in *Gan Eden,* and he passed it on to Chanoch. Chanoch gave it to Noach, who in turn gave it to Avraham. Avraham passed it along to Yitzchak, and Yitzchak gave it to Yaakov, who brought it with him to Egypt and gave it to Yosef. When Yosef died, it was put in Pharoah's palace. Yitro, who was one of Pharoah's three advisers, saw it and desired it very much. He took it and planted it in his garden. No one was able to remove it from there until Moshe came and stretched out his hand and took it. When Yitro saw this he was convinced that Moshe would be the one to redeem the Jewish people from Egypt, and he gave him his daughter Tziporah as a wife.

(פרקי דר' אליעזר פ"מ)

"ובאתות זה המטה"
"And with signs, this refers to the staff."

QUESTION: According to the *Midrash Rabbah* (*Shemot* 8:3), the staff weighed forty *se'ah*. What is the significance of this particular weight?

ANSWER: In describing the Jews' suffering in Egypt, the Torah says, *"Vayitnu aleinu avodah kashah"* — "They placed hard work upon us" (*Devarim* 26:6). Superficially, it should simply have said *"vaya'avidu otanu kashah"* — "they made us work very hard"?

ובאתות *"And with signs"* — this refers to the staff, as it is said:[1] "Take this staff in your hand, with which you shall perform the signs." *"And with wonders"* — this refers to the blood, as it is said:[2] "And I will show wonders in heaven and on earth:

1. *Shemot* 4:17.   2. *Joel* 3:3.

The *Gemara* (*Sotah* 34a) says that an average person can lift a weight of forty *se'ah*. The weight which one can raise upon his shoulder is one-third of the weight he can carry when others help him to set the burden upon his shoulder. Consequently, the average person can carry one hundred and twenty *se'ah* when others help him assume the burden. With the words *"vayitnu aleinu"* — "they placed upon us" — the Torah is emphasizing that they increased the weight of our workload threefold.

According to the *Gemara* (*Mo'eid Kattan* 18a) Pharaoh was a midget only one *amah* tall. Since the average person is three *amot* tall (see *Shabbat* 92a), Pharaoh could lift one-third of forty *se'ah* by himself and carry a load of forty *se'ah* with assistance. Because he tripled the workload of the Jewish people, he was punished through a staff of forty *se'ah*, which is three times his personal workload.

(הגש"פ מוצל מאש - בית אהרן - בברכות בחשבון)

"ואת המטה הזה תקח בידך אשר תעשה בו את האתת"
"Take this staff in your hand with which you shall perform the signs."

QUESTION: The word *"asher"* seems superfluous. It could have just said *"veta'aseh bo et ha'otot"* — "and perform with it the signs"?

ANSWER: The word *"asher"* (אשר) has the numerical value of 501, which is also the numerical value of the letters דצ"ך עד"ש באח"ב, which serve as an acronym for the ten plagues. Thus, Hashem was alluding that in addition to Moshe's using the staff to show "signs" that Hashem sent him, the Egyptians would receive 10 plagues, whose acronym adds up to 501, and some of which would be inflicted upon them through this staff.

* * *

באמירת דם ואש ותמרות עשן ישפוך ג' שפיכות ואין ליטול באצבע
לשפוך כ"א בכוס עצמו וישפוך לתוך כלי שבור (ויכוון שהכוס הוא
סוד המלכות ושופך מהיין שבתוכו סוד האף והזעם שבה ע"י כח
הבינה לתוך כלי שבור סוד הקליפה שנקראת ארור:

דָּם וָאֵשׁ וְתִמְרוֹת עָשָׁן:

Hashem struck Pharoah and the Egyptians with these plagues because His ways are measure for measure. When Moshe presented to Pharoah Hashem's request that he free the Jews, Pharoah arrogantly said, "Who is G-d 'asher eshma bekolo' — אשר אשמע בקולי — that I should heed His voice" (Shemot 5:2). Because Pharoah in his defiance said the word "asher" (אשר), which is superfluous (he could have just said "she'eshma" — "that I should listen") and numerically equivalent to five hundred and one, he was taught to heed Hashem through receiving the plagues whose acrostic has the numerical value of five hundred and one.

When Hashem gave the Jews the Torah, His first words were "I am G-d your G-d **Asher** hotzeiticha — Who took you out — of the land of Egypt" (Shemot 20:2). There, too, the word asher is superfluous. He could have said "shehotzeiticha." His message was that "I am G-d your G-d Who, through asher — the plagues whose acrostic adds up to 501 — took you out of Egypt."

(שמחת הרגל להחיד"א, ועי' לקוטי דבורים ע' תכ"ד
והגהות מיימוניות סוף הל' חו"מ ובהגש"פ ילקוט שמעוני)

* * *

According to the Midrash Rabbah (Shemot 5:6), on the staff were the acronyms דצ"ך עד"ש באח"ב (DeTzaCh, ADaSH, BeACHaB) which have the numerical value of five hundred and one. According to Rabbi Yose, in addition to the plagues delivered in Egypt there were an additional fifty plagues at the sea. According to Rabbi Eliezer there were an additional two hundred, and according to Rabbi Akiva there were an additional two hundred and fifty.

When saying the following words — 'blood, and fire, and pillars of smoke' — spill three times from the wine in the cup into a broken dish. Do not remove wine by dipping a finger, but by spilling from the cup itself. (Have in mind that the cup symbolizes the aspect of *malchut* which contains an aspect of 'anger and indignation.' By means of our faculty of *binah* [understanding] we pour out [that aspect of 'anger and indignation'] by spilling from the wine in the cup into a broken dish which represents *kelipah* i.e., that which is called accursed [the principle of evil]).

(When the Rebbe poured from his cup, the dish [not noticeably broken] was on the floor above a piece of paper — *Otzar Minhagei Chabad*.)

blood, and fire, and pillars of smoke."

The total number of the plagues of all three opinions is five hundred. These acronyms are thus an allusion to the five hundred plagues received at the ocean, and the extra one is to emphasize that they were all the work of the One and Only One — Hashem.

(הגש״פ עם פי׳ ילקוט שמעוני, בשם יבין שמועה מהרשב״ץ)

"דם ואש ותמרות עשן"
"Blood, and fire, and pillars of smoke."

QUESTION: Why do we pour off from the cup when reciting these three, the ten plagues and the three acronyms?

ANSWER: There is an opinion in the Jerusalem Talmud (*Pesachim* 10:1, see also *Midrash Rabbah, Bereishit* 88:5) that the four cups we drink at the *Seder* are an allusion to the four cups of wrath which Hashem will ultimately make the nations of the world drink. Pouring off drops from the cup symbolizes that what the Egyptians received is only a drop in comparison to what awaits the nations of the world in the future.

(הגש״פ עם פי׳ באר מרים מהרב ראובן ז״ל מרגליות)

Alternatively, the removal of the wine from the cup symbolizes the fact that after each plague the Egyptians lost a small portion of their resistance and strength.

(הגר״א)

דָּבָר אַחֵר בְּיָד חֲזָקָה שְׁתַּיִם. וּבִזְרוֹעַ נְטוּיָה שְׁתַּיִם. וּבְמוֹרָא גָּדוֹל שְׁתַּיִם. וּבְאֹתוֹת שְׁתַּיִם. וּבְמֹפְתִים שְׁתַּיִם:

אֵלּוּ עֶשֶׂר מַכּוֹת שֶׁהֵבִיא הַקָּדוֹשׁ בָּרוּךְ הוּא עַל הַמִּצְרִים בְּמִצְרַיִם. וְאֵלּוּ הֵן:

באמירת עשר מכות ישפוך עשר שפיכות מהכוס עצמו כנ"ל (ויכוון בשפיכה גם כן כנ"ל) ומה שנשאר בכוס (נעשה סוד יין המשמח) לכך לא ישפוך אלא יוסיף יין:

דָּם. צְפַרְדֵּעַ. כִּנִּים. עָרוֹב. דֶּבֶר. שְׁחִין. בָּרָד. אַרְבֶּה. חֹשֶׁךְ. מַכַּת בְּכוֹרוֹת:

"אלו עשר מכות...ואלו הן"
"These are the ten plagues ... they are"

QUESTION: Why is it necessary to list the names of the ten plagues?

ANSWER: According to the *Arizal,* there are 3280 avenging angels in heaven whose mission is to strike the wicked and punish them in *Geihinom*, and these angels also struck the wicked Pharoah and the Egyptians. An allusion to this is the verse, *"lehakot b'egrof resha"* — "to strike with a wicked fist" (Isaiah 58:4). The word *"resha"* (רֶשַׁע) — can also be read as *"Rasha"* (רָשָׁע) — "wicked person," and the word *"egrof"* (אגרף) — is an abbreviation for "ג' אלפים" — "three thousand" and "ר, פ" — "two hundred and eighty." The prophet is thus saying that through the three thousand two hundred and eighty angels, the wicked are smitten.

דבר Another explanation [associating each phrase with two plagues]:

"With a strong hand": two; *"and with an outstretched arm"*: two; *and with great manifestations"*: two; *"and with signs"*: two; *"and with wonders"*: two.

אלו These are the ten plagues which the Holy One, blessed be He, brought upon the Egyptians in Egypt: They are:

> When saying the ten plagues, spill from the cup itself ten times, as stated above (and again have in mind the mystical intention described above).

דם Blood, Frogs, Lice, Wild Beasts, Pestilence, Boils, Hail, Locusts, Darkness, Slaying of the Firstborn.

The total numerical value of the spelling of the names of the ten plagues adds up to three thousand, two hundred, and eighty, alluding to the number of wicked angels who struck Pharoah and the Egyptians. (Though *"kinim"* [כנים] — "lice" — is written in the *Haggadah* with a "יו", the first time it is mentioned in the Torah [*Shemot* 8:12] it is spelled without a "יו").

(ר' שמשון זצ"ל מאוסטרפליא)

Blood, Frogs, Lice — דם, צפרדע, כנים

QUESTION: The first three plagues were brought by Aharon. Moshe did not smite the waters or the earth because he personally benefited from the waters when he was cast into the river and he benefited from the earth when he killed the Egyptian and buried him in the sand. (*Shemot* 7:19, Rashi)

Why would these reasons preclude Moshe from initiating the plagues so many years later?

ANSWER: From this we can learn a very important lesson in *hakarat hatov* — showing gratitude — often, when someone does a favor, we forget it in the course of time. Hashem, by instructing

Aharon to bring these plagues, was conveying a lesson that one should remain thankful for a lifetime. Though the favor Moshe received from the water had happened 80 years earlier and Moshe had benefited from the earth approximately 70 years earlier, he was told to be appreciative and not hurt them in any way.

If this is true in regard to water and earth, which are inanimate, how much more so must this apply to a human being who does a favor.

Blood — דם

QUESTION: Regarding the plague of blood it is stated that "the fish in the river died" (Shemot 7:21). Isn't this statement superfluous since fish can only live in water?

ANSWER: The plague of blood might have happened in one of two ways: 1) All the waters became blood, turning back into water only when a Jew filled a glass. 2) There was no change in the water except that when an Egyptian filled a glass, it would become blood.

It was the latter that actually occurred. Consequently, the Egyptians received a double punishment: The fresh water turned into blood when used, and the fish died in the fresh water, making the water stink terribly.

It is necessary to explain it in this way because we are told that the Egyptians were compelled to purchase water from the Jews, who thus profited from the situation (Midrash Rabbah 9:9). If all the waters had been transformed to blood, the Jews would have been unable to charge the Egyptians for drinkable water, because it is forbidden to derive benefit from a miracle. (See Ta'anit 24a.)

(פרדס יוסף)

Frogs — צפרדע

QUESTION: Regarding the plague of frogs the Torah says, "The frog-infestation ascended and covered the land of Egypt. The magicians did the same and they brought up the frogs upon the land of Egypt" (Shemot 8:2-3). Why does the Torah repeat that the frogs were upon the land of Egypt?

ANSWER: At that time, there was a dispute between Egypt and its neighbors regarding their borders. The dispute was settled by the plague of the frogs who only "covered the land of Egypt," and did not go any further. The Egyptian magicians attempted to please Pharoah and endeavored to get the frogs to spread out further. However, the additional frogs made by their sorcery remained "upon the land of Egypt" and did not go any further than the frogs which were already brought by Aharon.

(מדרש רבה י:ב)

Wild beasts — ערוב

QUESTION: Regarding the wild beasts the Torah states that "The houses of Egypt shall be filled with the swarm of wild beasts and even the ground upon which they are" (*Shemot* 8:17). To which ground is this referring?

ANSWER: Among the animals of the world there is an extremely rare one found in the wild jungles of Africa and known as the *"adnei hasadeh."* It has the face of a person, long hands that reach to its knees, and a very unusual relationship to its habitat.

It is always connected to the ground through a string that comes out of its navel. Although it is very dangerous and kills anyone that comes within its reach, there is one way to capture it: by shooting arrows at the string. As soon as it becomes detached from the ground, it screams bitterly and dies immediately.

Hashem brought upon the Egyptians a mixture of all animals from the entire world, including the strange and vicious *"adnei hasadeh."* To keep them alive until they reached Egypt, they were brought together with the ground to which they were connected. Therefore, Moshe told Pharaoh, "The homes of the Egyptians shall be filled with the mixture of wild animals and also *'adnei hasadeh'* will come, together with the ground upon which they are [attached]."

(פנים יפות, ועי' כלאים פ"ח מ"ה ברע"ב ותפארת ישראל)

רַבִּי יְהוּדָה הָיָה נוֹתֵן בָּהֶם סִמָּנִים:
דְּצַ"ךְ. עֲדַ"שׁ. בְּאַחַ"ב:

Hail — ברד

QUESTION: When Pharoah asked Moshe to end the plague of hail, he responded, "When I go out of the city, I will spread my hands and pray to G-d" (*Shemot* 9:29). Why did Moshe insist on praying outside of the city only during the plague of hail, which was the seventh plague?

ANSWER: When Moshe warned Pharoah of the coming plague of hail, he told him that the Egyptians should take in all the cattle from the fields because any man or animal in the fields would die. The Egyptians who took the warning seriously brought their cattle into their houses. Others, who did not regard Hashem's words, left their servants and cattle out in the fields, where they were killed (*Shemot* 9:19-21).

Egypt worshipped the sheep. Therefore, during all other plagues, Moshe was willing to pray in the city since the sheep were out in the fields as usual. However, the city was filled with sheep during the plague of hail, and Moshe went out of the city to pray because he did not want to pray in a place filled with idols.

(ר' יהונתן ז"ל אייבשיץ)

Locusts — ארבה

QUESTION: Regarding the locusts the Torah states, "The locust swarm ascended over the entire land of Egypt, and it rested in the entire border of Egypt" (*Shemot* 10:14). Why does the Torah repeat "in the entire border of Egypt" after saying that the locusts "ascended over the *entire* land of Egypt"?

ANSWER: The Jews of Egypt lived in the city of Goshen and were not affected by the plague of hail (*Shemot* 9:26) that struck "all the herbs of the field and smashed every tree of the field" (9:25). The locusts were meant to "consume the remainder [of vegetation] that was left by the hail and all the trees that grow from the field" (10:5).

רבי Rabbi Yehudah referred to them by the acronyms:

Spill from the cup when saying each of these three acronyms:

detzach, adash, be'achav.

The wine remaining in the cup (will have become 'wine that causes joy' and thus) is not spilled, and other wine is added to it [to refill the cup].

Knowing that very shortly the Jewish people would be leaving Egypt, Hashem sent the locusts. They covered Egypt from border to border — including Goshen — in order to ensure that the Egyptians would have no benefit from the produce of the Jewish fields.

(ילקוט מעם לועז – שמות, הגש״פ מגדל עדר החדש בפי׳ כנפי נשרים)

Darkness — חשך

QUESTION: According to Rashi (*Shemot* 10:22), "For three days no man could see another, and during the succeeding three days the darkness was so thick that if an Egyptian was sitting, he was unable to stand up, and if he was standing, he was unable to sit down."

Every plague lasted seven days (except the plague of the firstborn). Why did the plague of darkness last only six days?

ANSWER: When the Jews left Egypt and traveled in the desert, clouds of glory accompanied them. During the day the clouds would clear a path in the desert, and at night a pillar of fire illuminated the camp. When the Egyptians pursued the Jews, the Torah says, "There was a cloud of darkness [for the Egyptians] and the night was illuminated [for the Jews through a pillar of fire]" (14:20). Thus, Hashem reserved the remaining seventh day of darkness to punish the Egyptians when they chased after the Jewish people.

(מדרש רבה שמות י״ד, ג')

"רבי יהודה היה נותן בהם סימנים דצ״ך עד״ש באח״ב"
"Rabbi Yehudah referred to them by the acronyms:
DeTzaCh, ADaSh, BeACHaB."

QUESTION: The *Haggadah* lists the ten plagues, and afterwards we are told that Rabbi Yehudah referred to them by acronyms: "דצ״ך, עד״ש, באח״ב."

Rabbi Yehudah was one of the great Sages of the Talmud. What genius is there in making an acrostic out of the first letters of the ten plagues?

ANSWER: In Psalms (136:10), Hashem is praised for *"lemakeih Mitzraim bivchoreihem"* — "striking the Egyptians through their firstborn." It does not say that Hashem struck the firstborn of Egypt, but rather that He struck the Egyptians *through* their firstborn. This is explained in the *Midrash (Yalkut Shimoni)* as follows:

Upon hearing that they would be victims of the last plague, the firstborn demanded from Pharaoh and their parents, the immediate release of the Jews. When their plea was refused, a civil war broke out and the desperate firstborn attacked and killed their parents and fellow Egyptians. Thus, the tenth plague dealt a double blow to Egypt, killing both firstborn and non-firstborn.

In the *Haggadah*, the ten plagues are listed as *"dam, tzefardei'a...makat bechorot"* — "blood, frogs...plague of the firstborn." The word *"makat"* is not mentioned for any of the plagues except for *"bechorot"* — why?

It can be explained that Rabbi Yehudah *argues* with the author of the *Haggadah* as to what was the major part of the double-blow plague. According to the author of the *Haggadah*, the main part was *"makat"* — the smiting of the Egyptians by *bechorot* — their own angry and violent firstborn.

Rabbi Yehudah's third acronym is "באח״בי". The final "בי" stands for *"bechorot."* He did not make the acronym "באח״מי," which would have meant *"Makat bechorot,"* because in his opinion the major part of the plague was *"bechorot"* — Hashem's slaying of the firstborn and not the smiting of the Egyptians by their own firstborn.

(הגש״פ צוף אמרים בשם יסוד התורה)

Years ago, blood libels were unfortunately prevalent. Around Pesach time the Catholics would accuse the Jewish people of killing a gentile child in order to mix his blood into the *matzot*. Once, a debate took place in which a priest claimed that in fact,

this vicious act is alluded to in the *Haggadah*. The priest went on to say that the letters "באח״בי עד״ש דצ״ך" are an acronym of;

"Dam tzerichim kulanu (דם צריכים כולנו) — We all need blood —
al devar sheharagnu (על דבר שהרגנו) — because we killed —
ben Ei-l chai bashamayim (בן א-ל חי בשמים) — the 'son' of the living G-d in heaven."

The Rabbi representing the Jews immediately told the priest that he had misinterpreted the code in the *Haggadah*. On the contrary, the words are a hint to

"Dovrim tzorereinu kazav (דוברים צוררינו כזב) — Our enemies talk falsehood —
alilat dam sheker (עלילת דם שקר) — blood libels are false —
b'nei Avraham chalilah bezot (בני אברהם חלילה בזאת) — the children of Avraham would never do such a thing."

(פון אונזער אלטען אוצר)

"דצ״ך. עד״ש. באח״ב"
"DeTzaCh (blood, frogs, lice); ADaSh (beasts, pestilence, boils); BeAChaB (hail, locust, darkness, firstborn)."

QUESTION: Why did Rabbi Yehudah group them in this way?

ANSWER: The third of each set shares an aspect in common with the third plagues of the other two sets. Firstly, all the plagues were preceded by a warning except these three: *"kinim"* — "lice" — *"shechin"* — "boils" — and *"choshech"* — "darkness" — for which there was no warning.

In addition, in each of these three there was a minor occurrence of the other two (for instance, there were minor plagues of boils and lice during the plague of darkness) although the main plague predominated. When one writes the name of these three *makot*, one beneath the other, a square is formed. Besides the names of the plagues, which can be read in the normal way, they can also be read vertically. This indicates their being intermingled.

(הגהות מיימוניות, רמב״ם הל׳ חמץ ומצה נוסח ההגדה, בשם ריב״א)

רַבִּי יוֹסֵי הַגְּלִילִי אוֹמֵר מִנַּיִן אַתָּה אוֹמֵר שֶׁלָּקוּ הַמִּצְרִים בְּמִצְרַיִם עֶשֶׂר מַכּוֹת וְעַל הַיָּם לָקוּ חֲמִשִּׁים מַכּוֹת. בְּמִצְרַיִם מַה הוּא אוֹמֵר וַיֹּאמְרוּ הַחַרְטֻמִּם אֶל־פַּרְעֹה אֶצְבַּע אֱלֹהִים הִיא. וְעַל הַיָּם מַה הוּא אוֹמֵר וַיַּרְא יִשְׂרָאֵל אֶת־הַיָּד הַגְּדוֹלָה אֲשֶׁר עָשָׂה יְהוָֹה בְּמִצְרַיִם וַיִּירְאוּ הָעָם אֶת־יְהוָֹה וַיַּאֲמִינוּ בַּיהוָֹה וּבְמֹשֶׁה עַבְדּוֹ: כַּמָּה לָקוּ בְאֶצְבַּע עֶשֶׂר מַכּוֹת. אֱמֹר מֵעַתָּה בְּמִצְרַיִם לָקוּ עֶשֶׂר מַכּוֹת. וְעַל הַיָּם לָקוּ חֲמִשִּׁים מַכּוֹת:

"רבי יוסי הגלילי אומר...במצרים לקו עשר מכות. ועל הים לקו חמשים מכות"
"Rabbi Yossi the Gallilean said... 'In Egypt they were struck by ten plagues, and at the sea they were struck by fifty plagues.' "

QUESTION: The *Haggadah* cites three opinions concerning how many plagues the Egyptians received in Egypt and how many at the sea.

Why is the number of plagues significant?

ANSWER: Hashem promised the Jewish people that if they will hearken diligently to His voice, then "Any of the diseases that I placed upon Egypt, I will not bring upon you, for I am G-d your Healer" (*Shemot* 15:26). Thus, a greater number of plagues is to our benefit because it means fewer ways for us to suffer.

(קול אליהו)

"ויאמרו החרטמים אל פרעה אצבע אלקים היא"
"And the magicians said to Pharaoh, 'This is the finger of G-d.' "

QUESTION: Why, after the plague of lice, did the magicians finally concede "This is the finger of G-d?"

ANSWER: The wicked Titus burned the *Beit Hamikdash* and blasphemed Hashem. While returning to his city, his boat was threatened by strong waves. Arrogantly he stated, "The power of the Jewish G-d is only over the water. Throughout history He has used water as a means of punishment. If He is really mighty, let Him meet me on dry land, and we shall see who will conquer." A voice emanating from heaven said, "Wicked one, son of the wicked, I have a small creature in my world called a *'yatush'* (a gnat) — come on dry land and we will see who is stronger!" Titus presumptuously came on dry land, and a *yatush* entered his nose and bore through his brain until he died (*Gittin* 56b).

רבי Rabbi Yossi the Gallilean said: How do you know that the Egyptians were struck by ten plagues in Egypt and were struck by fifty plagues at the Sea? Concerning [the plagues in] Egypt, it says:[1] "The magicians said to Pharaoh: 'This is the *finger* of God.'" And [concerning the plagues] at the sea, it says:[2] "And Israel saw the great *hand* which *Adonai* wielded against Egypt, the people feared *Adonai,* and they believed in *Adonai* and in Moshe His servant." With how many plagues were they struck by "the *finger*"? Ten plagues! Thus, we may conclude that in Egypt they were struck by ten plagues and at the sea they were struck by fifty plagues.

1. *Shemot* 8:15. 2. *Shemot* 14:31.

The first two plagues to hit Egypt were blood and frogs, which originated from the water. The magicians consoled Pharaoh, "Don't worry, it appears that their G-d is not omnipotent: His strength is limited to water." Therefore, Hashem struck them with the plague of lice, extremely minute creatures which come from the earth. Upon seeing this, the magicians were forced to concede, "This is the finger of G-d, and He is indeed omnipotent." (שער בת רבים - בשם ראשית בכורים)

"ויֵרא ישראל את היד הגדלה אשר עשה ה' במצרים...ויאמינו בה' ובמשה עבדו"
"And Israel saw the big hand which G-d wielded against Egypt...
and they believed in G-d and in Moshe His servant."

QUESTION: What "big hand" did they see that caused them to believe in Moshe?

ANSWER: Pharaoh ordered the drowning of newborn Jewish boys. When Moshe was born, his mother managed to keep his birth a secret for three months. Afterwards, she put him in a box and placed it at the river's edge.

Pharaoh's daughter came to bathe and noticed the box. The Torah (*Shemot* 2:5) relates that she sent *"amatah"* — "her handmaiden — to fetch the box. Rashi explains that *"amatah"* can also mean "her hand" so that the Torah is saying that when she stretched out her hand, it miraculously elongated and she was able to reach the box. When the Jewish people saw — i.e. learned about — the "big hand" which Hashem made many years ago in Egypt to save Moshe, they recognized his stature and had faith in Hashem and in Moshe, His servant.

(ילקוט האורים מר' משה אורי ז"ל קעללער בשם ספר לב ארי' עה"ת)

רַבִּי אֱלִיעֶזֶר אוֹמֵר מִנַּיִן שֶׁכָּל־מַכָּה וּמַכָּה שֶׁהֵבִיא הַקָּדוֹשׁ בָּרוּךְ הוּא עַל הַמִּצְרִים בְּמִצְרַיִם הָיְתָה שֶׁל אַרְבַּע מַכּוֹת שֶׁנֶּאֱמַר יְשַׁלַּח בָּם חֲרוֹן אַפּוֹ עֶבְרָה וָזַעַם וְצָרָה מִשְׁלַחַת מַלְאֲכֵי רָעִים: עֶבְרָה אַחַת. וָזַעַם שְׁתַּיִם. וְצָרָה שָׁלֹשׁ. מִשְׁלַחַת מַלְאֲכֵי רָעִים אַרְבַּע. אֱמֹר מֵעַתָּה בְּמִצְרַיִם לָקוּ אַרְבָּעִים מַכּוֹת. וְעַל הַיָּם לָקוּ מָאתַיִם מַכּוֹת:

רַבִּי עֲקִיבָא אוֹמֵר מִנַּיִן שֶׁכָּל־מַכָּה וּמַכָּה שֶׁהֵבִיא הַקָּדוֹשׁ בָּרוּךְ הוּא עַל הַמִּצְרִים בְּמִצְרַיִם הָיְתָה שֶׁל חָמֵשׁ מַכּוֹת. שֶׁנֶּאֱמַר יְשַׁלַּח בָּם חֲרוֹן אַפּוֹ עֶבְרָה וָזַעַם וְצָרָה מִשְׁלַחַת מַלְאֲכֵי רָעִים. חֲרוֹן אַפּוֹ אַחַת. עֶבְרָה שְׁתַּיִם. וָזַעַם שָׁלֹשׁ. וְצָרָה אַרְבַּע. מִשְׁלַחַת מַלְאֲכֵי רָעִים חָמֵשׁ. אֱמֹר מֵעַתָּה בְּמִצְרַיִם לָקוּ חֲמִשִּׁים מַכּוֹת. וְעַל הַיָּם לָקוּ חֲמִשִּׁים וּמָאתַיִם מַכּוֹת:

כַּמָּה מַעֲלוֹת טוֹבוֹת לַמָּקוֹם עָלֵינוּ:

אִלּוּ הוֹצִיאָנוּ מִמִּצְרַיִם וְלֹא עָשָׂה בָהֶם שְׁפָטִים   דַּיֵּנוּ:
אִלּוּ עָשָׂה בָהֶם שְׁפָטִים וְלֹא עָשָׂה בֵאלֹהֵיהֶם   דַּיֵּנוּ:

"כמה מעלות טובות למקום עלינו"
"How many levels of favors has the Omnipresent bestowed upon us."

QUESTION: Grammatically it should have said *"meihaMakom lanu"* — *"from* the Omnipresent"?

רבי Rabbi Eliezer said: Which source teaches that every plague that the Holy One, blessed be He, brought upon the Egyptians in Egypt consisted of four plagues? For it is said:[1] "He sent upon them His fierce anger: wrath, fury, trouble, and a band of emissaries of evil." "Wrath" [refers to] one plague; "fury" to a second; "trouble" to a third; and "a band of emissaries of evil" to a fourth. Thus, we may conclude that in Egypt they were struck by forty plagues and at the sea by two hundred plagues.

רבי Rabbi Akiva said: Which source teaches that every plague that the Holy One, blessed be He, brought upon the Egyptians consisted of five plagues? For it is said: "He sent upon them His fierce anger, wrath, fury, trouble, a band of emissaries of evil." "His fierce anger" [refers to] one plague; "wrath" to a second; "fury" to a third; "trouble" to a fourth; and "a band of emissaries of evil" to a fifth. Thus, we may conclude that in Egypt they were struck by fifty plagues and at the sea by two hundred and fifty plagues.

כמה How many levels of favors has the Omnipresent bestowed upon us:

> One does not interrupt the recital of the fourteen verses
> of *Dayeinu* — "It would have sufficed us."

אלו If He had brought us out of Egypt, and not executed judgments against them,   it would have sufficed us!

If He had executed judgments against them, and not against their gods,   it would have sufficed us!

1. *Psalms* 78:49.

ANSWER: Hashem's love for the Jewish people is like the love of a father for his only son and even greater. Just as a father loves to help and do favors for his child, so much more is Hashem happy when He has an opportunity to extend his goodness to the Jewish people. Therefore we say *"laMakom"* — *"to* the Omnipresent" — for He derives enjoyment through bestowing good things, *"aleinu"* — "upon us."

(קדושת לוי)

אִלּוּ עָשָׂה בֵאלֹהֵיהֶם וְלֹא הָרַג אֶת־בְּכוֹרֵיהֶם   דַּיֵּנוּ:

אִלּוּ הָרַג אֶת־בְּכוֹרֵיהֶם וְלֹא נָתַן לָנוּ אֶת־מָמוֹנָם   דַּיֵּנוּ:

אִלּוּ נָתַן לָנוּ אֶת־מָמוֹנָם וְלֹא קָרַע לָנוּ אֶת־הַיָּם   דַּיֵּנוּ:

"אלו הרג את בכוריהם ולא נתן לנו את ממונם"
"If He had slain their firstborn, and not given us their wealth."

QUESTION: Why did Hashem instruct that the borrowing of their wealth take place *after* the smiting of the first born?

ANSWER: The intention of plaguing the Egyptians was to force them to free the Jewish people. Hashem was very careful to prevent the Egyptians from deriving any personal gain from the plagues. Therefore, when they attempted to preserve the locusts for food, miraculously they flew away and disappeared from Egypt (*Shemot* 10:19, Rashi).

According to Egyptian laws of inheritance, all children were equal heirs of a father's estate. Thus, in a family with four children, the estate would be divided equally among the four. If one died during the father's lifetime, then the estate would be divided in three ways. Consequently, in Egypt when the firstborn were smitten, the survivors stood to profit. (Likewise, if there were no firstborn in the house, the head of the household was smitten and his survivors also stood to profit through inheritance.)

In order to avoid this from happening, immediately after the plague, Hashem instructed the Jews to borrow valuables from the Egyptians. Simultaneously, He gave the Jews favor in the eyes of the Egyptians (ibid. 12:36), and He gave the Egyptians the intuition to lend the Jews the exact amount they stood to gain through the death of the firstborn (or head of household) in each family. Thus after *He* killed the firstborns, *He* gave us *"mamonam"* — their wealth — i.e. the money which belonged to the firstborn.

(יריעות שלמה על הגש"פ לר' שלמה ז"ל קלוגער)

If He had executed judgments against their gods, and not slain their firstborn, it would have sufficed us!

If He had slain their firstborn, and not given us their wealth, it would have sufficed us!

If He had given us their wealth, and not split the sea for us, it would have sufficed us!

"אלו הרג את בכוריהם ולא נתן לנו את ממונם, דינו.
אלו נתן לנו את ממונם ולא קרע לנו את הים, דינו"

**"If He had slain their firstborn, and not given us their wealth,
it would have sufficed us. If He had given us their wealth,
and not split the sea for us, it would have sufficed us."**

QUESTION: The wealth obtained in Egypt after the killing of the first born was *borrowed,* so what wealth did He *give* us between the killing of the firstborn and the splitting of the sea?

ANSWER: In the days of Yosef a famine struck Egypt and the surrounding countries. From all over they came to Egypt to purchase food. "Yosef gathered all the money that was to be found in the land of Egypt and in the land of Canaan through selling provisions, and he brought it into Pharaoh's palace (*Bereishit* 47:14). Pharaoh instructed him to hide all the money in the idol of Tzefon. (*"Tzefon"* means "hidden," and the idol was named after its use as a hiding place.)

According to the *Midrash (Yalkut Shimoni, Shemot* 230), Hashem's promise of, "And afterwards they shall leave with great wealth," *(Bereishit* 15:13) does not refer to the gold and silver which they borrowed from the Egyptians; they were entitled to this as compensation for their slavery.

After the Jews left Egypt, Hashem told Moshe that they should turn back and encamp in front of Ba'al Tzefon *(Shemot* 14:2). Here they uncovered the vast hidden treasures, and thus the promise of "And afterwards they shall leave with great wealth" was realized. Consequently, the wealth referred to here came from a different source and was *given* to them outright.

(הגש"פ מוצל מאש - בית אהרן - בפי' רוח חדשה)

"אלו נתן לנו את ממונם ולא קרע לנו את הים"
"If He had given us their wealth and not split the sea for us."

QUESTION: Hashem did not *give* the Jewish people their wealth; He told them to ask for it as a loan?

אִלּוּ קָרַע לָנוּ אֶת־הַיָּם וְלֹא הֶעֱבִירָנוּ בְּתוֹכוֹ בֶּחָרָבָה   דַּיֵּנוּ:

אִלּוּ הֶעֱבִירָנוּ בְּתוֹכוֹ בֶּחָרָבָה וְלֹא שִׁקַּע צָרֵינוּ בְּתוֹכוֹ   דַּיֵּנוּ:

אִלּוּ שִׁקַּע צָרֵינוּ בְּתוֹכוֹ וְלֹא סִפֵּק צָרְכֵּנוּ בַּמִּדְבָּר
אַרְבָּעִים שָׁנָה   דַּיֵּנוּ:

אִלּוּ סִפֵּק צָרְכֵּנוּ בַּמִּדְבָּר אַרְבָּעִים שָׁנָה וְלֹא הֶאֱכִילָנוּ
אֶת־הַמָּן   דַּיֵּנוּ:

אִלּוּ הֶאֱכִילָנוּ אֶת־הַמָּן וְלֹא נָתַן לָנוּ אֶת־הַשַּׁבָּת   דַּיֵּנוּ:

אִלּוּ נָתַן לָנוּ אֶת־הַשַּׁבָּת וְלֹא קֵרְבָנוּ לִפְנֵי הַר־סִינַי   דַּיֵּנוּ:

ANSWER: The reason Hashem originally told the Jewish people to *borrow* gold, silver, and valuables from the Egyptians was to deceive them into thinking that the Jews would return after three days. Realizing that they were not returning, the Egyptians chased after the Jews to retrieve their money, and then Hashem drowned them in the sea as punishment for their decree to drown the Jewish children. Thus, we are proclaiming, "If He had *given* us their wealth and not told us to merely borrow it, (thus they would not have chased after us, and the sea would not be split in order to drown them) — it would have sufficed us."

(הגש"פ עם פי' ילקוט שמעוני)

"ולא שקע צרינו בתוכו"
"And had not drowned our oppressors in it."

QUESTION: Instead of *"shika"* which means causing to drown through a direct act, it should have said *"nishka'u"* — "they drowned"?

ANSWER: According to the *Midrash*, the *pasuk* "You broke the heads of sea giants on the water" (Psalms 74:13) refers to an event that took place when Hashem split the sea. The Egyptians were very accomplished in sorcery. When the waters of the sea began to close in on them, some used their arcane knowledge and came out alive from the sea. Hashem then sent the angel Michael, who seized them by their hair and threw them back into the sea. Thus, *"shika tzareinu"* — He *drowned* our oppressors in the sea.

(ילקוט מעם לועז על הגש"פ)

If He had split the sea for us, and not led us through it on dry land, it would have sufficed us!

If He had led us through it on dry land, and not drowned our oppressors in it, it would have sufficed us!

If He had drowned our oppressors in it, and not provided for our needs in the wilderness for forty years, it would have sufficed us!

If He had provided for our needs in the wilderness for forty years, and not sustained us with the manna, it would have sufficed us!

If He had sustained us with the manna, and not given us the *Shabbat*, it would have sufficed us!

If He had given us the *Shabbat*, and not brought us before Mount Sinai, it would have sufficed us!

"אלו שקע צרינו בתוכו ולא ספק צרכינו במדבר ארבעים שנה דיינו"
"If He had drowned our oppressors in it, but had not provided for our needs in the wilderness for forty years, it would have sufficed us."

QUESTION: What is the connection between these two?

ANSWER: Prior to leaving Egypt the Jews borrowed the Egyptians' wealth. At this point it was only borrowed and did not belong to them, and in fact, the Egyptians pursued them to retrieve it. It ultimately became theirs when the Egyptians were drowned in the sea. Thus, we are proclaiming, "If He had drowned our oppressors in it, it would have sufficed us, and He would not have needed to provide our sustenance miraculously for forty years. For with this great wealth we could have easily purchased food in the wilderness, even at enormous cost."

(הגש"פ מוצל מאש - בית אהרן - בפי' רוח חדשה)

"אלו האכילנו את המן ולא נתן לנו את השבת"
"If He had fed us the manna, and had not given us the *Shabbat*."

QUESTION: 1) The Jews were already commanded to observe *Shabbat* while in Marah (*Shemot* 15:25, Rashi), and afterwards they began to receive the manna. So it should have said the reverse: "If he had given us the *Shabbat* and not fed us the manna"?

2) What is the connection between manna and *Shabbat*?

אִלּוּ קֵרְבָנוּ לִפְנֵי הַר־סִינַי וְלֹא נָתַן לָנוּ אֶת־הַתּוֹרָה דַּיֵּנוּ:
אִלּוּ נָתַן לָנוּ אֶת־הַתּוֹרָה וְלֹא הִכְנִיסָנוּ לְאֶרֶץ יִשְׂרָאֵל דַּיֵּנוּ:
אִלּוּ הִכְנִיסָנוּ לְאֶרֶץ יִשְׂרָאֵל וְלֹא בָנָה לָנוּ
אֶת־בֵּית־הַבְּחִירָה דַּיֵּנוּ:

ANSWER: The Torah (*Shemot* 16:22) relates that on *Shabbat* the the manna did not descend, and on Friday the Jews gathered *"lechem mishneh"* — "a double portion." Rashi quotes a *Midrash* to read *"lechem meshuneh"* (לחם מְשֻׁנֶּה) — "different bread." On *Shabbat* the manna tasted better and smelled better. Thus the *Haggadah* is saying, "If he had fed us the manna in the same form throughout the entire week and not given us the *Shabbat* — a special *Shabbat* manna which tasted even better — *dayeinu* — it would have sufficed us."

(הגש״פ עם פי׳ קהלת משה בשם ר׳ פנחס זצ״ל מקאריץ)

Alternatively, this follows the opinion that the precept of *Shabbat* was given in Alush (Jerusalem Talmud *Beitzah* 2:1).

Alternatively, this follows the commentators who say that the precept was indeed given in Marah, but Moshe forgot to instruct the people until they came to Alush.

(הגש״פ עם לקוטי טעמים ומנהגים)

"אלו קרבנו לפני הר סיני ולא נתן לנו את התורה דינו"
"If He had brought us before Mount Sinai and had not given us the Torah, it would have sufficed us."

QUESTION: What benefit would have come from just being brought before Mount Sinai and not being given the Torah?

ANSWER: When the Jews encamped at Mount Sinai, the Torah tells us *"Vayichan sham Yisrael neged hahar"* — "Israel encamped there opposite the mountain" (*Shemot* 19:2). It says *"vayichan"* in the singular, and not *"vayachanu"* in the plural, to emphasize that they were united like one person with one heart (Rashi). The unparalleled unity and *ahavat Yisrael* which prevailed at Mount Sinai would have sufficed, even if it were not followed by the giving of the Torah.

(הגדה של פסח צוף אמרים)

Alternatively, The Torah consists of 613 *mitzvot*. The word Torah (תורה) has the numerical value of 611 to indicate that the first two commandments were uttered by Hashem Himself and the rest of the Torah was given through Moshe (*Makkot* 23b). Thus, we proclaim, "If He had brought us before Mount Sinai only to hear the

If He had brought us before Mount Sinai, and not given us the Torah,   it would have sufficed us!

If He had given us the Torah, and not brought us into *Eretz Yisrael,*   it would have sufficed us!

If He had brought us into *Eretz Yisrael,* **and not built for us the** *Beit Habechirah* **[the chosen house, i.e. the** *Beit Hamikdash***]**   it would have sufficed us!

---

first two commandments directly from Hashem and not given us the Torah, i.e. the other 611 *mitzvot*, it would have sufficed us."

(הגש״פ ברכת השיר)

Alternatively, the *Gemara* (*Shabbat* 146a) says that when the serpent seduced Chavah to eat from the Tree of Knowledge, they also had marital relations, and he cast impurity into her which she then passed on to future generations. When the Jews stood at Mount Sinai to receive the Torah, their impurity was removed and they were returned to their original uncontaminated state as at the time of creation. (The souls of *all* Jews were present at Mount Sinai including those of converts.) The impurity of the idolaters, however, who did not stand at Mount Sinai, was not removed and it thus persists to this day.

Hence, Hashem's deed of bringing us to Mount Sinai to receive the Torah was of great benefit to us even without the giving of the Torah.

(יבין שמועה מהרשב״ץ, שו״ת הראב״ד סי׳ י״א)

"אלו נתן לנו את התורה ולא הכניסנו לארץ ישראל דיינו"

"If He had given us the Torah and not brought us into
***Eretz Yisrael* — it would have sufficed us."**

QUESTION: Why don't we say the reverse — "If He had brought us into *Eretz Yisrael* and not given us the Torah, it would have sufficed us"?

ANSWER: Hashem gave the Torah in the wilderness prior to the entry of the Jews into *Eretz Yisrael* to emphasize the Torah's superiority over land. The nations of the world who refused to accept the Torah became extinct with the loss of their lands. The Jews, however, exist forever, even without a land, as long as they keep the Torah.

Jews and Torah are inseparable, which is not the case with Jews and *Eretz Yisrael*. We can suffice with a Torah even without having *Eretz Yisrael*, but *Eretz Yisrael* in itself, without Torah, is of no value to the Jews.

(מצאתי בכתבי זקני הרב צבי הכהן ז״ל קאפלאן)

עַל־אַחַת כַּמָּה וְכַמָּה טוֹבָה כְפוּלָה וּמְכֻפֶּלֶת לַמָּקוֹם עָלֵינוּ. שֶׁהוֹצִיאָנוּ מִמִּצְרַיִם. וְעָשָׂה בָהֶם שְׁפָטִים. וְעָשָׂה בֵאלֹהֵיהֶם. וְהָרַג אֶת־בְּכוֹרֵיהֶם. וְנָתַן לָנוּ אֶת־מָמוֹנָם. וְקָרַע לָנוּ אֶת־הַיָּם. וְהֶעֱבִירָנוּ בְתוֹכוֹ בֶּחָרָבָה. וְשִׁקַּע צָרֵינוּ בְּתוֹכוֹ. וְסִפֵּק צָרְכֵּינוּ בַּמִּדְבָּר אַרְבָּעִים שָׁנָה. וְהֶאֱכִילָנוּ אֶת־הַמָּן. וְנָתַן לָנוּ אֶת־הַשַּׁבָּת. וְקֵרְבָנוּ לִפְנֵי הַר־סִינָי. וְנָתַן לָנוּ אֶת־הַתּוֹרָה. וְהִכְנִיסָנוּ לְאֶרֶץ יִשְׂרָאֵל. וּבָנָה לָנוּ אֶת בֵּית־הַבְּחִירָה לְכַפֵּר עַל כָּל־עֲוֹנוֹתֵינוּ:

רַבָּן גַּמְלִיאֵל הָיָה אוֹמֵר כָּל־שֶׁלֹּא אָמַר שְׁלֹשָׁה דְבָרִים אֵלּוּ בַּפֶּסַח לֹא יָצָא יְדֵי חוֹבָתוֹ. וְאֵלּוּ הֵן: פֶּסַח, מַצָּה, וּמָרוֹר: פֶּסַח שֶׁהָיוּ אֲבוֹתֵינוּ אוֹכְלִים בִּזְמַן שֶׁבֵּית־הַמִּקְדָּשׁ קַיָּם, עַל־שׁוּם מָה. עַל־שׁוּם שֶׁפָּסַח הַמָּקוֹם עַל־בָּתֵּי אֲבוֹתֵינוּ בְּמִצְרַיִם.

"והאכילנו את המן" — "And fed us the manna."

QUESTION: In the wilderness, all the needs of the Jewish people were provided by Hashem. Food came from heaven, and their clothing grew with them. How was one able to fulfill the *mitzvah* of *tzedakah* (helping those in need)?

ANSWER: When the Jews ate the manna, they were able to enjoy the taste of any food they imagined (*Yoma* 75a). Since many poor people had never tasted expensive foods, the *tzedakah* of a rich person was to recommend to a poor person what to have in mind while eating so that his palate would enjoy hitherto untasted delicacies.

(פון אונזער אלטען אוצר, דברים)

"רבן גמליאל היה אומר כל שלא אמר שלשה דברים אלו בפסח לא יצא ידי חובתו ואלו הן: פסח. מצה. ומרור"
"Rabbi Gamliel used to say: "Whoever has not explained the following three things on *Pesach*, has not fulfilled his obligation, namely: *Pesach*, matzah and maror."

QUESTION: What obligation is Rabban Gamliel referring to?

ANSWER: According to many opinions one who has not explained the reason for these three things adequately has not properly fulfilled the *mitzvah* of *sipur yetziat Mitzrayim* — relating the Exodus from Egypt.

That is, whoever does not explain these three *mitzvot* "has not fulfilled his obligation" in an *ideal manner*, though the basic Biblical

על Thus, how much more so [do we owe thanks] to the Omnipresent for the repeated and manifold favors He bestowed upon us: He brought us out of Egypt; He executed judgments against them; He executed judgments against their gods; He slew their firstborn; He gave us their wealth; He split the sea for us; He led us through it on dry land; He drowned our oppressors in it; He provided for our needs in the wilderness for forty years; He sustained us with the manna; He gave us the *Shabbat;* He brought us before Mount Sinai; He gave us the Torah; He brought us into *Eretz Yisrael;* He built for us the *Beit Habechirah* to atone for all our sins.

רבן Rabban Gamliel would say: "Whoever has not explained the following three things on *Pesach* [at the *Seder*] has not fulfilled his obligation: They are *Pesach* (the *Pesach*-offering), *matzah* (the unleavened bread), and *maror* (the bitter herbs)."

When reciting the following passage, one should not point to the *zero'a* (shankbone) on the *Seder* plate.

פסח The *Pesach*-offering that our fathers ate during the period when the *Beit Hamikdash* stood — what is its reason? Because the Omnipresent passed over the houses of our fathers in

---

obligation would have been discharged even by a mere mention (see p. 79).

(אברבנאל, וכן מוכח מהרמב״ם שהביא דברי רבן גמליאל בפ״ז מהל׳ חו״מ ומיירי שם במצות סיפור יציאת מצרים, ועי׳ ר״ן פסחים קט״ז)

Some hold that Rabban Gamliel is referring to the *mitzvot* of eating *pesach, matzah* and *maror,* and instructing that an explanation of each *mitzvah* must precede the eating for the *mitzvah* to be fulfilled properly.

(אבודרהם, כל בו, מהרש״א פסחים קט״ז ע״ב)

"פסח מצה ומרור" — *"Pesach, Matzah and Maror."*

QUESTION: In the Rambam (*Chameitz Umatzah* 8:4) the order is *pesach, maror, matzah.* Why in our *Haggadah* do we discuss *matzah* before *maror?*

ANSWER: The Rambam follows chronological order; therefore, *maror* is mentioned before *matzah* because it represents the period when *"mareru et chayeihem"* — their lives were embittered through Egyptian bondage. This is followed by *matzah,* which alludes to the redemption from Egypt.

The prevalent custom is to mention *matzah* first, however, because it is eaten before the *maror,* and also because in contemporary times *matzah* is a Biblical obligation while *maror* is only *miderabanan* — a Rabbinic ordinance.

(הגש״פ חזון עובדיה, ועי׳ צל״ח עמ״ס פסחים קט״ז ע״ב)

שֶׁנֶּאֱמַר וַאֲמַרְתֶּם זֶבַח פֶּסַח הוּא לַיהוָה אֲשֶׁר פָּסַח עַל־בָּתֵּי בְנֵי יִשְׂרָאֵל בְּמִצְרַיִם בְּנָגְפּוֹ אֶת־מִצְרַיִם וְאֶת־בָּתֵּינוּ הִצִּיל וַיִּקֹּד הָעָם וַיִּשְׁתַּחֲווּ:

נוֹטֵל הַפְּרוּסָה בְּיָדוֹ וְיֹאמַר:

מַצָּה זוֹ שֶׁאָנוּ אוֹכְלִים עַל־שׁוּם מָה. עַל־שׁוּם שֶׁלֹּא הִסְפִּיק בְּצֵקֶת שֶׁל אֲבוֹתֵינוּ לְהַחֲמִיץ עַד שֶׁנִּגְלָה עֲלֵיהֶם מֶלֶךְ מַלְכֵי־הַמְּלָכִים הַקָּדוֹשׁ בָּרוּךְ הוּא וּגְאָלָם. שֶׁנֶּאֱמַר וַיֹּאפוּ אֶת־הַבָּצֵק אֲשֶׁר הוֹצִיאוּ מִמִּצְרַיִם עֻגֹת מַצּוֹת כִּי לֹא חָמֵץ כִּי גֹרְשׁוּ מִמִּצְרַיִם וְלֹא יָכְלוּ לְהִתְמַהְמֵהַּ וְגַם צֵדָה לֹא עָשׂוּ לָהֶם:

נוֹטֵל הַמָּרוֹר בְּיָדוֹ וְיֹאמַר:

מָרוֹר זֶה שֶׁאָנוּ אוֹכְלִים עַל־שׁוּם מָה. עַל־שׁוּם שֶׁמֵּרְרוּ הַמִּצְרִים אֶת־חַיֵּי אֲבוֹתֵינוּ בְּמִצְרָיִם שֶׁנֶּאֱמַר וַיְמָרְרוּ אֶת־חַיֵּיהֶם בַּעֲבֹדָה קָשָׁה בְּחֹמֶר וּבִלְבֵנִים וּבְכָל־עֲבוֹדָה בַּשָּׂדֶה אֵת כָּל־עֲבֹדָתָם אֲשֶׁר עָבְדוּ בָהֶם בְּפָרֶךְ:

"אֲשֶׁר פָּסַח עַל בָּתֵּי בְנֵי יִשְׂרָאֵל בְּמִצְרַיִם
בְּנָגְפּוֹ אֶת מִצְרַיִם וְאֶת בָּתֵּינוּ הִצִּיל"
"Because He passed over the houses of the Children
of Israel in Egypt when He struck the Egyptians
with a plague, and He saved our houses."

QUESTION: The words *"ve'et bateinu hitzil"* — "and He saved our houses" — are superfluous since it already says that He skipped over the Jewish homes when He struck the Egyptians?

הַגָּדָה שֶׁל פֶּסַח   166

Egypt, as it is said:[1] "You shall say, 'It is a *Pesach*-offering for *Adonai* because He passed over the houses of the Children of Israel in Egypt, when He struck the Egyptians with a plague, and He saved our houses,' and the people bowed and prostrated themselves."

While we recite the following paragraph, it is the prevailing Lubavitch custom to hold the middle and lower *matzot* and their covering until the second time the phrase *al shum* ("Because") is recited.

מצה This *matzah* that we eat — what is its reason? Because the dough of our fathers did not have time to rise before the King of kings, the Holy One, blessed be He, revealed Himself to them and redeemed them, as it is said:[2] "They baked the dough that they had brought out of Egypt into *matzah* cakes, because it had not fermented, for they were driven out of Egypt and could not delay; nor had they prepared any [other] provisions for themselves."

While reciting the following paragraph, it is the prevailing Lubavitch custom to rest one's hand on the *maror*, as well as on the *maror* to be used for the *koreich* until the second time the phrase *"al shum"* ("Because") is mentioned.

מרור This *maror* that we eat — what is its reason? Because the Egyptians embittered the lives of our fathers in Egypt, as it is said:[3] "They embittered their lives with harsh labor, with mortar and with bricks, as well as with all kinds of labor in the field; all the toil which they made them serve was with rigor."

1. *Shemot* 12:27. 2. *Shemot* 12:39. 3. *Shemot* 1:14.

ANSWER: According to the *Midrash Rabbah* (*Shemot* 18:2), when the Egyptians were warned of the oncoming plague of the killing of the firstborn, some thought they would outsmart Hashem by putting their firstborn in Jewish homes. This was of no avail because there, too, the Egyptian firstborn were killed. Thus, the *pasuk* is saying that this is a *Pesach*-offering to Hashem because 1) He passed over the houses of the Jews when He struck the Egyptian homes, and 2) *"Et bateinu hitzil"* — our household, i.e. the Jewish firstborn, were saved when He would enter a Jewish house to kill an Egyptian firstborn.

(הגש״פ מגדל עדר החדש בפי׳ דובר שלום)

KI YISHALCHA BINCHA

בְּכָל־דּוֹר וָדוֹר חַיָּב אָדָם לִרְאוֹת אֶת־עַצְמוֹ כְּאִלּוּ הוּא יָצָא מִמִּצְרַיִם. שֶׁנֶּאֱמַר וְהִגַּדְתָּ לְבִנְךָ בַּיּוֹם הַהוּא לֵאמֹר בַּעֲבוּר זֶה עָשָׂה יהוה לִי בְּצֵאתִי מִמִּצְרָיִם: לֹא אֶת־אֲבוֹתֵינוּ בִּלְבָד גָּאַל הַקָּדוֹשׁ בָּרוּךְ הוּא מִמִּצְרַיִם אֶלָּא אַף אוֹתָנוּ גָּאַל עִמָּהֶם. שֶׁנֶּאֱמַר וְאוֹתָנוּ הוֹצִיא מִשָּׁם לְמַעַן הָבִיא אוֹתָנוּ לָתֶת לָנוּ אֶת־הָאָרֶץ אֲשֶׁר נִשְׁבַּע לַאֲבֹתֵינוּ:

יכסה את הפת ויגביה את הכוס
ואוחזו בידו עד סיום ברכת אשר גאלנו:

לְפִיכָךְ אֲנַחְנוּ חַיָּבִים לְהוֹדוֹת לְהַלֵּל לְשַׁבֵּחַ לְפָאֵר לְרוֹמֵם לְהַדֵּר לְבָרֵךְ לְעַלֵּה וּלְקַלֵּס, לְמִי שֶׁעָשָׂה לַאֲבוֹתֵינוּ וְלָנוּ אֶת־כָּל־הַנִּסִּים הָאֵלּוּ, הוֹצִיאָנוּ מֵעַבְדוּת לְחֵרוּת, מִיָּגוֹן לְשִׂמְחָה, וּמֵאֵבֶל לְיוֹם טוֹב, וּמֵאֲפֵלָה לְאוֹר גָּדוֹל, וּמִשִּׁעְבּוּד לִגְאֻלָּה, וְנֹאמַר לְפָנָיו הַלְלוּיָהּ:

"בכל דור ודור אדם חייב לראות את עצמו כאלו הוא יצא ממצרים"
**"In every generation a person is obligated
to regard himself as if he had gone out of Egypt."**

QUESTION: Since it says, *"ke'ilu hu yatza mimitzrayim"* — "as if *he* had gone out of Egypt." The words *"et atzmo"* — "himself" — are superfluous.

ANSWER: Though Hashem had told Avraham that the Jews would be in Egypt for 400 years, in reality they were there for 210. According to the *Zohar*, the missing years are made up by Hashem, who was there in Egypt together with the Jewish people, as He said to Yaakov, "I shall descend with you to Egypt and I shall also surely bring you up" (*Bereishit* 46:4). The words *"et atzmo"* — "himself" — refer to Hashem (see p. 95). Hence, the *Haggadah* is saying that in every generation one is obligated to regard *"et Atzmo"* — Hashem — as if He had come out of Egypt.

(צבי לצדיק)

בכל In every generation, a person is obligated to regard himself as if he had gone out of Egypt, as it is said:[1] "And you shall tell your son on that day, saying: 'It is because of this that *Adonai* did for me when I went out of Egypt.'" It was not only our fathers whom the Holy One, blessed be He, redeemed from Egypt; He redeemed us as well, as it is said:[2] "He brought us out from there, so that He might bring us to give us the land He swore to our fathers."

The *matzot* are covered and the cup is raised.

לפיכך Therefore, we are obliged to thank, praise, laud, glorify, exalt, honor, bless, extol, and acclaim the One who performed for our fathers and for us all these miracles. He took us out from slavery to freedom, from sorrow to joy, from mourning to festivity, from deep darkness to great light, and from servitude to redemption. Therefore, let us say before Him: *Halleluyah* — praise God.

1. *Shemot* 13:8. 2. *Devarim* 6:23.

"לפיכך אנחנו חיבים להודות להלל"

"Therefore, we are obliged to thank, to praise."

QUESTION: For what reason is there an introduction explaining why it is proper to say *Hallel* this night?

ANSWER: The *Gemara* (*Arachin* 10b) says that *Hallel* is not said over a miracle which took place outside of *Eretz Yisrael*. If so, the *Gemara* asks, why do we say *Hallel* on *Pesach*? The *Gemara* answers that this rule took effect only in regard to miracles that occurred after the Jews entered *Eretz Yisrael,* but if the miracle occurred prior, it was appropriate to say *Hallel* even though it occurred outside of *Eretz Yisrael.*

This passage of the *Haggadah* is offering another reason why it is appropriate to recite *Hallel* for the Exodus, though it occurred outside of *Eretz Yisrael.*

The *Maharsha* (ibid.) explains that the difference between a miracle which occurs in *Eretz Yisrael* and one which occurs in any other land is that the former is performed through Hashem Himself while the latter is through an angel.

Previously the *Haggadah* states clearly that the miraculous redemption from Egypt was entirely through Hashem and no one else. Consequently, we say *"lefichach"* — "therefore" — it is proper to offer praise to the One who personally performed miracles on our behalf, even though the miracles were outside of *Eretz Yisrael.*

(הגש״פ קבוץ חכמים מרב עבדאל סומך ז״ל מבגדאד)

הַלְלוּיָהּ | הַלְלוּ עַבְדֵי יְהֹוָה הַלְלוּ אֶת־שֵׁם יְהֹוָה: יְהִי שֵׁם יְהֹוָה מְבֹרָךְ מֵעַתָּה וְעַד־עוֹלָם: מִמִּזְרַח־שֶׁמֶשׁ עַד־מְבוֹאוֹ מְהֻלָּל שֵׁם יְהֹוָה: רָם עַל־כָּל־גּוֹיִם | יְהֹוָה עַל־הַשָּׁמַיִם כְּבוֹדוֹ: מִי כַּיהֹוָה אֱלֹהֵינוּ הַמַּגְבִּיהִי לָשָׁבֶת: הַמַּשְׁפִּילִי לִרְאוֹת בַּשָּׁמַיִם וּבָאָרֶץ: מְקִימִי מֵעָפָר דָּל מֵאַשְׁפֹּת יָרִים אֶבְיוֹן: לְהוֹשִׁיבִי עִם־נְדִיבִים עִם נְדִיבֵי עַמּוֹ: מוֹשִׁיבִי | עֲקֶרֶת הַבַּיִת אֵם־הַבָּנִים שְׂמֵחָה הַלְלוּיָהּ:

"Praise G-d." — "הללוי־ה"

QUESTION: *Hallel* is usually recited standing and with a *berachah*. Why tonight do we omit the *berachah* and recite it sitting?

ANSWER: The *berachah* is omitted because the *Hallel* is divided into two parts, separated by the festive meal. The reason for this is that the first two chapters of *Hallel* are related to the Exodus from Egypt, the splitting of the sea, and the giving of the Torah, which are events of the past. Therefore, after these two Psalms, we recite the blessing for the redemption and eat the *matzah* in commemoration of the Exodus. The later Psalms refer to future events (the resurrection of the dead and the "birth pangs" of *Mashiach*, see *Pesachim* 118a).

It is recited while sitting because we do things on *Pesach* in a manner which demonstrates freedom.

(הגש״פ עם לקוטי טעמים ומנהגים)

* * *

Alternatively, the *Gemara* (*Pesachim* 36a) explains the reason why *matzah* is called *"lechem oni"* is because it is *"lechem she'onin alav devarim harbeh"* — "Bread upon which one declares many things." Rashi explains that "the many things declared are the *Haggadah* and complete *Hallel*. Thus, the *Hallel* recited at the *Seder* is not similar to all the others, which are recited primarily to thank Hashem for miracles, but rather it relates to the fulfillment of the *mitzvah* of eating *lechem oni* — *matzah*.

In addition, the *Hallel* recited tonight is unique. It is a part of the fulfillment of the *mitzvah* of *sipur yetziat mitzraim* — relating of

הללויה *Halleluyah* — Praise God! Offer praise you servants of *Adonai*, praise the Name of *Adonai*. May the Name of *Adonai* be blessed from now until eternity. From the rising of the sun until its setting, praised is the Name of *Adonai*. Exalted above all nations is *Adonai*, above the heavens is His glory. Who is like *Adonai*, our God, who dwells on high, yet lowers Himself to look upon the heaven and the earth? He raises the poor from the dust; He lifts the needy from the dunghill, to seat them with nobles, with the nobles of His people. He restores the barren woman into a household, into a joyful mother of children, *Halleluyah* — praise God.[1]

1. Psalm 113.

---

the Exodus — and praising Hashem for the favor He did us (see Rambam, *Sefer Hamitzvot* 157 (Me'erie, *Pesachim* 95a)). Consequently, the laws which apply to the *Hallel* recited on the eighteen occasions discussed by the *Gemara* (*Arachin* 10a) do not apply tonight.

(אורות הפסח מהרב שלמה הלוי וואָרמאַן סי' מ"ב, מ"ג)

ובזה מובן מדוע הרמב"ם כתב אודות אמירת הלל בתוך הסדר בהל' חו"מ פ"ח הל' ה' ואילו בפ"ג מהלכות חנוכה כ' הלכות הלל ומנה הי"ח ימים שגומרין בהן את ההלל ולא הזכיר ההלל שאומרים בהגש"פ.

"ממזרח שמש עד מבואו מהלל שם ה'"
"From the rising of the sun to its setting, G-d's name is praised."

QUESTION: Instead of "From the rising of the sun to its setting," it could have simply said, "The entire day"?

ANSWER: The rising of the sun is an allusion to periods of affluence and success when everything is "shining" for the individual. On the other hand, the setting of the sun alludes to periods of darkness when, G-d forbid, the opposite prevails. King David is saying that in whatever situation a person may find himself, regardless of whether things are shining for him or the opposite, Hashem should be praised.

(שי לחגים ומועדים)

בְּצֵאת יִשְׂרָאֵל מִמִּצְרָיִם בֵּית יַעֲקֹב מֵעַם לֹעֵז: הָיְתָה
יְהוּדָה לְקָדְשׁוֹ יִשְׂרָאֵל מַמְשְׁלוֹתָיו: הַיָּם רָאָה וַיָּנֹס הַיַּרְדֵּן
יִסֹּב לְאָחוֹר: הֶהָרִים רָקְדוּ כְאֵילִים גְּבָעוֹת כִּבְנֵי צֹאן: מַה־לְּךָ
הַיָּם כִּי תָנוּס הַיַּרְדֵּן תִּסֹּב לְאָחוֹר: הֶהָרִים תִּרְקְדוּ כְאֵילִים
גְּבָעוֹת כִּבְנֵי־צֹאן: מִלִּפְנֵי אָדוֹן חוּלִי אָרֶץ מִלִּפְנֵי אֱלוֹהַּ
יַעֲקֹב: הַהֹפְכִי הַצּוּר אֲגַם־מָיִם חַלָּמִישׁ לְמַעְיְנוֹ־מָיִם:

"The sea saw and fled." — "הים ראה וינוס"

QUESTION: According to the *Midrash* (*Shochar Tov* 114) when
the sea saw Yosef's coffin, it fled. What exactly was it that influenced
the sea?

ANSWER: The *Midrash Rabbah* (*Shemot* 21:6) says that when the
Jews approached the sea, it refused to split for them, saying, "I am
older than man; you all should honor me and not expect me to split
for you." (Oceans and seas were created on the third day of creation,
and man was created on the sixth day.)

However, seeing the coffin of Yosef, the sea agreed to split for
the following reason:

Though Yosef was one of the youngest of Yaakov's sons, the
brothers gave him all the honors befitting a firstborn. They were
convinced that he was fit to be their king because of the high level of
kedushah — holiness — he maintained while living in Egypt. Even
when he became the viceroy to Pharaoh, he remained a *tzaddik*.
Seeing Yosef's coffin, the sea realized that qualitative years are
superior to quantitative ones. Therefore, though the sea was older, it
deferred to the Jews' lofty spiritual qualities and divided its waters
to accommodate them as they were en route to receiving the Torah.

(הדרש והעיון, שמות מאמר קכ"ד)

"הים ראה וינס הירדן יסב לאחור"
"The sea saw and fled, the Jordan turned backward."

QUESTION: There is a *Midrash Peli'ah* (wondrous *Midrash*)
that asks, "What did the sea see?" The *Midrash* answers, "It saw
the *Bereita* (Talmudic statement) of Rabbi Yishmael."

What did the sea learn from Rabbi Yishmael?

בצאת When Israel went out of Egypt, the House of Yaakov from a people of a alien language, Judah became His holy one, Israel His dominion. The sea saw and fled; the Jordan turned backward. The mountains skipped like rams, the hills like young lambs. What is with you, O sea, that you flee? Jordan, that you turn backward? Mountains, [why] do you skip like rams; hills, like young lambs? [We do so] before the Master, the Creator of the earth, before the God of Yaakov; Who turns the rock into a pool of water, the flintstone into a spring of water.[1]

1. Psalm 114.

ANSWER: Rabbi Yishmael says, "Through thirteen rules the Torah is elucidated." One is *"kal vachomer"* — a conclusion inferred from a lenient law to a strict one and vice versa (*Sifra*, Introduction). Originally, the sea was reluctant to go against its nature and split. However, when it realized that later on in history the Jordan river would split for Yehoshua when he would lead the Jews into *Eretz Yisrael* (Joshua 3:16), the sea used a *kal vachomer*, saying, "If the Jordan will split for the student, then how much more should I agree to split for Moshe, the teacher."

This fits in very well with the words *"Hayam ra'ah vayanos —* the sea saw and fled [because] *hayardein —* the Jordan — *yisov —* will turn backwards (future tense)."

(שער בת רבים פ׳ ואתחנן)

Alternatively, according to *halachah* if one chases after a person intending to kill him, all bystanders are obligated to rescue the one being chased, even if it is necessary to kill the pursuer. The *Gemara* (*Sanhedrin* 73a) bases this *halachah* on a teaching of Rabbi Yishmael regarding a *na'arah me'orasah* (betrothed girl).

When the sea saw the Egyptians chasing the Jewish people, it was hesitant to split so that the Jews could be saved and then return to its full strength to drown the Egyptians. Why should the Jews receive better treatment than the Egyptians? However, when it realized that the Egyptians pursued the Jews intending to kill them, it "saw the teaching of Rabbi Yishmael" and concluded that it was obligated to save the Jews and kill the Egyptians.

בָּרוּךְ אַתָּה יְהֹוָה אֱלֹהֵינוּ מֶלֶךְ הָעוֹלָם אֲשֶׁר גְּאָלָנוּ
וְגָאַל אֶת־אֲבוֹתֵינוּ מִמִּצְרַיִם, וְהִגִּיעָנוּ הַלַּיְלָה הַזֶּה לֶאֱכָל־
בּוֹ מַצָּה וּמָרוֹר, כֵּן יְהֹוָה אֱלֹהֵינוּ וֵאלֹהֵי אֲבוֹתֵינוּ יַגִּיעֵנוּ
לְמוֹעֲדִים וְלִרְגָלִים אֲחֵרִים הַבָּאִים לִקְרָאתֵנוּ לְשָׁלוֹם
שְׂמֵחִים בְּבִנְיַן עִירֶךָ וְשָׂשִׂים בַּעֲבוֹדָתֶךָ, וְנֹאכַל שָׁם מִן
הַזְּבָחִים וּמִן הַפְּסָחִים (במוצאי שבת: מִן הַפְּסָחִים וּמִן
הַזְּבָחִים) אֲשֶׁר יַגִּיעַ דָּמָם עַל קִיר מִזְבַּחֲךָ לְרָצוֹן, וְנוֹדֶה
לְךָ שִׁיר חָדָשׁ עַל גְּאֻלָּתֵנוּ וְעַל פְּדוּת נַפְשֵׁנוּ: בָּרוּךְ אַתָּה
יְהֹוָה גָּאַל יִשְׂרָאֵל:

ומברך ושותה בהסיבה:

בָּרוּךְ אַתָּה יְהֹוָה אֱלֹהֵינוּ מֶלֶךְ הָעוֹלָם בּוֹרֵא פְּרִי הַגָּפֶן:

"וְנֹאכַל שָׁם מִן הַזְּבָחִים וּמִן הַפְּסָחִים (במוצאי שבת מִן הַפְּסָחִים וּמִן הַזְּבָחִים)"
"There we shall eat of the sacrifices and *Pesach*-offerings
(when *Pesach* falls on the conclusion of *Shabbat*: **of the**
Pesach-offerings and of the sacrifices)."

QUESTION: Why is the order changed on *"motza'ei Shabbat"*
— "the conclusion of the *Shabbat*"?

ANSWER: In the time of the *Beit Hamikdash* on *Erev Pesach*, a
karban Chagigah — Festival-offering — was offered in addition to
the *karban Pesach* — *Pesach*-offering. At the *Seder* they would
partake first of the festival-offering so that the *Pesach*-offering
would be eaten *"al hasovah"* — to reach satiation — i.e. like desert
at the end of the meal. Thus, the order of first "sacrifices" and then
"*Pesach*-offerings."

When *Pesach* fell on *motza'ei Shabbat*, the *Pesach*-offering was
offered even though it was *Shabbat*, and the *Chagigah* was not
offered till the next day — Sunday. Therefore on *motza'ei Shabbat* we
reverse the order and mention the *Pesach*-offering first and then the
sacrifices, i.e. the *Chagigah*, which will be offered the next day.

According to others, there is no difference in the text, even if
the *Seder* is on *motza'ei Shabbat*, because we are expressing the
wish that Hashem redeem us so that we will have the opportunity
next year to be in Jerusalem and eat there of the sacrifices which
will be brought in the *Beit Hamikdash*. Even if according to our pre-

The cup of wine is raised and held until the
conclusion of the blessing over the wine.

ברוך **Blessed are You, *Adonai*, our God, King of the universe, Who redeemed us and redeemed our fathers from Egypt, and Who has enabled us to reach this night so that we may eat *matzah* and *maror*. So too, *Adonai*, our God and God of our fathers, enable us to reach other holidays and festivals that will come to us in peace, gladdened in the rebuilding of Your city and rejoicing in Your service. There we shall eat of the sacrifices and of the *Pesach*-offerings** {when Pesach falls on Saturday night: **of the *Pesach*-offerings and the sacrifices}** **whose blood shall be sprinkled on the wall of Your altar, to be graciously accepted, and we shall give thanks to You with a new song for our redemption and for the deliverance of our souls. Blessed are You, *Adonai*, Who redeemed Israel.**

After reciting the following blessing,
we drink the second cup **reclining on the left side.**

ברוך **Blessed are You, *Adonai*, our God, King of the universe, Who created the fruit of the vine.**

---

calculated calendar, next year *Pesach* will fall on *motza'ei Shabbat*, nevertheless, when the *Beit Hamikdash* will be rebuilt we will return to establishing the calendar based on the testimony of witnesses, and it is possible that *Pesach* will not fall on *Shabbat*. (שו״ע הרב סי׳ תע״ג, סמ״ט)

"ונודה לך שיר חדש"
"And we shall give thanks to You with a new song."

QUESTION: Why does it say *"shir chadash"* — "a new song" — in masculine, and not the common *"shirah chadashah"* in feminine?

ANSWER: The word *"shirah"* in feminine, suggests that just as a woman conceives and gives birth again and again, always experiencing the pangs of childbirth, so too, all miracles — and their songs — are followed by new trials and tribulations and new deliverances. In the Messianic age, however, there will no longer be any troubles. At that time, therefore, they will recite a *"shir"* — "song" (in masculine) — which suggests that just as a man does not suffer birth pangs, so too the Jewish people will not suffer anymore. In other words, the ultimate miracle and redemption will be complete and ever-lasting. (פסחים דף קט״ז ע״ב תוד״ה ונאמר)

רָחְצָה

וְאַחַר כָּךְ נוֹטֵל יָדָיו וּמְבָרֵךְ עַל נְטִילַת יָדַיִם:

מוֹצִיא

וְיִקַּח הַמַּצּוֹת כְּסֵדֶר שֶׁהִנִּיחָם הַפְּרוּסָה בֵּין שְׁתֵּי הַשְּׁלֵמוֹת
וְיֹאחֲזֵם בְּיָדוֹ וִיבָרֵךְ:

בָּרוּךְ אַתָּה יְהוָֹה אֱלֹהֵינוּ מֶלֶךְ הָעוֹלָם הַמּוֹצִיא לֶחֶם מִן הָאָרֶץ:

מַצָּה

וְלֹא יִבְצַע מֵהֶן אֶלָּא יַנִּיחַ הַמַּצָּה הַשְּׁלִישִׁית לְהִשָּׁמֵט מִיָּדוֹ וִיבָרֵךְ עַל
הַפְּרוּסָה עִם הָעֶלְיוֹנָה טֶרֶם יְשַׁבְּרֵם בְּרָכָה זוֹ. וִיכַוֵּין לִפְטוֹר גַּ"כ אֲכִילַת
הַכְּרִיכָה שֶׁמַּמַּצָּה הַשְּׁלִישִׁית וְגַם אֲכִילַת הָאֲפִיקוֹמָן יִפְטוֹר בִּבְרָכָה זוֹ:

בָּרוּךְ אַתָּה יְהוָֹה אֱלֹהֵינוּ מֶלֶךְ הָעוֹלָם אֲשֶׁר קִדְּשָׁנוּ בְּמִצְוֹתָיו וְצִוָּנוּ עַל אֲכִילַת מַצָּה:

וְאַחַר כָּךְ יִבְצַע כְּזַיִת מִכָּל אֶחָד מִשְּׁתֵּיהֶן וְיֹאכְלֵם בְּיַחַד וּבַהֲסִבָּה:

MATZAH

QUESTION: Why do we bake our *matzot* round?

ANSWER: It was *Pesach* when the three angels visited Avraham (see *Rosh Hashanah* 11a, *Tosafot*). After they accepted his invitation to eat with him, he told Sarah to quickly get flour and *"lushi va'asi ugot"* — "kneed and make cakes" (*Bereishit* 18:6). In Hebrew the word *"ugah"* means a circle (see *Ta'anit* 23a, Rashi). Since Avraham baked round *matzot* on *Pesach*, we follow suit.

QUESTION: What is the significance of round *matzah*?

ANSWER: In the olden days paganism was prevalent. It was common practice for one to worship more than one deity or idol, and the people would indicate through the bread they baked how many gods they had. If, for instance, one had two gods, he made his bread with two points, and if one had five gods, his bread was shaped to have five corners. In order to accentuate our belief in one G-d, it was Avraham's practice, and also the practice of our fathers in Egypt, to make round bread, indicating that we believe in only one G-d and that He has no beginning or end.

(שו"ת יהודה יעלה - מהר"י אסאד - או"ח סי' קנ"ז)

RACHTZAH
WASHING THE HANDS

The hands are washed in preparation for partaking of the *matzah*. The blessing *"Al netilat yada'im"* is recited:

MOTZI
RECITING THE BLESSING *"HAMOTZI"*

Take the *matzot* in the order that they are lying on the tray — the broken piece between the two whole *matzot;* hold them in your hand and recite the following blessing:

ברוך **Blessed are You,** *Adonai,* **our God, King of the universe, Who brought forth bread from the earth.**

MATZAH
RECITING THE BLESSING
"AL ACHILAT MATZAH" AND EATING THE *MATZAH*

Do not break anything off the *matzot*. First put down the third *matzah* (the bottom one), and recite the following blessing over the broken *matzah* and the top one. When reciting the blessing have in mind that it refers also to the eating of the 'sandwich' of *koreich* — which will be made with the third *matzah* — and also to the eating of the *afikoman*. Though one should avoid any irrelevant talk before eating the *koreich,* it is not the prevailing Lubavitch custom to extend this stringency until the eating of the *afikoman*.

It is a positive commandment to eat *matzah* on the *Seder* night. To fulfill one's obligation, one must eat a *kezayit* (a measure formally described as the size of an olive and traditionally determined as one ounce, 27 grams). This amount of *matzah* must be eaten *bichedei achilat p'ras* (half the standard Mishnaic loaf of bread). The precise definition of this time period is a matter of debate among the Rabbis. The accepted figure with regard to eating *matzah* is four minutes (see p. 36).

ברוך **Blessed are You,** *Adonai,* **our God, King of the universe, Who has sanctified us with His commandments and commanded us concerning the eating of** *matzah.*

Now break off a *kezayit* from the upper *matzah*, and a *kezayit* from the middle *matzah*. We eat these two pieces **simultaneously** and **while reclining on the left side.** The prevailing Lubavitch custom is not to dip the *matzah* in salt.

Usually, the *matzot* of the *Seder* plate are not large enough to provide everyone with portions of the desired size. Therefore, other *matzah* is taken in addition.

מָרוֹר

ואחר כך יקח כזית מרור ויטבל בחרוסת וינער החרוסת מעליו כדי
שלא יתבטל טעם המרירות ויברך ברכה זו:

בָּרוּךְ אַתָּה יְהוָה אֱלֹהֵינוּ מֶלֶךְ הָעוֹלָם אֲשֶׁר קִדְּשָׁנוּ בְּמִצְוֹתָיו וְצִוָּנוּ עַל אֲכִילַת מָרוֹר:

ויאכלנו בלי הסיבה:

כּוֹרֵךְ

ואח"כ יקח מצה הג' וחזרת עמה כשיעור כזית ויטבול בחרוסת ויכרכם
ביחד ויאמר זה:

כֵּן עָשָׂה הִלֵּל בִּזְמַן שֶׁבֵּית הַמִּקְדָּשׁ הָיָה קַיָּם הָיָה כּוֹרֵךְ פֶּסַח מַצָּה וּמָרוֹר וְאוֹכֵל בְּיַחַד, כְּמוֹ שֶׁנֶּאֱמַר עַל מַצּוֹת וּמְרוֹרִים יֹאכְלֻהוּ:

ואוכלם ביחד (ובהסיבה. טוש"ע סימן תע"ה.
הגהה מסדור אדמו"ר בעל צ"צ זלל"ה:

"כמו שנאמר על מצות ומרורים יאכלהו"
"As it is said: "With *matzot* and *maror* they shall eat it.""

QUESTION: This *pasuk* is from *Bamidbar* (9:11), and it refers to the second *Pesach*-offering, which was brought one month later by those who were unable to bring it in the proper time. Why doesn't the *Haggadah* quote the *pasuk* in *Shemot* (12:8), which refers to the first *Pesach* and which states, *"Ve'achlu et habasar balailah hazeh tzeli eish umatzot al merorim yochluhu"* — "They shall eat the flesh on that night — roasted over the fire — and *matzot*; with bitter herbs shall they eat it"?

ANSWER: The word *"matzot"* in the *pasuk* in *Shemot* can be explained as being connected to the earlier part, namely, that at night they should eat the meat with *matzot*. Then the *pasuk* continues to command another separate obligation, namely, that the meat should also be eaten with bitter herbs. Hence, there is no proof from the *pasuk* that all three, *Pesach*, *matzah*, and *maror*, are to be *combined* and eaten together. This is only clear in the second *pasuk*, which states that "They shall eat it with *matzot* and *maror*."

(רמב"ן, ועי' הדרש והעיון – שמות, ושו"ת חתם סופר או"ח סי' ק"מ)

MAROR
EATING THE BITTER HERBS

Now take a *kezayit* of the *maror*, dip it into the *charoset*. Before that, the *charoset* should be softened with wine. One should not dip the entire *maror* into the *charoset*, so that its bitter taste will not be neutralized. For the same reason one should shake off the *charoset*.

The blessing *"al achilat maror"* should not be recited until the *maror* is dipped into the *charoset*, so that the *mitzvah* of eating the *maror* will follow it immediately. When reciting this blessing, one should bear in mind the *maror* of *koreich* as well. **One does *not* recline while eating the *maror*.**

* * *

In the present age, eating *maror* fulfills a Rabbinic commandment. In this instance as well, one must eat a *kezayit bichedei achilat p'ras* — four minutes. When it is difficult for a person to eat a full ounce of *maror*, he may rely on the more lenient opinions that consider a *kezayit* to be ¾ of an ounce. Similarly, in such circumstances, one may consider *kedei achilat p'ras* to be six or seven minutes. The romaine lettuce and the horseradish are both included in the measure of a *kezayit*.

ברוך **Blessed are You, *Adonai*, our God, King of the universe, Who has sanctified us with His commandments and commanded us concerning the eating of *maror*.**

KOREICH
EATING A SANDWICH OF *MATZAH* AND BITTER HERBS

The *koreich* is a sandwich including a *kezayit* from the third *matzah* and a *kezayit* of *maror*. It must also be eaten *bichedei achilat p'ras* — four minutes. In this instance as well, if necessary, one may rely on the more lenient opinions that consider a *kezayit* to be ¾ of an ounce and *kedai achilat p'ras* to be six or seven minutes.

The *chazeret* alone is dipped into the *charoset*, but not the *matzah*. The prevailing Lubavitch custom is not to dip the *chazeret* in the *charoset*, but to put some dry *charoset* on the *chazeret*, and then to shake it off. The sandwich should be **eaten while reclining on the left side.**

Before partaking of the sandwich, the following passage is recited:

כן **Thus did Hillel at the time when the *Beit Hamikdash* was standing; He would combine the *Pesach*-offering, *matzah*, and *maror* and eat them together, as it is said:**[1] **"They shall eat it with *matzot* and *maror*."**

1. *Bamidbar* 9:11.

שֻׁלְחָן עוֹרֵךְ

ואחר כך אוכל ושותה כדי צרכו
ויכול לשתות יין בין כוס ב' לג':

צָפוּן

ואח"כ יקח האפיקומן ויחלקו לכל בני ביתו
לכל אחד כזית ויזהר שלא ישתה אחר אפיקומן
ויאכל בהסיבה וצריך לאכלו קודם חצות:

שלחן עורך
Eating the festive meal

QUESTION: Why is it customary to eat an egg at the beginning of the meal?

ANSWER: It is customary for a mourner to eat eggs. Hence, an egg is eaten for the last meal before the fast on *Tishah B'Av,* when we mourn the destruction of the *Beit Hamikdash.* Similarly, on *Pesach* the fact that we do not have the *Pesach*-offering reminds of us the destruction of the *Beit Hamikdash.* Thus, we place an egg on the *Seder* plate and eat it at the start of the meal.

It is interesting to note that every year the first *seder* and *Tishah B'Av* take place on the same day of the week.

(רמ"א סי' תע"ו, ב', ועי' ט"ז)

Alternatively, the Egyptians were strict vegetarians. They did not eat meat or fish or anything which came from the animal kingdom, such as blood, milk, or eggs. Due to this lifestyle, shepherds were "abhorrent to Egyptians" (*Bereishit* 46:34), and they despised anyone who ate animal derivatives (see Ibn Ezra, *Shemot* 22:8).

Hence, to demonstrate that we are emancipated from Egypt and have no fear of the Egyptians or respect for their practices, we eat an egg at the outset of the festive meal and follow it up with fish, meat, and all the dainties.

(אוצר כל מנהגי ישרון מר' אברהם אליעזר ז"ל הירשאוויץ)

SHULCHAN OREICH
EATING THE FESTIVE MEAL

It is customary to begin the festive meal by eating the egg from the *Seder* plate after it is dipped in salt-water to recall the *Chagigah* sacrifice offered in the *Beit Hamikdash*. The *zero'a* should not be eaten. The prevailing custom in Lubavitch is to eat the meal without reclining.

Particular care should be taken to avoid wetting the *matzah*. For this reason, the *matzot* on the table are kept covered, so that no drop of water should fall on them, and so that no *matzah* crumbs should fall into any water or soup. Likewise, before pouring water or liquids containing water into a cup or plate, one should check for any crumbs of *matzah*. The prevailing Lubavitch custom is not to eat *matzah* together with fish or meat lest it become wet.

One may drink wine between the second and third cup without reservation.

Roasted or broiled meat or chicken, including pot roast, should not be eaten at the *Seder* since the *Pesach*-offering, which we do not have at present, had to be roasted.

TZAFUN
EATING THE AFIKOMAN

The *afikoman* is the half of the middle *matzah* that was hidden away to be eaten at the conclusion of the meal. There is an unresolved question as to whether the *afikoman* is intended to commemorate the *Pesach*-offering or the *matzah* that was eaten together with it. Therefore, ideally one should eat two *kezeitim*. This is the prevailing Lubavitch custom.

Some find this difficult and therefore eat only one *kezayit*. In such an instance, the person should have the intent that the *matzah* serve to commemorate whichever of the above two subjects is the one requiring commemoration.

Portions of the desired size should be given to everyone. The *afikoman* that was hidden away usually is not large enough to provide everyone with enough. Therefore, other *matzah* is taken in addition.

The *afikoman* should be **eaten reclining on the left side,** without pause or interruption, and must be eaten *bichedei achilat p'ras* (see p. 36). At the first *Seder*, the *afikoman* should be eaten before midnight. With the exception of the remaining two of the four cups of wine drunk at the *Seder*, after the *afikoman,* nothing should be eaten or drunk for the remainder of the night so that the taste of the *matzah* will remain in one's mouth.

בָּרֵךְ

ואח״כ מוזגין כוס שלישי ואומר עליו בהמ״ז:

שִׁיר הַמַּעֲלוֹת בְּשׁוּב יְהוָֹה אֶת־שִׁיבַת צִיּוֹן הָיִינוּ
כְּחֹלְמִים: אָז יִמָּלֵא שְׂחוֹק פִּינוּ וּלְשׁוֹנֵנוּ רִנָּה אָז יֹאמְרוּ
בַגּוֹיִם הִגְדִּיל יְהוָֹה לַעֲשׂוֹת עִם־אֵלֶּה: הִגְדִּיל יְהוָֹה לַעֲשׂוֹת
עִמָּנוּ הָיִינוּ שְׂמֵחִים: שׁוּבָה יְהוָֹה אֶת־שְׁבִיתֵנוּ כַּאֲפִיקִים
בַּנֶּגֶב: הַזֹּרְעִים בְּדִמְעָה בְּרִנָּה יִקְצֹרוּ: הָלוֹךְ יֵלֵךְ | וּבָכֹה נֹשֵׂא
מֶשֶׁךְ־הַזָּרַע בֹּא יָבֹא בְרִנָּה נֹשֵׂא אֲלֻמֹּתָיו:

לִבְנֵי־קֹרַח מִזְמוֹר שִׁיר יְסוּדָתוֹ בְּהַרְרֵי־קֹדֶשׁ: אֹהֵב יְהוָֹה
שַׁעֲרֵי צִיּוֹן מִכֹּל מִשְׁכְּנוֹת יַעֲקֹב: נִכְבָּדוֹת מְדֻבָּר בָּךְ עִיר
הָאֱלֹהִים סֶלָה: אַזְכִּיר | רַהַב וּבָבֶל לְיֹדְעָי הִנֵּה פְלֶשֶׁת וְצוֹר
עִם כּוּשׁ זֶה יֻלַּד־שָׁם: וּלְצִיּוֹן | יֵאָמַר אִישׁ וְאִישׁ יֻלַּד־בָּהּ
וְהוּא יְכוֹנְנֶהָ עֶלְיוֹן: יְהוָֹה יִסְפֹּר בִּכְתוֹב עַמִּים זֶה יֻלַּד־שָׁם
סֶלָה: וְשָׁרִים כְּחֹלְלִים כֹּל מַעְיָנַי בָּךְ:

אֲבָרְכָה אֶת־יְהוָֹה בְּכָל־עֵת תָּמִיד תְּהִלָּתוֹ בְּפִי: סוֹף דָּבָר
הַכֹּל נִשְׁמָע אֶת־הָאֱלֹהִים יְרָא וְאֶת־מִצְוֹתָיו שְׁמוֹר כִּי־זֶה כָּל־
הָאָדָם: תְּהִלַּת יְהוָֹה יְדַבֶּר־פִּי וִיבָרֵךְ כָּל־בָּשָׂר שֵׁם קָדְשׁוֹ
לְעוֹלָם וָעֶד: וַאֲנַחְנוּ נְבָרֵךְ | יָהּ מֵעַתָּה וְעַד־עוֹלָם הַלְלוּיָהּ:

קודם מים אחרונים יאמר פסוק זה:

זֶה | חֵלֶק־אָדָם רָשָׁע מֵאֱלֹהִים וְנַחֲלַת אִמְרוֹ מֵאֵל:

ואחר מים אחרונים יאמר פסוק זה:

וַיְדַבֵּר אֵלַי זֶה הַשֻּׁלְחָן אֲשֶׁר לִפְנֵי יְהוָֹה:

כוס של ברכה — Cup of Blessing

QUESTION: The *Gemara* (*Pesachim* 119b) says that when the resurrection takes place, Hashem will make a feast for the *tzaddikim*, and when Avraham will be given the Cup of Blessing he will say, "I am unfit to recite the blessing because I had a son Yishmael." Yitzchak will say, "I am unfit because Eisav was my

182

BEIRACH — RECITING GRACE

The third cup of wine is filled, and the Blessing After the Meal is recited over it.

שיר A Song of Ascents. When *Adonai* returns the exiles of Zion, it will be as if we had been dreaming. Then, our mouth will be filled with laughter and our tongue with songs of joy. Then they will declare among the nations: "*Adonai* has done great things for these." *Adonai* has done great things for us; we have been joyful. Bring back, *Adonai*, our exiles as streams in the desert. Those who sow in tears will reap with joyous song. He who goes along weeping, carrying the bag of seed, will return singing joyously, carrying his sheaves.[1]

לבני By the sons of Korach, a psalm, a song whose theme is [praise for] the holy mountains [of Zion and Jerusalem]. *Adonai* loves the gates of Zion more than all the dwelling places of Yaakov. Glorious things are spoken of you, eternal city of God. I will make mention of Rahav (Egypt) and Babylon to those who know me; behold there are Philistia, Tyre, as well as Cush; [their call to fame is] "This one [great person] was born there." But of Zion it can be said; "Man after man [many men of greatness] were born in her," and He will establish her as supreme. *Adonai* will count in the register of people, "This one was born there"; *Selah*. Singers and dancers [will praise Jerusalem,] chanting: "All my inner thoughts are of you."[2]

אברכה I will bless *Adonai* at all times; His praise shall always be in my mouth.[3] The ultimate conclusion, all having been heard: Fear God, and observe His commandments, for this is the whole purpose of man.[4] My mouth will utter the praise of *Adonai*, and let all flesh bless His holy name forever and ever.[5] And we will bless God from now until eternity, *Halleluyah* — praise God.[6]

Before *mayim acharonim* — rinsing of the fingers — the following is said. [In contrast to the custom throughout the year, the wet fingers are not passed over one's lips.]

זה This is the portion of a wicked man from God, and the heritage assigned to him by the Almighty.[7]

After rinsing the fingers, the following is said:

וידבר And he said to me: 'This is the table that is before *Adonai*.'"[8]

Grace is said over a cup of wine or grape juice. The cup is held in the palm of one's right hand. It is held three handbreadths (approx. ten inches) above the table until one concludes the blessing *"Boneh berachamav Yerushalayim, Amein"* ("Who rebuilds Jerusalem in His mercy, *Amein*"), at which time it is placed on the table. It is raised again at the conclusion of Grace, for the blessing: *"Borei pri hagafen"* ("Who created the fruit of the vine").

1. Psalm 126. 2. Psalm 87. 3. *Psalms* 34:2. 4. *Ecclesiastes* 12:13. 5. *Psalms* 145:21. 6. *Psalms* 115:18. 8. *Job* 20:29.

אִם מְבָרְכִין בְּזִמּוּן אוֹמֵר הַמְבָרֵךְ:

הַב לָן וְנִבְרִיךְ: (או בל״א) רַבּוֹתַי מִיר וֶועלִין בֶּענְטְשִׁין:

וְעוֹנִין הַמְסוּבִּין:

יְהִי שֵׁם יְהֹוָה מְבֹרָךְ מֵעַתָּה וְעַד עוֹלָם:

הַמְבָרֵךְ אוֹמֵר:

בִּרְשׁוּת מָרָנָן וְרַבָּנָן וְרַבּוֹתַי נְבָרֵךְ (במנין אֱלֹהֵינוּ) שֶׁאָכַלְנוּ מִשֶּׁלּוֹ:

וְעוֹנִין הַמְסוּבִּין:

בָּרוּךְ (במנין אֱלֹהֵינוּ) שֶׁאָכַלְנוּ מִשֶּׁלּוֹ וּבְטוּבוֹ חָיִינוּ:

מִי שֶׁלֹּא אָכַל עִמָּהֶם עוֹנֶה:

בָּרוּךְ (במנין אֱלֹהֵינוּ) וּמְבֹרָךְ שְׁמוֹ תָּמִיד לְעוֹלָם וָעֶד:

בָּרוּךְ אַתָּה יְהֹוָה אֱלֹהֵינוּ מֶלֶךְ הָעוֹלָם הַזָּן אֶת־הָעוֹלָם כֻּלּוֹ בְּטוּבוֹ בְּחֵן בְּחֶסֶד וּבְרַחֲמִים, הוּא־נוֹתֵן לֶחֶם לְכָל־בָּשָׂר כִּי לְעוֹלָם חַסְדּוֹ: וּבְטוּבוֹ הַגָּדוֹל עִמָּנוּ תָּמִיד לֹא־חָסֵר לָנוּ וְאַל יֶחְסַר־לָנוּ מָזוֹן לְעוֹלָם וָעֶד: בַּעֲבוּר שְׁמוֹ הַגָּדוֹל כִּי הוּא אֵל זָן וּמְפַרְנֵס לַכֹּל וּמֵטִיב לַכֹּל וּמֵכִין מָזוֹן לְכָל־בְּרִיּוֹתָיו אֲשֶׁר בָּרָא כָּאָמוּר פּוֹתֵחַ אֶת־יָדֶךָ וּמַשְׂבִּיעַ לְכָל־חַי רָצוֹן: בָּרוּךְ אַתָּה יְהֹוָה הַזָּן אֶת הַכֹּל:

נוֹדֶה לְךָ יְהֹוָה אֱלֹהֵינוּ עַל שֶׁהִנְחַלְתָּ לַאֲבוֹתֵינוּ אֶרֶץ חֶמְדָּה טוֹבָה וּרְחָבָה, וְעַל שֶׁהוֹצֵאתָנוּ יְהֹוָה אֱלֹהֵינוּ מֵאֶרֶץ מִצְרַיִם וּפְדִיתָנוּ מִבֵּית עֲבָדִים, וְעַל־בְּרִיתְךָ שֶׁחָתַמְתָּ בִּבְשָׂרֵנוּ, וְעַל תּוֹרָתְךָ שֶׁלִּמַּדְתָּנוּ, וְעַל חֻקֶּיךָ שֶׁהוֹדַעְתָּנוּ, וְעַל חַיִּים חֵן וָחֶסֶד שֶׁחוֹנַנְתָּנוּ, וְעַל אֲכִילַת מָזוֹן שָׁאַתָּה זָן וּמְפַרְנֵס אוֹתָנוּ תָּמִיד בְּכָל־יוֹם וּבְכָל־עֵת וּבְכָל־שָׁעָה:

son." Yaakov will turn it down, "Because I married two sisters, which the Torah will later forbid." Moshe will say, "I cannot be the one to recite the blessing because I was not privileged to enter *Eretz Yisrael*," and Yehoshua will decline it saying, "I am unfit, for I did not merit to have a son." He will then say to David, "Take the cup and recite the blessing," and David will respond, "I will do so, and it is fitting for me, as it is stated, 'I shall raise the cup of salvations, and the Name of Hashem I shall invoke.'" (Psalms 106:13)

When there are three or more adult males eating at the *Seder,*
Grace is introduced as follows:

רבותי (Leader:) **Gentlemen, let us say Grace.**

(The others respond:) **May the Name of *Adonai* be blessed from now and forever.**

(The leader repeats that response and continues:) **With your permission, masters, teachers, and gentlemen, let us bless Him** (if ten or more adult males are present, he substitutes **"our God"** for **"Him"**) **of Whose bounty we have eaten.**

(The others respond:) **Blessed be He** (if ten or more adult males are present, they substitute **"our God"** for **"He"**) **of Whose bounty we have eaten and through His goodness we live.**

(The leader repeats this response.)

(Those present who did not partake of the meal respond:) **Blessed be He** (if ten or more adult males are present, they substitute **"our God"** for **"He"**) **and praised be His Name continually forever and ever.**

ברוך **Blessed are You, *Adonai*, our God, King of the universe Who, in His goodness, nourishes the entire world with grace, kindness, and mercy. He gives food to all flesh, for His kindness is eternal. Through His great goodness to us continuously we do not lack [food], and may we never lack food forever and ever for the sake of His great Name. For He is the Almighty, Who nourishes and sustains all, and does good to all, and prepares food for all His creatures which He has created, as is said:**[1] **"You open Your hand and satisfy the desire of every living being." Blessed are You, *Adonai*, Who provides food for all.**

נודה **We thank You, *Adonai*, our God, for having given as a heritage to our fathers, a precious, good, and spacious land, and for taking us out, *Adonai*, our God, from the land of Egypt and for redeeming us from the house of bondage; for Your covenant which You sealed in our flesh; for Your Torah which You taught us, and for Your statutes which You made known to us; for the life, favor, and kindness which You have graciously bestowed upon us; and for the food we eat with which You constantly feed and sustain us every day, at all times, and at every hour.**

1. *Psalms* 145:16.

Why will David consider himself so qualified for the honor?

ANSWER: The *Gemara* (*Berachot* 46a) rules that, *"Ba'al habayit botzei'a ve'orei'ach mevareich"* — "The host breaks the bread [makes the *Hamotzi*] and the guest recites the Blessing After Meal."

וְעַל הַכֹּל יהוה אֱלֹהֵינוּ אֲנַחְנוּ מוֹדִים לָךְ, וּמְבָרְכִים אוֹתָךְ,
יִתְבָּרֵךְ שִׁמְךָ בְּפִי כָּל חַי תָּמִיד לְעוֹלָם וָעֶד: כַּכָּתוּב וְאָכַלְתָּ
וְשָׂבָעְתָּ וּבֵרַכְתָּ אֶת־יהוה אֱלֹהֶיךָ עַל־הָאָרֶץ הַטּוֹבָה אֲשֶׁר נָתַן־
לָךְ: בָּרוּךְ אַתָּה יהוה עַל־הָאָרֶץ וְעַל־הַמָּזוֹן:

רַחֵם יהוה אֱלֹהֵינוּ עַל־יִשְׂרָאֵל עַמֶּךָ וְעַל־יְרוּשָׁלַיִם עִירֶךָ,
וְעַל צִיּוֹן מִשְׁכַּן כְּבוֹדֶךָ וְעַל מַלְכוּת בֵּית דָּוִד מְשִׁיחֶךָ וְעַל־
הַבַּיִת הַגָּדוֹל וְהַקָּדוֹשׁ שֶׁנִּקְרָא שִׁמְךָ עָלָיו: אֱלֹהֵינוּ אָבִינוּ רוֹעֵנוּ
זוֹנֵנוּ פַּרְנְסֵנוּ וְכַלְכְּלֵנוּ וְהַרְוִיחֵנוּ וְהַרְוַח לָנוּ יהוה אֱלֹהֵינוּ
מְהֵרָה מִכָּל־צָרוֹתֵינוּ: וְנָא אַל־תַּצְרִיכֵנוּ יהוה אֱלֹהֵינוּ. לֹא
לִידֵי מַתְּנַת בָּשָׂר וָדָם וְלֹא לִידֵי הַלְוָאָתָם, כִּי אִם לְיָדְךָ הַמְּלֵאָה
הַפְּתוּחָה הַקְּדוֹשָׁה וְהָרְחָבָה שֶׁלֹּא נֵבוֹשׁ וְלֹא נִכָּלֵם לְעוֹלָם וָעֶד:

בשבת:

רְצֵה וְהַחֲלִיצֵנוּ יהוה אֱלֹהֵינוּ בְּמִצְוֹתֶיךָ, וּבְמִצְוַת יוֹם הַשְּׁבִיעִי
הַשַּׁבָּת הַגָּדוֹל וְהַקָּדוֹשׁ הַזֶּה כִּי יוֹם זֶה גָּדוֹל וְקָדוֹשׁ הוּא לְפָנֶיךָ
לִשְׁבָּת־בּוֹ וְלָנוּחַ־בּוֹ בְּאַהֲבָה כְּמִצְוַת רְצוֹנֶךָ. וּבִרְצוֹנְךָ הָנִיחַ לָנוּ
יהוה אֱלֹהֵינוּ שֶׁלֹּא תְהֵא צָרָה וְיָגוֹן וַאֲנָחָה בְּיוֹם מְנוּחָתֵנוּ.
וְהַרְאֵנוּ יהוה אֱלֹהֵינוּ בְּנֶחָמַת צִיּוֹן עִירֶךָ, וּבְבִנְיַן יְרוּשָׁלַיִם עִיר
קָדְשֶׁךָ, כִּי אַתָּה הוּא בַּעַל הַיְשׁוּעוֹת וּבַעַל הַנֶּחָמוֹת:

King David was destined to be stillborn. Fortunately, Adam
gave him as a gift 70 years of his life and, thus, he lived in the
world for 70 years (see *Zohar* 1:168a).

A guest is one who is dependent on the favor of others. Thus,
King David, who really was not supposed to be in this world and
consequently not supposed to have anything to do with the
resurrection of the dead, considered himself a guest in the world
and also at the resurrection feast. Hence, being the guest, it is
halachically proper that when the Host — Hashem — makes the
meal, he should be the one to take the Cup of Blessing and recite
the Blessing After Meal.

(הרי״ף על עין יעקב)

ועל For all this, *Adonai*, our God, we thank You and bless You. May Your Name be blessed by the mouth of every living being constantly and forever, as it is written:[1] "When you have eaten and are satiated, you shall bless *Adonai*, your God, for the good land which He has given you." Blessed are You, *Adonai*, for the land and for the food.

רחם Have mercy, *Adonai*, our God, on Israel Your people, on Jerusalem Your city, on Zion the dwelling of Your glory, on the kingship of the House of David Your anointed, and on the great and holy house upon which Your Name is called. Our God, our Father, our Shepherd, feed us, nourish us, sustain us, and provide us with comfort, and speedily, *Adonai*, our God, grant us relief from all our afflictions. Please, *Adonai*, our God, do not make us dependent on the gifts of mortals nor upon their loans, but only upon Your full, open, holy, and generous hand, that we may not be shamed or disgraced forever and ever.

{On the *Shabbat,* the following paragraph is added:}

רצה May it please You *Adonai*, our God, to strengthen us through Your commandments and through the commandment of the seventh day, this great and holy *Shabbat*. For this day is great and holy before You, to refrain from work and to rest on it with love, in accordance with the commandment of Your will. And in Your will grant us tranquility *Adonai*, our God, that there be no distress, grief, or sorrow on the day of our rest. And show us, *Adonai*, our God, the consolation of Zion Your city, and the rebuilding of Jerusalem Your holy city, for You are the Master of deliverances and the Master of consolations.

1. *Devarim* 8:10.

"לידך המלאה הפתוחה הקדושה והרחבה"

"Your full, open, holy, and generous hand."

QUESTION: It should have said, *"yadecha hakedoshah"* — "Your holy hand" — before describing His benevolence? It does not seem to fit between the descriptions of "open" and "generous"?

ANSWER: In the *Ba'al Shem Tov's* hand-written *Siddur*, which was acquired by the sixth *Lubavitcher Rebbe*, Rabbi Yosef Yitzchak Schneersohn, and is currently in the library of *Agudat Chassidei Chabad*, instead of *"hakedoshah"* — "holy" — it says *"hegedushah"* — "overflowing" — (as in *"maleih vegadush"* — "full and overflowing").

(עי' ספר ברוך שאמר, וערוך השלחן קפ"ז:ו)

אֱלֹהֵינוּ וֵאלֹהֵי אֲבוֹתֵינוּ. יַעֲלֶה וְיָבֹא. וְיַגִּיעַ וְיֵרָאֶה וְיֵרָצֶה. וְיִשָּׁמַע וְיִפָּקֵד וְיִזָּכֵר. זִכְרוֹנֵנוּ וּפִקְדוֹנֵנוּ. וְזִכְרוֹן אֲבוֹתֵינוּ. וְזִכְרוֹן מָשִׁיחַ בֶּן־דָּוִד עַבְדֶּךָ. וְזִכְרוֹן יְרוּשָׁלַיִם עִיר קָדְשֶׁךָ. וְזִכְרוֹן כָּל־עַמְּךָ בֵּית יִשְׂרָאֵל לְפָנֶיךָ לִפְלֵיטָה לְטוֹבָה. לְחֵן וּלְחֶסֶד וּלְרַחֲמִים וּלְחַיִּים טוֹבִים וּלְשָׁלוֹם. בְּיוֹם חַג הַמַּצּוֹת הַזֶּה. בְּיוֹם טוֹב מִקְרָא קֹדֶשׁ הַזֶּה זָכְרֵנוּ יְהֹוָה אֱלֹהֵינוּ בּוֹ לְטוֹבָה. וּפָקְדֵנוּ בּוֹ לִבְרָכָה וְהוֹשִׁיעֵנוּ בּוֹ לְחַיִּים טוֹבִים: וּבִדְבַר יְשׁוּעָה וְרַחֲמִים חוּס וְחָנֵּנוּ וְרַחֵם עָלֵינוּ וְהוֹשִׁיעֵנוּ כִּי אֵלֶיךָ עֵינֵינוּ. כִּי אֵל מֶלֶךְ חַנּוּן וְרַחוּם אָתָּה:

וּבְנֵה יְרוּשָׁלַיִם עִיר הַקֹּדֶשׁ בִּמְהֵרָה בְיָמֵינוּ. בָּרוּךְ אַתָּה יְהֹוָה בֹּנֵה בְרַחֲמָיו יְרוּשָׁלָיִם אָמֵן:

בָּרוּךְ אַתָּה יְהֹוָה אֱלֹהֵינוּ מֶלֶךְ הָעוֹלָם, הָאֵל. אָבִינוּ מַלְכֵּנוּ. אַדִּירֵנוּ בּוֹרְאֵנוּ גּוֹאֲלֵנוּ יוֹצְרֵנוּ. קְדוֹשֵׁנוּ קְדוֹשׁ יַעֲקֹב רוֹעֵנוּ רוֹעֵה יִשְׂרָאֵל הַמֶּלֶךְ הַטּוֹב וְהַמֵּטִיב לַכֹּל בְּכָל יוֹם וָיוֹם, הוּא הֵיטִיב לָנוּ. הוּא מֵטִיב לָנוּ. הוּא יֵיטִיב לָנוּ. הוּא גְמָלָנוּ הוּא גוֹמְלֵנוּ הוּא יִגְמְלֵנוּ לָעַד. לְחֵן וּלְחֶסֶד וּלְרַחֲמִים וּלְרֶוַח הַצָּלָה וְהַצְלָחָה. בְּרָכָה וִישׁוּעָה. נֶחָמָה פַּרְנָסָה וְכַלְכָּלָה וְרַחֲמִים וְחַיִּים וְשָׁלוֹם וְכָל־טוֹב וּמִכָּל־טוּב לְעוֹלָם אַל יְחַסְּרֵנוּ:

* אֵין עוֹנִין אָמֵן אַחַר "אַל יְחַסְּרֵנוּ" עי׳ אג״ק כ״ק אד״ש ח״ז ע׳ רכח, ורשימות כ״ק אדמו״ר חוברת קפ״ב.

"לחן ולחסד ולרחמים...וכל טוב"
"Grace and kindness and mercy... and all good"

QUESTION: Why do we beseech Hashem to bestow upon us fifteen Divine favors specifically?

ANSWER: According to the *Gemara* (*Shabbat* 117b) it is customary to eat two meals daily, one in the morning and one in the evening, and on *Shabbat* there is an additional meal. In keeping with this custom, the *Gemara* says that the charity fund is required to provide the impoverished with fifteen meals, which would last one for the entire week. Thus, during a period of a week, one recites the Grace After Meals fifteen times. In merit of this, we ask Hashem to bless us with fifteen acts of Divine kindness.

(בהמ״ז עם פירושו של ר׳ נתן ז״ל שפירא, נדפס לראשונה בלובלין בשנת של״ה)

הגדה של פסח

188

During the following passage, the person leading the Grace should raise his voice slightly when reciting the phrase *"Zachreinu A-donai"* ("Remember us *A-donai"*). Those assembled should answer *Amein* after the words *"letovah"* ("for good"), *"liverachah"* ("for blessing"), and *"lechayim tovim"* ("and for good life").

אלהינו Our God and the God of our fathers, may there ascend, come, reach, be seen, accepted, be heard, be recalled, and be remembered before You, the remembrance and recollection of us, the remembrance of our fathers, the remembrance of *Mashiach*, the son of David Your servant, the remembrance of Jerusalem, Your holy city, and the remembrance of Your entire people the House of Israel, for deliverance, well-being, grace, kindness, mercy, good life, and peace, on this day of the Festival of *Matzot*, on this day of holy convocation.

Remember us, *Adonai*, our God, thereon, for good, recollect us thereon for blessing, help us thereon for a good life. And in accord with the promise of deliverance and mercy, have compassion on us and be gracious to us; have mercy on us and deliver us, for our eyes are directed to You, for You, Almighty, are a gracious and merciful King.

ובנה And rebuild Jerusalem, the holy city, speedily in our days. Blessed are You, *Adonai*, Who in His mercy rebuilds Jerusalem. *Amein.*

The cup of wine is put on the table.

ברוך Blessed are You, *Adonai*, our God, King of the universe, the Almighty, our Father, our King, our Might, our Creator, our Redeemer, our Maker, our Holy One, the Holy One of Yaakov, our Shepherd, the Shepherd of Israel, the King who is good and does good to all each and every day. He has done good for us, He does good for us, He will do good for us. He has bestowed, He bestows, He will forever bestow upon us grace and kindness and mercy; and relief, salvation, and success; blessing and help; consolation, sustenance and nourishment and compassion and life and peace and all good, and may He never deprive us of all good things.*

* *Amein* is not responded after "All good things"

"וכל טוב ומכל טוב לעולם אל יחסרנו"
"...and all goodness, and may He never deprive us of all good things."

QUESTION: This request sounds redundant?

ANSWER: There are people who have received Hashem's blessings of goodness in abundant measure. They have a beautiful family, plenty of food and a wardrobe full of clothing. However, due to their poor health they are unable to enjoy His blessings. Thus, we pray that He give us all good things and the opportunity to enjoy them in good health.

(סי' אוצר התפלות בפי' עיון תפלה)

הָרַחֲמָן הוּא יִמְלוֹךְ עָלֵינוּ לְעוֹלָם וָעֶד:

הָרַחֲמָן הוּא יִתְבָּרֵךְ בַּשָּׁמַיִם וּבָאָרֶץ:

הָרַחֲמָן הוּא יִשְׁתַּבַּח לְדוֹר דּוֹרִים וְיִתְפָּאֵר בָּנוּ לָעַד וּלְנֵצַח נְצָחִים וְיִתְהַדַּר בָּנוּ לָעַד וּלְעוֹלְמֵי עוֹלָמִים:

הָרַחֲמָן הוּא יְפַרְנְסֵנוּ בְּכָבוֹד:

הָרַחֲמָן הוּא יִשְׁבּוֹר עוֹל* גָּלוּת מֵעַל צַוָּארֵנוּ וְהוּא יוֹלִיכֵנוּ קוֹמְמִיּוּת לְאַרְצֵנוּ:

הָרַחֲמָן הוּא יִשְׁלַח בְּרָכָה מְרֻבָּה בְּבַיִת זֶה וְעַל שֻׁלְחָן זֶה שֶׁאָכַלְנוּ עָלָיו:

הָרַחֲמָן הוּא יִשְׁלַח לָנוּ אֶת אֵלִיָּהוּ הַנָּבִיא זָכוּר לַטּוֹב וִיבַשֶּׂר־לָנוּ בְּשׂוֹרוֹת טוֹבוֹת יְשׁוּעוֹת וְנֶחָמוֹת:

כמה מהחסידים נוהגים לומר

הָרַחֲמָן הוּא יְבָרֵךְ אֶת־אֲדוֹנֵנוּ מוֹרֵנוּ וְרַבֵּנוּ:

הָרַחֲמָן הוּא יְבָרֵךְ אֶת־אָבִי מוֹרִי בַּעַל הַבַּיִת הַזֶּה וְאֶת־אִמִּי מוֹרָתִי בַּעֲלַת הַבַּיִת הַזֶּה אוֹתָם וְאֶת־בֵּיתָם וְאֶת־זַרְעָם וְאֶת־כָּל־אֲשֶׁר לָהֶם אוֹתָנוּ וְאֶת־כָּל־אֲשֶׁר לָנוּ: כְּמוֹ שֶׁבֵּרַךְ אֶת־אֲבוֹתֵינוּ אַבְרָהָם יִצְחָק וְיַעֲקֹב בַּכֹּל מִכֹּל כֹּל כֵּן יְבָרֵךְ אוֹתָנוּ (בני ברית) כֻּלָּנוּ יַחַד בִּבְרָכָה שְׁלֵמָה וְנֹאמַר אָמֵן:

* צ״ל עול הגוים (ראה שערי הלכה ומנהג ח״א ע׳ ריב).

"הרחמן...והוא יוליכנו קוממיות לארצנו"

"May the Merciful One...and may He lead us upright to our land."

QUESTION: How can this be reconciled with the *Gemara* (*Kedushin* 31a) that says it is forbidden for a person to walk four cubits *"bekomah zekufah"* — "with an erect posture"?

ANSWER: *Eretz Yisrael* is our holy land, and all Jews yearn to live there. Those who do not reach it during their lifetime will ultimately come there in the days of *techiyat hameitim* — the

הרחמן May the Merciful One reign over us forever and ever. May the Merciful One be blessed in heaven and on earth. May the Merciful One be praised for all generations, and be glorified through us forever and all eternity, and may He be honored through us for eternity. May the Merciful One provide us our livelihood with honor. May the Merciful One break the yoke of exile (alt. "the yoke of [the] nations") from our necks and may He lead us upright to our land. May the Merciful One send abundant blessing into this house and upon this table at which we have eaten. May the Merciful One send us Eliyahu the Prophet, of blessed memory, and may he announce good tidings to us, salvations, and consolations.

Many of the *Chassidim,* add the following.

הרחמן May the Merciful One bless our master, our teacher, and our Rebbe.

The following is recited even if one's parent is deceased.

הרחמן May the Merciful One bless my father, my teacher, the master of this house and my mother, my teacher, the mistress of this house, them, their household, their children, and all that is theirs; ourselves and all that is ours. Just as He blessed our fathers Avraham, Yitzchak, and Yaakov "with everything,"[1] "from everything,"[2] and with "everything,"[3] so may He bless all of us (when a gentile is present: the children of the Covenant) together with a perfect blessing and let us say: *Amein.*

1. *Bereishit* 24:1. 2. *Ibid.* 27:31 3. *Ibid.* 33:11.

---

resurrection. However, they will have to roll through tunnels under the earth until they reach the holy land (see *Bereishit* 47:29, Rashi).

Our prayer to Hashem that He "lead us upright to our land" asks that we merit to come to *Eretz Yisrael* happily and healthily during our lifetime and not, G-d forbid, have to roll through underground tunnels to reach it.

(מצאתי בכתבי אבי הרב שמואל פסח ז"ל באגאמילסקי)

מִמָּרוֹם יְלַמְּדוּ עָלָיו וְעָלֵינוּ זְכוּת שֶׁתְּהֵא לְמִשְׁמֶרֶת שָׁלוֹם וְנִשָּׂא בְרָכָה מֵאֵת יְהֹוָה וּצְדָקָה מֵאֱלֹהֵי יִשְׁעֵנוּ וְנִמְצָא חֵן וְשֵׂכֶל טוֹב בְּעֵינֵי אֱלֹהִים וְאָדָם:

בשבת:

הָרַחֲמָן הוּא יַנְחִילֵנוּ לְיוֹם שֶׁכֻּלּוֹ שַׁבָּת וּמְנוּחָה לְחַיֵּי הָעוֹלָמִים:

ביום טוב:

הָרַחֲמָן הוּא יַנְחִילֵנוּ לְיוֹם שֶׁכֻּלּוֹ טוֹב:

הָרַחֲמָן הוּא יְזַכֵּנוּ לִימוֹת הַמָּשִׁיחַ וּלְחַיֵּי הָעוֹלָם הַבָּא. מִגְדֹּל יְשׁוּעוֹת מַלְכּוֹ וְעֹשֶׂה חֶסֶד לִמְשִׁיחוֹ לְדָוִד וּלְזַרְעוֹ עַד עוֹלָם: עֹשֶׂה שָׁלוֹם בִּמְרוֹמָיו הוּא יַעֲשֶׂה שָׁלוֹם עָלֵינוּ וְעַל כָּל־יִשְׂרָאֵל וְאִמְרוּ אָמֵן:

יְראוּ אֶת־יְהֹוָה קְדֹשָׁיו כִּי־אֵין מַחְסוֹר לִירֵאָיו: כְּפִירִים רָשׁוּ וְרָעֵבוּ וְדֹרְשֵׁי יְהֹוָה לֹא־יַחְסְרוּ כָל־טוֹב: הוֹדוּ לַיהֹוָה כִּי־טוֹב כִּי לְעוֹלָם חַסְדּוֹ: פּוֹתֵחַ אֶת־יָדֶךָ וּמַשְׂבִּיעַ לְכָל־חַי רָצוֹן: בָּרוּךְ הַגֶּבֶר אֲשֶׁר יִבְטַח בַּיהֹוָה וְהָיָה יְהֹוָה מִבְטַחוֹ:

ומברך על הכוס ושותה בהסיבה:

בָּרוּךְ אַתָּה יְהֹוָה אֱלֹהֵינוּ מֶלֶךְ הָעוֹלָם בּוֹרֵא פְּרִי הַגָּפֶן:

"ממרום ילמדו עליו ועלינו"
"From On High, may there be invoked upon him and upon us."
QUESTION: To what is *"alav"* — "upon him" — referring?
ANSWER: In the physical food there are *"nitzotzot"* — "Divine sparks of G-dliness" — which are elevated when the Jew eats *l'sheim Shamayim* — for the sake of Heaven — i.e. to have strength to serve Hashem in learning and prayer, each one according to his level.

Thus we pray that "From On High, may there be invoked *alav* — upon him — i.e. the food being elevated, and *aleinu* — upon us — the Jews who eat for the sake of serving Hashem, such merit which will bring enduring peace.

(אגרת קדש כ״ק אדמו״ר מוהריי״צ ח״א ע׳ ר״ד)

"כי אין מחסור ליראיו"
"Those who fear Him suffer no want."
QUESTION: Do those who fear Him have so much?

ממרום From On High, may there be invoked upon him and upon us such merit which will bring an enduring peace. May we receive blessing from *Adonai* and just kindness from God our deliverer. May we find grace and good understanding in the eyes of God and man.

הרחמן {On the *Shabbat*, the following line is added:} **May the Merciful One cause us to inherit the day which will be completely *Shabbat* and rest for eternal life.**

הרחמן May the Merciful One cause us to inherit the day which is all good.

הרחמן May the Merciful One grant us the privilege of reaching the days of *Mashiach* and the life of the World to Come. He is a tower of salvations for His king and bestows kindness upon His anointed, to David and his descendants forever.[1] He Who makes peace in His heights, may He make peace for us and for all Israel, and say: *Amein.*

יראו Fear *Adonai*, you His holy ones, for those who fear Him suffer no want. Young lions are in need and go hungry, but those who seek *Adonai* shall not lack any good.[2] Give thanks to *Adonai* for He is good, for His kindness is everlasting.[3] You open Your hand and satisfy the desire of every living being.[4] Blessed is the man who trusts in *Adonai*, and *Adonai* will be His security.[5]

The following blessing is now recited over the cup of wine, and we drink it reclining on the left side.

ברוך Blessed are You, *Adonai*, our God, King of the universe, Who created the fruit of the vine.

1. *II Samuel* 22:15.　2. *Psalms* 34:10-11.　3. *Psalms* 107:1.　4. *Psalms* 145:16.　5. *Jeremiah* 17:7.

ANSWER: When Yaakov met Eisav and presented him with a gift, Eisav said, *"Yeish li rav"* — "I have plenty." Yaakov continued urging him to take the gift and said, "Please accept my gift because *yeish li kol* — I have everything" (*Bereishit* 33:9-11).

The reason that Yaakov stated "I have everything" while Eisav said "I have plenty" is that the wicked are never fully satisfied. They are not content with what they have and always want more. On the other hand, the righteous are happy with whatever Hashem gives them, which they consider to be "everything." Hence, the G-d fearing suffer no want, for they are happy with what Hashem has allotted them and they do not torment themselves over any perceived deficiency.

(סי' אוצר התפלות בפי' ענף יוסף)

כוס של אליהו
Cup of Eliyahu

QUESTION: Why do we add a cup for Eliyahu when we celebrate the *Pesach seder?*

ANSWER: Eliyahu once complained to Hashem that the Jewish people were not faithfully observing the *mitzvah* of circumcision. Hashem did not receive this complaint very well and told Eliyahu, "My children are trustworthy, and from now on you will be present at every Jewish *brit* to witness their dedication." Thus, at every *brit* a special chair is set aside for Eliyahu (*Pirkei DeRabbi Eliezer* 20).

The Torah states (*Shemot* 12:48), "No uncircumcised male may eat of it [the *Pesach*-offering]." Therefore, Eliyahu, who is present at all *britim,* appears in each home to testify that the participants of the *seder* are all eligible to eat from the *Pesach*-offering, and a cup is prepared in his honor.

(הר"מ חאגיז בספר ברכת אליהו)

כוס של אליהו הנביא
Cup of Eliyahu the Prophet

QUESTION: Why is it called the "Cup of Eliyahu the *Prophet"* (see *Shulchan Aruch Harav* 480:5 and *Mishneh Berurah* 480:10) and not just the "Cup of Eliyahu"?

ANSWER: Eliyahu is the one who will eventually clarify all unresolved questions in halachic matters. He will not do this through prophetic powers because, "Torah is not in heaven" (see *Bava Metzia* 59b; and Rambam, *Yesodei Hatorah* 9:1). Rather it is through his vast knowledge of Torah that he will have all the answers. However, as a *navi* — prophet — he will prophesy to the Jewish people the coming of *Mashiach*, as stated in Malachi (3:23), "Behold I will send you Eliyahu the prophet before the coming of the great and awesome day of Hashem (revelation of *Mashiach*)."

At the *Seder* we open the door for Eliyahu to invite him to visit with us and bring us the good tidings that *Mashiach* is on his way. In his honor and in eager anticipation of the fulfillment of his prophecy, we pour a cup of wine, representing the *"kos yeshu'ot"* —

The fourth cup is filled. An additional cup of wine, *The Cup of Eliyahu the Prophet* is filled now.

(The Rebbe would fill the cup of Eliyahu before reciting Grace After Meals *(Otzar Minhagei Chabad,* p. 192.)

The prevailing Lubavitch custom is that all the doors between the room where the *Seder* is conducted and the outside are then opened. The passage beginning *"Shefoch"* — "Pour out" — is then said; those sent to open the doors recite it at the front door. When *Pesach* takes place on a weekday, a lighted candelabrum is taken in hand. There is no need to stand while reciting this passage.

"cup of salvations" — of the ultimate redemption, which he will announce — even tonight.

(כ"ק אדמו"ר, פסח תשכ"ג - הגש"פ דברי נגידים למהר"ל)

כוס של אליהו הנביא — Cup of Eliyahu the Prophet

QUESTION: At the *Seder* table we drink four cups of wine in honor of the four expressions of redemption (*Shemot* 6:6-7). Why don't we drink a fifth cup for the fifth expression (ibid. 6:8), *"veheiveiti"* — "I shall bring you"?

ANSWER: The first four expressions of redemption, *"Vehotzeiti"* — "I shall take you out." *"Vehitzalti"* — "I shall rescue you." *"Vega'alti"* — "I shall redeem you," and *"Velakachti"* — "I shall take you" — are addressed to the entire Jewish community. However, the fifth expression, "I will bring you to the land...and I shall give it to you as a heritage" (ibid. 6:8), refers to the giving of *Eretz Yisrael* to the Jewish people and does not apply to the tribe of Levi, because they did not have their own portion of *Eretz Yisrael*. They only had 42 cities plus the six cities of refuge which were given to them by the other tribes (*Bamidbar* 35:6). Since "I shall bring you" does not apply to everyone, we do not drink a fifth cup.

Nevertheless, *Kohanim* and *Levi'im* drink four cups at the *Seder,* because they were only exempt from the *"avodat perach"* — extremely difficult slave labor — (see *Midrash Rabbah, Shemot* 5:16), but they too definitely felt the pressure and wickedness of the Egyptians, and eagerly awaited the Exodus from Egypt.

* * *

Though we do not drink a fifth cup for *veheiveiti,* an additional cup is placed on the table and called *"kos shel Eliyahu Hanavi"* be-

KI YISHALCHA BINCHA

cause he is the prophet who will announce the coming of *Mashiach*. When *Mashiach* comes, *Eretz Yisrael* will be divided into 13 portions, including one for the tribe of Levi. The tribes of Ephraim and Menashe will jointly possess the one portion of the tribe of Yosef, and the 13th portion will be for *Mashiach* (*Bava Batra* 122a).

Hence, it is appropriate to associate Eliyahu with this cup, because when he heralds the coming of *Mashiach*, *all* the Jews will be given a heritage in the land and drink a fifth cup for "*Veheiveiti*" — "I will bring you to *Eretz Yisrael* — and give it to you as a heritage."

(הדרש והעיון - שמות)

* * *

Incidentally, the word "*veheiveiti*" (והבאתי) has the numerical value of 424, which is also the numerical value of *Mashiach ben David* (משיח בן דוד), whose revelation will be heralded by Eliyahu the Prophet.

(אמרי נועם)

פותחין הדלת — Open the door

QUESTION: Why do we open the door after eating the *afikoman*?

ANSWER: The episode related in the Torah regarding Yaakov's receiving the *berachot* from Yitzchak took place on the night of *Pesach*, when we perform the *Seder*. The two goats which Rivkah and Yaakov prepared for Yitzchak represented the *Pesach*-offering and the *Chagigah*-offering, and the angel Michael sent along wine for the four cups (*Bereishit* 27:9, Rashi. *Da'at Zekeinim Miba'alei Hatosafot* 27:25).

Yitzchak concluded the meal with eating the *afikoman*. This is evident from his telling Eisav, "Your brother came '*bemirmah*' — with wisdom — and took away your blessing" (ibid. 27:35). The word "*bemirmah*" (במרמה) has the numerical value of two hundred and eighty-seven, which is also the numerical value of the word "*afikoman*" (אפיקומן). Yitzchak told Eisav, "Your brother is indeed very wise. He gave me the *afikoman* before you arrived, and thus, I am forbidden to eat any more food tonight."

The *Midrash Rabbah* (*Bereishit* 66:5) explains the *pasuk* "And Yaakov had scarcely left from the presence of Yitzchak his father when Eisav his brother came back from his hunt" (ibid. 27:30) to mean that Eisav swung open the door to the tent and Yaakov stood behind the open door until Eisav came in and then he

הגדה של פסח

196

quietly departed behind his back. To commemorate Yaakov's being saved through escaping via the open door after Yitzchak ate the *afikoman*, we too open the door after eating the *afikoman*.

(מנחם ציון מר׳ מנחם מענדל זצ״ל מרימונב, פרדס יוסף בראשית כ״ז, כ״ה)

* * *

Alternatively, the door is opened to recall that it is *"leil shimurim"* — "a night of protection" — and that we are not afraid of anything. In merit of this *emunah* — faith — *Mashiach* will come and Hashem will pour his wrath upon the nations (*Shulchan Aruch Harav* 480:4).

QUESTION: What is the connection with *delet* — door — and *Mashiach*?

ANSWER: The numerical value of *"delet"* (דלת) is 434, the same as *Mashiach ben David* (משיח בן דויד). (Throughout the book of Chronicles the name David is spelled with a *yud* — see also *Veyevareich David* in the daily *Shacharit*.)

פותחין הדלת — Open the door

QUESTION: The Rebbe in his notes on the *Haggadah* writes that one of the reasons for opening the door is so that "Eliyahu should come in and bring the tidings of redemption."

Eliyahu comes to the *brit* of every Jewish boy and also to every *Seder* on the night of *Pesach*. Why do we only have the custom of opening the door for him at the *Seder*?

ANSWER: When the Baal Shem Tov entered the heavenly abode of *Mashiach* and asked him, "When will the Master come?" he responded, "When your well-springs will spread forth on the outside." To hasten the coming of *Mashiach*, the Rebbe has dedicated his entire lifetime to spreading the teachings of Torah and *Chassidut* to the "outside world."

Since the pouring of the extra cup is an expression of prayer that the prophet Eliyahu speedily proclaim the coming of *Mashiach*, we open the door to indicate that the Torah spirit which prevails in our home should also emanate to those who are on the outside, and through this we will merit Eliyahu's arrival to announce the good tidings that *Mashiach* is coming.

(שמעתי מאחי הרב שמואל פסח שי׳ באגאמילסקי, וע״י בקובץ שאלות פירושים וביאורים חי״ג)

שְׁפֹךְ חֲמָתְךָ אֶל-הַגּוֹיִם אֲשֶׁר לֹא
יְדָעוּךָ. וְעַל מַמְלָכוֹת אֲשֶׁר בְּשִׁמְךָ לֹא
קָרָאוּ: כִּי אָכַל אֶת-יַעֲקֹב וְאֶת-נָוֵהוּ
הֵשַׁמּוּ: שְׁפָךְ-עֲלֵיהֶם זַעְמֶךָ וַחֲרוֹן
אַפְּךָ יַשִּׂיגֵם: תִּרְדֹף בְּאַף וְתַשְׁמִידֵם
מִתַּחַת שְׁמֵי יְהֹוָה:

"שפוך חמתך אל הגוים"
"Pour out Your wrath upon the nations."

QUESTION: When asking Hashem to pour out His wrath upon the nations who have "devoured Yaakov" and destroyed the *Beit Hamikdash*, why is it necessary to mention, *"asher lo yeda'ucha"* — "that do not acknowledge You" — and *"asher beshimecha lo kara'u"* — "that do not call upon Your Name"?

ANSWER: Rabbi Shimon bar Yochai says that it is a *halachah* and a known fact that Eisav hates Yaakov (*Bereishit* 33:4, Rashi). He uses the term *"halachah"* to emphasize that just as *halachah* is not based necessarily on reason, likewise Eisav's hatred for Yaakov is inherent in him and not dictated by reason, logic, or rationale.

Thus, we ask Hashem, "Pour out Your wrath upon the nations who have made the Jewish people suffer." They cannot justify their actions by claiming they did them *l'sheim shamayim* — for Hashem's Name — i.e. to punish the Jews for their abandonment of Torah, since "they do not acknowledge You and do not call upon Your Name." This proves that they were not motivated by the desire to fulfill Hashem's wish, but simply by hatred.

(פון אונזער אלטען אוצר בשם ר' מרדכי ז"ל בנעט אב"ד ניקלשבורג)

הגדה של פסח   198

שפוך **Pour out Your wrath upon the nations that do not acknowledge You, and upon the kingdoms that do not call upon Your Name, for he has devoured Yaakov and destroyed his habitation.**[1] **Pour out Your anger against them, and let the wrath of Your fury overtake them.**[2] **Pursue them with anger and destroy them from beneath the heavens of *Adonai*.**[3]

We wait for those who were sent to open the doors to return, and then begin the *Hallel*.

1. *Psalms 79:6-7.* 2. *Psalms 69:25.* 3. *Lamentations 3:66.*

"שפוך חמתך אל הגוים...כי אכל את יעקב"
"Pour out Your wrath upon the nations...
For he has devoured Yaakov."

QUESTION: Since the verse begins with *"goyim"* — "nations" — in plural, instead of *"achal"* — *"he* devoured" — it should have said *"achlu"* — *"they* have devoured"?

ANSWER: The world consists of many nations. Each has its selfish interests and aspirations, and often one competes against the other. The common denominator which unites them all, however, is their hatred for the Jewish people. When it comes to harming the Jews, suddenly they all unite, forming one entity. Thus, the verse states, *"achal et Yaakov"* — "he has devoured Yaakov."

(הגש"פ עם פי' ילקוט שמעוני)

הַלֵּל נִרְצָה

לֹא לָנוּ יְהֹוָה לֹא לָנוּ כִּי לְשִׁמְךָ תֵּן כָּבוֹד עַל־חַסְדְּךָ
עַל־אֲמִתֶּךָ: לָמָּה יֹאמְרוּ הַגּוֹיִם אַיֵּה נָא אֱלֹהֵיהֶם:
וֵאלֹהֵינוּ בַשָּׁמָיִם כֹּל אֲשֶׁר חָפֵץ עָשָׂה: עֲצַבֵּיהֶם כֶּסֶף וְזָהָב
מַעֲשֵׂי יְדֵי אָדָם: פֶּה לָהֶם וְלֹא יְדַבֵּרוּ עֵינַיִם לָהֶם וְלֹא
יִרְאוּ: אָזְנַיִם לָהֶם וְלֹא יִשְׁמָעוּ אַף לָהֶם וְלֹא יְרִיחוּן:
יְדֵיהֶם | וְלֹא יְמִישׁוּן רַגְלֵיהֶם וְלֹא יְהַלֵּכוּ לֹא יֶהְגּוּ
בִּגְרוֹנָם: כְּמוֹהֶם יִהְיוּ עֹשֵׂיהֶם כֹּל אֲשֶׁר בֹּטֵחַ בָּהֶם: יִשְׂרָאֵל
בְּטַח בַּיהֹוָה עֶזְרָם וּמָגִנָּם הוּא: בֵּית אַהֲרֹן בִּטְחוּ בַיהֹוָה
עֶזְרָם וּמָגִנָּם הוּא: יִרְאֵי יְהֹוָה בִּטְחוּ בַיהֹוָה עֶזְרָם וּמָגִנָּם הוּא:

"עצביהם כסף וזהב מעשה ידי אדם"
"Their idols are of silver and gold, the work of human hands."

QUESTION: The common word for idol is *"pesel."* Why is the term *"atzabeihem"* used here?

ANSWER: The word *"atzabeihem"* (עצביהם) is derived from the same root word as *"atzvut"* (עצבות) — "sadness and grief." When Rabbi DovBer Schneerson, the second Lubavitcher Rebbe, was a young boy, he noticed a group of *chassidim* who appeared to be sad. Upon learning that they were experiencing financial difficulties, he remarked, "'*Atzabeihem*' — 'their sadness' — pertains to matters of *'kesef vezahav'* — 'gold and silver' — i.e. material concerns." Unfortunately, some people think that affluence is *'ma'asei yedei adam'* — something which a person accomplishes on his own — and worship it as 'their idols.'"

(לקוטי דיבורים ח"א ע' ק"ע)

"פה להם ולא ידברו...אזנים להם ולא ישמעו... ידיהם ולא ימישון רגליהם ולא יהלכו"
"They have a mouth, but cannot speak... they have ears, but cannot hear... Their hands cannot feel; their feet cannot walk."

QUESTION: Why is the word *"lahem"* — "to them" — used in the phrases about mouths, eyes, ears, and noses, but omitted in the phrase about hands and feet?

Hallel Nirtzah
Reciting Hallel, Psalms of Praise;
The *Seder* is Accepted Favorably by G-d

לא Not for our sake, *Adonai*, not for our sake, but for Your Name's sake give glory for the sake of Your kindness and for Your truth. Why should the nations say, "Where now is their God?" Our God is in heaven, whatever He desires He does. Their idols are silver and gold, the work of human hands. They have a mouth, but cannot speak; they have eyes, but cannot see. They have ears, but cannot hear; they have a nose, but cannot smell. Their hands cannot feel; their feet cannot walk; they can make no sounds with their throats. Like them shall be their makers, everyone that trusts in them. Israel trust in *Adonai*, their help and their shield is He. House of Aharon trust in *Adonai*, their help and their shield is He. *Adonai*-fearing trust in *Adonai*, their help and their shield is He.[1]

1. *Psalms* 115:1-11.

ANSWER: According to the *Gemara* (*Avodah Zarah* 41a) pieces broken off an idol are not considered idols and may be used for other purposes. However, since some originally make a hand or foot as an idol, hands or feet, even when broken off from an idol, are still considered idols and forbidden to be used. Thus, the mouth, the eyes, and the nose have idol-status only as long as they are *"lahem"* — "to them" — i.e. connected to the idol itself, unlike the hands and feet which have idol status even when they have been severed.

(חנוכת התורה)

"ישראל בטח בה' עזרם ומגנם הוא"
"Israel, trust in G-d; their help and their shield is He."

QUESTION: Since King David is commanding the Jews to trust in Hashem, he should have concluded *"ezrechem umaginechem"* — *"your* help and *your* shield [is He]"?

ANSWER: Throughout history the Jewish people have been oppressed and tortured by the nations of the world, and at times it has appeared, G-d forbid, that we were on the brink of annihilation. King David is saying to the Jewish people, "Trust in Hashem and have no fear, because in reality *ezram umaginam Hu* — Hashem is *their* shield — i.e. your enemies' — and without Him they are powerless. Rest assured He will not permit them to destroy you."

(שמעתי מזקני הרב צבי הכהן ז"ל קאפלאן)

יְהוָֹה זְכָרָנוּ יְבָרֵךְ יְבָרֵךְ אֶת בֵּית יִשְׂרָאֵל יְבָרֵךְ אֶת בֵּית אַהֲרֹן:
יְבָרֵךְ יִרְאֵי יְהוָֹה הַקְּטַנִּים עִם הַגְּדֹלִים: יֹסֵף יְהוָֹה עֲלֵיכֶם
וְעַל בְּנֵיכֶם: בְּרוּכִים אַתֶּם לַיהוָֹה עֹשֵׂה שָׁמַיִם וָאָרֶץ: הַשָּׁמַיִם
שָׁמַיִם לַיהוָֹה וְהָאָרֶץ נָתַן לִבְנֵי אָדָם: לֹא הַמֵּתִים יְהַלְלוּ יָהּ וְלֹא
כָּל יֹרְדֵי דוּמָה: וַאֲנַחְנוּ | נְבָרֵךְ יָהּ מֵעַתָּה וְעַד עוֹלָם הַלְלוּיָהּ:

אָהַבְתִּי כִּי יִשְׁמַע | יְהוָֹה אֶת קוֹלִי תַּחֲנוּנָי: כִּי הִטָּה אָזְנוֹ לִי
וּבְיָמַי אֶקְרָא: אֲפָפוּנִי | חֶבְלֵי מָוֶת וּמְצָרֵי שְׁאוֹל מְצָאוּנִי צָרָה
וְיָגוֹן אֶמְצָא: וּבְשֵׁם יְהוָֹה אֶקְרָא אָנָּה יְהוָֹה מַלְּטָה נַפְשִׁי: חַנּוּן
יְהוָֹה וְצַדִּיק וֵאלֹהֵינוּ מְרַחֵם: שֹׁמֵר פְּתָאִים יְהוָֹה דַּלּוֹתִי וְלִי
יְהוֹשִׁיעַ: שׁוּבִי נַפְשִׁי לִמְנוּחָיְכִי כִּי יְהוָֹה גָּמַל עָלָיְכִי: כִּי חִלַּצְתָּ
נַפְשִׁי מִמָּוֶת אֶת עֵינִי מִן דִּמְעָה אֶת רַגְלִי מִדֶּחִי: אֶתְהַלֵּךְ לִפְנֵי
יְהוָֹה בְּאַרְצוֹת הַחַיִּים: הֶאֱמַנְתִּי כִּי אֲדַבֵּר אֲנִי עָנִיתִי מְאֹד: אֲנִי
אָמַרְתִּי בְחָפְזִי כָּל הָאָדָם כֹּזֵב:

מָה אָשִׁיב לַיהוָֹה כָּל תַּגְמוּלוֹהִי עָלָי: כּוֹס־יְשׁוּעוֹת אֶשָּׂא
וּבְשֵׁם יְהוָֹה אֶקְרָא: נְדָרַי לַיהוָֹה אֲשַׁלֵּם נֶגְדָה־נָּא לְכָל עַמּוֹ:
יָקָר בְּעֵינֵי יְהוָֹה הַמָּוְתָה לַחֲסִידָיו: אָנָּה יְהוָֹה כִּי אֲנִי עַבְדֶּךָ אֲנִי
עַבְדְּךָ בֶּן אֲמָתֶךָ פִּתַּחְתָּ לְמוֹסֵרָי: לְךָ אֶזְבַּח זֶבַח תּוֹדָה וּבְשֵׁם
יְהוָֹה אֶקְרָא: נְדָרַי לַיהוָֹה אֲשַׁלֵּם נֶגְדָה־נָּא לְכָל עַמּוֹ: בְּחַצְרוֹת
| בֵּית יְהוָֹה בְּתוֹכֵכִי יְרוּשָׁלָיִם הַלְלוּיָהּ:

"וְהָאָרֶץ נָתַן לִבְנֵי אָדָם... וַאֲנַחְנוּ נְבָרֵךְ יָ-הּ"
"The earth He gave to the children of man...But we bless Hashem..."

QUESTION: What is the connection between these two statements?

ANSWER: The *Gemara* (*Berachot* 35a) asks, how can the *pasuk* "to Hashem belongs the earth and its fullness" (Psalms 24:1), which implies that man's use of the world would constitute trespass on Hashem's property, be reconciled with the *pasuk* "The earth He gave to the children of man," which implies the earth is man's to use?

יהוה *Adonai*, who is ever-mindful of us, will bless, He will bless the House of Israel. He will bless the House of Aharon. He will bless those who fear *Adonai*, the small with the great. May *Adonai* increase [His blessings on] you, to you and to your children. You are blessed to *Adonai*, Maker of heaven and earth. The heaven is the heaven of *Adonai*, but the earth He gave to the children of man. The dead do not praise God, nor do those who descend to silence. But we will bless God, from now and forever. *Halleluyah* — praise God![1]

אהבתי I love *Adonai* for He hears my voice, my supplications. For He turned His ear to me, all my days I will call [upon Him]. I am encompassed with the pangs of death; the agony of the grave found me; I found trouble and sorrow. And upon the Name of *Adonai* I called, "I implore you *Adonai*, save my soul." Gracious is *Adonai* and righteous; and our God is merciful. *Adonai* guards the simpletons; I was brought low, but He saved me. Return, my soul, to your rest, for *Adonai* has dealt kindly with you. For You have delivered my soul from death, my eyes from tears, my feet from stumbling. I will walk before *Adonai* in the world of the living. I had faith even when I said: "I suffer so greatly," [even when] I said in my haste, "All men are deceitful."[2]

מה What can I repay to *Adonai* for all His kindness to me? I will lift up the cup of salvations and call upon the Name of *Adonai*. I will pay my vows to *Adonai*, now, in the presence of all His people. Grievous in the eyes of *Adonai* is the death of His pious ones. I thank You, *Adonai*, for I am Your servant; I am Your servant, the son of Your maidservant; You have loosened my bonds. To you I will offer a thanksgiving sacrifice, and upon the Name of *Adonai* I will call. I will pay my vows to *Adonai*, now, in the presence of all His people. In the courtyards of the House of *Adonai*, in your midst, Jerusalem, *Halleluyah* — praise God![3]

1. *Psalms* 116:1-11.   2. *Psalms* 116:12-19.   3. Psalm 117.

The *Gemara* answers that there is no contradiction because the first *pasuk* refers to *before* reciting a *berachah* while the second *pasuk* refers to *after* one recites a *berachah*, at which point He gives the earth to man for his use.

The passage in *Hallel* goes on to allude to the *Gemara's* discussion. We may wonder how we can say that the earth was given to man when another *pasuk* says the opposite. The answer is that *"ve'anachnu nevareich Y-ah"* — we bless Hashem — and for making a *berachah* He graciously gives the earth to man.

(ארץ החיים על תהלים מר' חיים ב"ר שלמה ז"ל ממאהלוב)

הַלְלוּ אֶת יְהֹוָה כָּל גּוֹיִם שַׁבְּחוּהוּ כָּל הָאֻמִּים: כִּי
גָבַר עָלֵינוּ | חַסְדּוֹ וֶאֱמֶת יְהֹוָה לְעוֹלָם הַלְלוּיָהּ:

הוֹדוּ לַיהֹוָה כִּי טוֹב	כִּי לְעוֹלָם חַסְדּוֹ:
יֹאמַר נָא יִשְׂרָאֵל	כִּי לְעוֹלָם חַסְדּוֹ:
יֹאמְרוּ נָא בֵית אַהֲרֹן	כִּי לְעוֹלָם חַסְדּוֹ:
יֹאמְרוּ נָא יִרְאֵי יְהֹוָה	כִּי לְעוֹלָם חַסְדּוֹ:

מִן־הַמֵּצַר קָרָאתִי יָהּ עָנָנִי בַמֶּרְחָב יָהּ: יְהֹוָה לִי לֹא
אִירָא מַה יַּעֲשֶׂה לִי אָדָם: יְהֹוָה לִי בְּעֹזְרָי וַאֲנִי אֶרְאֶה

"הללו את ה' כל גוים... כי גבר עלינו חסדו"
"Praise G-d all nations... For His kindness was mighty over us."

QUESTION: Why should all the nations praise Hashem because of His overpowering kindness to the Jews?

ANSWER: The Jews in exile are oppressed by the nations of the world, but ultimately Hashem will punish their tormentors (*Devarim* 32:43, Ezekiel 25:14). In truth, the Jewish people may deserve to suffer even more, G-d forbid, for their misdeeds; however, Hashem loves them and does not permit the nations to treat the Jews with their full viciousness and hatred. Thus, the nations should praise Hashem for His overwhelming kindness to the Jewish people since, in turn, it limits the extent of their ultimate punishment.

* * *

Perhaps the reason for describing Hashem's kindness with the word *"gavar"* (גבר) — "mighty" — is that it serves as an acronym for גומלי חסדים, **ב**ישנים, **ר**חמנים — benevolent, bashful and merciful — which, according to the *Gemara* (*Yevamot* 79a), are the three unique characteristics by which the Jewish people are distinguished. In merit of *"gavar"* — our unique character traits — Hashem reciprocates with bestowing His kindness upon us in a *"gavar"* — "mighty" — fashion.

(ארץ החיים על תהלים, ועי' פסחים קי"ח ע"ב)

הללו Praise *Adonai* all nations: Laud Him all the peoples; For His kindness was mighty over us, and the truth of *Adonai* is everlasting. *Halleluyah* — praise God!

The following verses are recited responsively. The leader begins by reciting: "Give thanks to *A-donai*..." and the others respond: "Give thanks to *A-donai*... Let Israel declare..." The leader, having repeated the verse "Give thanks to *A-donai*..." together with the assembled, then says the second verse: "Let Israel declare...." Those present again respond by saying "Give thanks to *A-donai*..." and proceed: "Let the House of Aharon declare..." The same procedure applies to the remaining two verses.

הודו Give thanks to *Adonai* for He is good; for His kindness is everlasting.

Let Israel declare: for His kindness is everlasting.

Let the House of Aharon declare: for His kindness is everlasting.

Let those who fear *Adonai* declare: for His kindness is everlasting.[1]

מן Out of the narrow confines I called to God; God answered me with abounding relief. *Adonai* is with me, I shall not fear; what can man do to me? *Adonai* is with me through my helpers;

1. *Psalms* 118:1-4.

"ה' לי בעזרי ואני אראה בשנאי"
"G-d is with me through my helpers, and I can face my enemies."

QUESTION: Since there is nothing a person can really do without Hashem's help, King David's statement is enigmatic: If Hashem is on the side of his helpers, obviously he will conquer his enemies?

ANSWER: Man often has to deal with two sorts of enemies. One appears to be a friend, but when the one who trusted him is not alert, he will knife him in the back. The other is an outright enemy. The former is worse than the latter because of his deception.

King David is saying that as mortal man he is limited and unable to read man's thoughts; therefore, he is beseeching Hashem "be with me *be'ozrai* — among my helpers — i.e. the enemies who masquerade as my 'friendly helper's' — *v'ani er'eh* — I myself will know to beware of and vanquish those who are *sonai* — my outright foes."

(מדרש שמואל על פרקי אבות, א:ז)

Appropriately, King Yanai extended the following advice to his wife Salome on his deathbed, "Do not fear the Pharisees for they are righteous people and will not do you any harm. Do not fear the non-Pharisees, for they are wicked and are my friends. Fear the hypocrites who are not in reality as they appear — outwardly they appear righteous, but inwardly they are wicked" (*Sotah* 22b).

KI YISHALCHA BINCHA

בְּשִׂנְאָי: טוֹב לַחֲסוֹת בַּיהוָֹה מִבְּטֹחַ בָּאָדָם: טוֹב לַחֲסוֹת בַּיהוָֹה מִבְּטֹחַ בִּנְדִיבִים: כָּל־גּוֹיִם סְבָבוּנִי בְּשֵׁם יְהוָֹה כִּי אֲמִילַם: סַבּוּנִי גַם־סְבָבוּנִי בְּשֵׁם יְהוָֹה כִּי אֲמִילַם: סַבּוּנִי כִדְבֹרִים דֹּעֲכוּ כְּאֵשׁ קוֹצִים בְּשֵׁם יְהוָֹה כִּי אֲמִילַם: דָּחֹה דְּחִיתַנִי לִנְפֹּל וַיהוָֹה עֲזָרָנִי: עָזִּי וְזִמְרָת יָה וַיְהִי־לִי לִישׁוּעָה: קוֹל | רִנָּה וִישׁוּעָה בְּאָהֳלֵי צַדִּיקִים יְמִין יְהוָֹה עֹשָׂה חָיִל: יְמִין יְהוָֹה רוֹמֵמָה יְמִין יְהוָֹה עֹשָׂה חָיִל: לֹא־אָמוּת כִּי אֶחְיֶה וַאֲסַפֵּר מַעֲשֵׂי יָהּ: יַסֹּר יִסְּרַנִּי יָּהּ וְלַמָּוֶת לֹא נְתָנָנִי: פִּתְחוּ־לִי שַׁעֲרֵי צֶדֶק אָבֹא־בָם אוֹדֶה יָהּ: זֶה־הַשַּׁעַר לַיהוָֹה צַדִּיקִים יָבֹאוּ בוֹ:

אוֹדְךָ כִּי עֲנִיתָנִי וַתְּהִי־לִי לִישׁוּעָה: אודך.

אֶבֶן מָאֲסוּ הַבּוֹנִים הָיְתָה לְרֹאשׁ פִּנָּה: אבן.

מֵאֵת יְהוָֹה הָיְתָה זֹּאת הִיא נִפְלָאת בְּעֵינֵינוּ: מאת.

זֶה־הַיּוֹם עָשָׂה יְהוָֹה נָגִילָה וְנִשְׂמְחָה בוֹ: זה.

"אבן מאסו הבונים היתה לראש פנה"
"The stone despised by the builders has become the cornerstone."

QUESTION: Which stone did the builders despise?

ANSWER: The Jewish people are the "cornerstone" of Hashem's design for the world. Ironically, "the builders" — the rulers of the countries of the world — never appreciated our essential role in their survival. Moreover, they despised the Jews and sought their annihilation. Their popular condemnation of our people is that we do not contribute to society, but only are here to take. When *Mashiach* arrives, all the nations of the world will realize their mistake. At that time, "the builders" — the rulers of the world — who have despised the Jewish people will realize that we are the "cornerstone" of the world and properly appreciate our contribution to society at large.

(רד"ק)

I can face [see the downfall of] my enemies. It is better to take refuge in *Adonai* than to trust in man. It is better to take refuge in *Adonai* than to trust in nobles. All nations surround me; in the Name of *Adonai* I cut them down. They encircle me and surround me; in the Name of *Adonai* I cut them down. They encircle me like bees; they are extinguished like flaming thorns; in the Name of *Adonai* I cut them down. You [my foes] pushed me again and again to fall, but *Adonai* helped me. God is my strength and song, and this has been my salvation. The sound of rejoicing and salvation is in the tents of the righteous: "The right hand of *Adonai* performs deeds of valor. The right hand of *Adonai* is exalted; the right hand of *Adonai* performs deeds of valor!" I shall not die, for I shall live and relate the deeds of God. God chastised me repeatedly, but He did not hand me over to death. Open for me the gates of righteousness; I will enter and thank God. This is the gate of *Adonai*; the righteous shall enter it. I thank You for You answered me, and you have become my salvation. (Repeat this verse) **The stone which the builders despised has become the cornerstone.** (Repeat this verse) **This is from *Adonai*; it is wondrous in our eyes.** (Repeat this verse) **This day *Adonai* has made, let us be glad and rejoice on it.**[1] (Repeat this verse)

1. *Psalms* 118:5-24.

Alternatively, the *Gemara* (*Megillah* 15a) says that the four most beautiful women in the world were Sarah, Rachav, Abigail, and Esther. *Tosafot* asks, why isn't Chavah also counted, since the *Gemara* (*Bava Batra* 58a) says that Sarah compared to Chavah was like an ape compared to a person? *Tosafot* answers that the *Gemara* is only counting those who were born from a woman.

The *pasuk* is alluding to this by saying, "The stone" — Chavah — who was the foundation and mother of all living (*Bereishit* 3:20), "was despised by the builders" — *talmidei chachamim*, i.e. the Sages of the *Gemara*, (see *Berachot* 64a) — and not listed among the most beautiful women of the world because, unlike all of them, she was unique in the fact that *"mei'eit Hashem hayetah zot"* — "she was created by G-d."

(חנוכת התורה)

Alternatively, the stone refers to Yosef (see *Bereishit* 49:24, *Ohr Hachaim*) who was despised by the builders — his brothers the great scholars, (see *Berachot* 64a), and ultimately "has become the cornerstone" — the ruler over Egypt and the source of sustenance for the entire people during the famine.

(הגש״פ תהילה לשאול מר׳ שאול ואקנין, קאלי, קולמבי״ה)

אָנָּא יְהֹוָה הוֹשִׁיעָה נָּא:

אָנָּא יְהֹוָה הוֹשִׁיעָה נָּא:

אָנָּא יְהֹוָה הַצְלִיחָה נָּא:

אָנָּא יְהֹוָה הַצְלִיחָה נָּא:

בָּרוּךְ הַבָּא בְּשֵׁם יְהֹוָה בֵּרַכְנוּכֶם מִבֵּית יְהֹוָה: ברוך: אֵל |
יְהֹוָה וַיָּאֶר לָנוּ אִסְרוּ־חַג בַּעֲבֹתִים עַד קַרְנוֹת הַמִּזְבֵּחַ:
אל. אֵלִי אַתָּה וְאוֹדֶךָ אֱלֹהַי אֲרוֹמְמֶךָּ: אלי. הוֹדוּ לַיהֹוָה
כִּי־טוֹב כִּי לְעוֹלָם חַסְדּוֹ: הודו.

יְהַלְלוּךָ יְהֹוָה אֱלֹהֵינוּ (עַל) כָּל מַעֲשֶׂיךָ וַחֲסִידֶיךָ
צַדִּיקִים עוֹשֵׂי רְצוֹנֶךָ וְכָל עַמְּךָ בֵּית יִשְׂרָאֵל בְּרִנָּה יוֹדוּ
וִיבָרְכוּ וִישַׁבְּחוּ וִיפָאֲרוּ וִירוֹמְמוּ וְיַעֲרִיצוּ וְיַקְדִּישׁוּ
וְיַמְלִיכוּ אֶת שִׁמְךָ מַלְכֵּנוּ כִּי לְךָ טוֹב לְהוֹדוֹת וּלְשִׁמְךָ
נָאֶה לְזַמֵּר כִּי מֵעוֹלָם וְעַד עוֹלָם אַתָּה אֵל:

כִּי לְעוֹלָם חַסְדּוֹ:	הוֹדוּ לַיהֹוָה כִּי־טוֹב
כִּי לְעוֹלָם חַסְדּוֹ:	הוֹדוּ לֵאלֹהֵי הָאֱלֹהִים
כִּי לְעוֹלָם חַסְדּוֹ:	הוֹדוּ לַאֲדֹנֵי הָאֲדֹנִים
כִּי לְעוֹלָם חַסְדּוֹ:	לְעֹשֵׂה נִפְלָאוֹת גְּדֹלוֹת לְבַדּוֹ
כִּי לְעוֹלָם חַסְדּוֹ:	לְעֹשֵׂה הַשָּׁמַיִם בִּתְבוּנָה

The Great *Hallel* — הלל הגדול

QUESTION: Why in the *Hallel Hagadol* — the Great *Hallel* —
which describes 26 aspects of Hashem's goodness and which
repeats the refrain, "For His kindness in everlasting" for each one,
is there no mention of His giving the Torah to the Jewish people?

ANSWER: According to Rabbi Yehoshua ben Levi (*Pesachim*
118a) the 26 verses correspond to the 26 generations of humanity
from Adam to Moshe that Hashem created in His world and sus-

אנא We implore you, *Adonai*, help us now!

We implore you, *Adonai*, help us now!

We implore you, *Adonai*, grant us success now!

We implore you, *Adonai*, grant us success now![1]

ברוך Blessed is He who comes in the Name of *Adonai*; we bless you from the House of *Adonai*. (Repeat this verse) The Almighty is *Adonai*; He illuminated for us, bind the festival offering with cords until [you bring it to] the corners of the altar. (Repeat this verse) You are my Almighty and I will thank You; my God, I will exalt You. (Repeat this verse) Give thanks to *Adonai* for He is good, for His kindness is everlasting.[2] (Repeat this verse)

יהללוך All Your works shall praise You, *Adonai*, our God. And Your pious ones, the righteous who do Your will, and all Your people, the House of Israel, with joyous song will thank, bless, praise, glorify, exalt, extol, sanctify, and proclaim the sovereignty of Your Name, our King. For to you it is good to give thanks, and to Your Name it is pleasant to sing praise, for from [the highest] world to [the lowest] world You are Almighty.

> The following Psalm is referred to as the "Great *Hallel.*" It contains 26 verses, the numerical equivalent of the Four-Letter Name of Hashem. The custom is to bear in mind the letter י [which equals ten] while reading the first ten verses, the letter ה [five] while reading the next five verses, the letter ו [six] while reading the next six verses, and the letter ה [five] while reading the final five verses.

הודו Give thanks to *Adonai* for He is good,for His kindness is everlasting.
Give thanks to the God of the angels,   for His kindness is everlasting.
Give thanks to the Master of masters (i.e. heavenly hosts),
        for His kindness is everlasting.
Who does great wonders alone,   for His kindness is everlasting.
Who made the heavens with understanding,
        for His kindness is everlasting.

1. *Psalms* 118:25. 2. *Psalms* 118:26-29.

---

tained through His mercy, although there was no Torah and the world lacked the merit of the fulfillment of *mitzvot*. Consequently, there is no mention of Torah in this Psalm, which corresponds to the period prior to the revelation at Sinai.

(הגש״פ מוצל מאש - בית אהרן - בפי׳ רוח חדשה)

כִּי לְעוֹלָם חַסְדּוֹ:		לְרוֹקַע הָאָרֶץ עַל הַמָּיִם
כִּי לְעוֹלָם חַסְדּוֹ:		לְעֹשֵׂה אוֹרִים גְּדֹלִים
כִּי לְעוֹלָם חַסְדּוֹ:		אֶת־הַשֶּׁמֶשׁ לְמֶמְשֶׁלֶת בַּיּוֹם
כִּי לְעוֹלָם חַסְדּוֹ:		אֶת־הַיָּרֵחַ וְכוֹכָבִים לְמֶמְשְׁלוֹת בַּלָּיְלָה
כִּי לְעוֹלָם חַסְדּוֹ:	יְ	לְמַכֵּה מִצְרַיִם בִּבְכוֹרֵיהֶם
כִּי לְעוֹלָם חַסְדּוֹ:		וַיּוֹצֵא יִשְׂרָאֵל מִתּוֹכָם
כִּי לְעוֹלָם חַסְדּוֹ:		בְּיָד חֲזָקָה וּבִזְרוֹעַ נְטוּיָה
כִּי לְעוֹלָם חַסְדּוֹ:		לְגֹזֵר יַם סוּף לִגְזָרִים
כִּי לְעוֹלָם חַסְדּוֹ:		וְהֶעֱבִיר יִשְׂרָאֵל בְּתוֹכוֹ
כִּי לְעוֹלָם חַסְדּוֹ:	הָ	וְנִעֵר פַּרְעֹה וְחֵילוֹ בְיַם־סוּף
כִּי לְעוֹלָם חַסְדּוֹ:		לְמוֹלִיךְ עַמּוֹ בַּמִּדְבָּר
כִּי לְעוֹלָם חַסְדּוֹ:		לְמַכֵּה מְלָכִים גְּדֹלִים
כִּי לְעוֹלָם חַסְדּוֹ:		וַיַּהֲרֹג מְלָכִים אַדִּירִים
כִּי לְעוֹלָם חַסְדּוֹ:		לְסִיחוֹן מֶלֶךְ הָאֱמֹרִי
כִּי לְעוֹלָם חַסְדּוֹ:		וּלְעוֹג מֶלֶךְ הַבָּשָׁן
כִּי לְעוֹלָם חַסְדּוֹ:	וַ	וְנָתַן אַרְצָם לְנַחֲלָה
כִּי לְעוֹלָם חַסְדּוֹ:		נַחֲלָה לְיִשְׂרָאֵל עַבְדּוֹ
כִּי לְעוֹלָם חַסְדּוֹ:		שֶׁבְּשִׁפְלֵנוּ זָכַר לָנוּ
כִּי לְעוֹלָם חַסְדּוֹ:		וַיִּפְרְקֵנוּ מִצָּרֵינוּ
כִּי לְעוֹלָם חַסְדּוֹ:		נֹתֵן לֶחֶם לְכָל־בָּשָׂר
כִּי לְעוֹלָם חַסְדּוֹ:	הָ	הוֹדוּ לְאֵל הַשָּׁמָיִם

Og king of Bashan — עוג מלך הבשן

QUESTION: The first time Og is mentioned in the Torah he is called *"Hapalit"* — "the fugitive" (*Bereishit* 14:13, Rashi). How did he get the name "Og"?

ANSWER: He happened to come to the home of Avraham and he found him busy making *"ugot"* — "round unleavened cakes" — to fulfill the *mitzvah* of eating *matzot* on *Pesach*. (See ibid. 18:6.

הגדה של פסח

210

Who stretched out the earth over the waters,

for His kindness is everlasting.

Who made the great lights, for His kindness is everlasting.

The sun to rule by day, for His kindness is everlasting.

The moon and the stars to rule by night,

for His kindness is everlasting.

Who struck Egypt through their firstborn, (י)

for His kindness is everlasting.

And brought Israel out of their midst,for His kindness is everlasting.

With a strong hand and with an outstretched arm,

for His kindness is everlasting.

Who split the Sea of Reeds into sections,

for His kindness is everlasting.

And led Israel through it, for His kindness is everlasting.

And who cast Pharaoh and his army into the Sea of Reeds, (ה)

for His kindness is everlasting.

Who led His people through the wilderness,

for His kindness is everlasting.

Who struck down great kings, for His kindness is everlasting.

And slew mighty kings, for His kindness is everlasting.

Sichon, king of the Amorites, for His kindness is everlasting.

And Og, king of Bashan, for His kindness is everlasting.

And gave their land as a heritage, (ו) for His kindness is everlasting.

A heritage for Israel, His servant, for His kindness is everlasting.

In our lowliness He remembered us, for His kindness is everlasting.

And delivered us from our oppressors,

for His kindness is everlasting.

He gives food to all flesh, for His kindness is everlasting.

Give thanks to the Almighty of heaven, (ה)

for His kindness is everlasting.[1]

1. Psalm 136.

Avraham fulfilled all the *mitzvot* of the Torah even before they were promulgated, *Yoma* 28b.) After inquiring about what Avraham was doing, he expressed scorn and ridicule. (See p. 176) Thus, he was nicknamed "Og" — "round cake" — as punishment for making fun of Avraham and the precept of *matzot*.

(מדרש רבה בראשית מ"ב ה' ועי' בפירוש מהרד"ו)

נִשְׁמַת כָּל־חַי תְּבָרֵךְ אֶת שִׁמְךָ יְהֹוָה אֱלֹהֵינוּ. וְרוּחַ כָּל־בָּשָׂר תְּפָאֵר וּתְרוֹמֵם זִכְרְךָ מַלְכֵּנוּ תָּמִיד. מִן הָעוֹלָם וְעַד־הָעוֹלָם אַתָּה אֵל. וּמִבַּלְעָדֶיךָ אֵין לָנוּ מֶלֶךְ גּוֹאֵל וּמוֹשִׁיעַ פּוֹדֶה וּמַצִּיל וּמְפַרְנֵס וְעוֹנֶה וּמְרַחֵם בְּכָל־עֵת צָרָה וְצוּקָה אֵין לָנוּ מֶלֶךְ אֶלָּא אַתָּה: אֱלֹהֵי הָרִאשׁוֹנִים וְהָאַחֲרוֹנִים אֱלוֹהַּ כָּל־בְּרִיּוֹת אֲדוֹן כָּל־תּוֹלָדוֹת הַמְהֻלָּל בְּרֹב הַתִּשְׁבָּחוֹת. הַמְנַהֵג עוֹלָמוֹ בְּחֶסֶד וּבְרִיּוֹתָיו בְּרַחֲמִים. וַיהֹוָה הִנֵּה לֹא יָנוּם וְלֹא יִישָׁן. הַמְעוֹרֵר יְשֵׁנִים וְהַמֵּקִיץ נִרְדָּמִים וְהַמֵּשִׂיחַ אִלְּמִים וְהַמַּתִּיר אֲסוּרִים וְהַסּוֹמֵךְ נוֹפְלִים וְהַזּוֹקֵף כְּפוּפִים. לְךָ לְבַדְּךָ אֲנַחְנוּ מוֹדִים. אִלּוּ פִינוּ מָלֵא שִׁירָה כַּיָּם וּלְשׁוֹנֵנוּ רִנָּה כַּהֲמוֹן גַּלָּיו וְשִׂפְתוֹתֵינוּ שֶׁבַח כְּמֶרְחֲבֵי רָקִיעַ וְעֵינֵינוּ מְאִירוֹת כַּשֶּׁמֶשׁ וְכַיָּרֵחַ וְיָדֵינוּ פְרוּשׂוֹת כְּנִשְׁרֵי שָׁמָיִם וְרַגְלֵינוּ קַלּוֹת כָּאַיָּלוֹת: אֵין אָנוּ מַסְפִּיקִים לְהוֹדוֹת לְךָ יְהֹוָה אֱלֹהֵינוּ וֵאלֹהֵי אֲבוֹתֵינוּ וּלְבָרֵךְ אֶת־שְׁמֶךָ עַל אַחַת מֵאֶלֶף אַלְפֵי אֲלָפִים וְרִבֵּי רְבָבוֹת פְּעָמִים הַטּוֹבוֹת נִסִּים וְנִפְלָאוֹת שֶׁעָשִׂיתָ עִמָּנוּ וְעִם־אֲבוֹתֵינוּ מִלְּפָנִים: מִמִּצְרַיִם גְּאַלְתָּנוּ יְהֹוָה אֱלֹהֵינוּ. מִבֵּית עֲבָדִים פְּדִיתָנוּ. בְּרָעָב זַנְתָּנוּ וּבְשָׂבָע כִּלְכַּלְתָּנוּ מֵחֶרֶב הִצַּלְתָּנוּ וּמִדֶּבֶר מִלַּטְתָּנוּ

"בְּרָעָב זַנְתָּנוּ וּבְשָׂבָע כִּלְכַּלְתָּנוּ"

"In famine You fed us and in times of plenty You sustained us."

QUESTION: To feed us when the entire world is hungry is praiseworthy, but what is so special about sustaining us if the entire world is experiencing plenty?

נשמת The soul of every living being shall bless Your Name, *Adonai*, our God, and the spirit of all flesh shall always glorify and exalt Your remembrance, our King. From the [highest] world to the [lowest] world, You are Almighty, and other than You, we have no king who redeems and helps; who delivers and rescues and sustains and answers; and is merciful in all times of trouble and distress, we have no King but You. [You are] the God of the first and last [generations]; God of all creatures, Master of all events, who is extolled with manifold praises, who leads His world with kindness and His creatures with mercy. And *Adonai*, behold, neither slumbers nor sleeps, He arouses those who sleep, and awakens those who slumber, gives speech to the mute, and releases the bound, supports the fallen, and raises up those who are bowed. To You alone we give thanks. Even if our mouths were filled with song like the sea, and our tongues filled with joyous song like the roar of its waves, and our lips were filled with praise like the breadth of the sky, and our eyes were radiant as the sun and the moon, and our hands were spread out like the eagles of the sky, and our feet as swift as a deer — we would still be unable to sufficiently thank You, *Adonai*, our God, and God of our fathers, and bless Your Name for even one of the innumerable thousands of millions and myriads of favors, miracles, and wonders You have done for us and our fathers before us. From Egypt You redeemed us, *Adonai*, our God, and from the house of bondage You liberated us; in famine You fed us and in [times of] plenty You sustained us; from the sword You saved us; from the pestilence you delivered us

---

ANSWER: In the *Gemara* (*Bava Batra* 91b) Rabbi Yochanan says, "I recall when there was an abundance of flour in the world and it was inexpensive, and yet there were many people who were swollen due to the hunger because of lack of money with which to purchase it."

We thank Hashem that in times of plenty He provided us with the means to purchase food with ease and enjoy the abundance with which the world has been blessed.

(ברוך שאמר)

וּמֵחֳלָיִם רָעִים וְנֶאֱמָנִים דִּלִּיתָנוּ: עַד־הֵנָּה עֲזָרוּנוּ רַחֲמֶיךָ וְלֹא־עֲזָבוּנוּ חֲסָדֶיךָ. וְאַל־תִּטְּשֵׁנוּ יְהֹוָה אֱלֹהֵינוּ לָנֶצַח: עַל־כֵּן אֵבָרִים שֶׁפִּלַּגְתָּ בָּנוּ וְרוּחַ וּנְשָׁמָה שֶׁנָּפַחְתָּ בְּאַפֵּנוּ וְלָשׁוֹן אֲשֶׁר שַׂמְתָּ בְּפִינוּ: הֵן הֵם יוֹדוּ וִיבָרְכוּ וִישַׁבְּחוּ וִיפָאֲרוּ וִירוֹמְמוּ וְיַעֲרִיצוּ וְיַקְדִּישׁוּ וְיַמְלִיכוּ אֶת שִׁמְךָ מַלְכֵּנוּ: כִּי כָל פֶּה לְךָ יוֹדֶה וְכָל לָשׁוֹן לְךָ תִשָּׁבַע. וְכָל־עַיִן לְךָ תְצַפֶּה וְכָל־בֶּרֶךְ לְךָ תִכְרַע וְכָל קוֹמָה לְפָנֶיךָ תִשְׁתַּחֲוֶה. וְכָל הַלְּבָבוֹת יִירָאוּךְ וְכָל־קֶרֶב וּכְלָיוֹת יְזַמְּרוּ לִשְׁמֶךָ. כַּדָּבָר שֶׁכָּתוּב כָּל־עַצְמוֹתַי תֹּאמַרְנָה יְהֹוָה מִי כָמוֹךָ. מַצִּיל עָנִי מֵחָזָק מִמֶּנּוּ וְעָנִי וְאֶבְיוֹן מִגֹּזְלוֹ: מִי יִדְמֶה־לָּךְ וּמִי יִשְׁוֶה־לָּךְ וּמִי יַעֲרָךְ־לָךְ. הָאֵל הַגָּדוֹל הַגִּבּוֹר וְהַנּוֹרָא אֵל עֶלְיוֹן קֹנֵה שָׁמַיִם וָאָרֶץ: נְהַלֶּלְךָ וּנְשַׁבֵּחֲךָ וּנְפָאֶרְךָ וּנְבָרֵךְ אֶת־שֵׁם קָדְשֶׁךָ. כָּאָמוּר לְדָוִד בָּרְכִי נַפְשִׁי אֶת יְהֹוָה וְכָל־קְרָבַי אֶת שֵׁם קָדְשׁוֹ:

הָאֵל בְּתַעֲצֻמוֹת עֻזֶּךָ. הַגָּדוֹל בִּכְבוֹד שְׁמֶךָ. הַגִּבּוֹר לָנֶצַח וְהַנּוֹרָא בְּנוֹרְאוֹתֶיךָ. הַמֶּלֶךְ הַיּוֹשֵׁב עַל כִּסֵּא רָם וְנִשָּׂא:

"הָאֵ-ל בְּתַעֲצֻמוֹת עֻזֶּךָ"

"The A-mighty, by virtue of Your strength."

QUESTION: Why does this statement follow the prayer of *Nishmat*?

ANSWER: In the final sentence of *Nishmat* we declare that no one is equal or comparable to Hashem, for He is 1) The A-mighty, 2) The Great, 3) The Powerful, and 4) The Awesome. Thus, we now explain the four unique qualities which only He possesses. 1) He is "The A-mighty" by virtue of His might — it is not depend-

and from severe and lingering sicknesses you spared us. Until now, Your mercies have helped us, and Your kindness has not forsaken us, and do not abandon us, *Adonai*, our God, forever. Therefore, the limbs You have arranged within us, and the spirit and soul You breathed into our nostrils, the tongue that You placed in our mouths — they all shall thank, bless, praise, glorify, exalt, extol, sanctify and proclaim the sovereignty of Your Name, our King. For every mouth shall thank You, every tongue shall swear allegiance to You, every eye shall look to You, every knee shall bend to You, all who stand erect shall prostrate before You, all hearts shall fear You, and all innards and kidneys shall sing to Your Name, as it is written:[1] "All my bones shall say: '*Adonai*, who is like You? Savior of the poor from one stronger than he, the poor and destitute from those who would rob him.' " Who resembles You, who is equal to You, who can be compared to You, the Almighty, the Great, the Powerful and the Awesome. Almighty the Most High, Maker of heaven and earth! We shall laud You, praise You, glorify You, and bless Your holy Name, as it is said:[2] "[A Psalm] by David; My soul bless *Adonai*, and all that is within me [bless] His holy Name."

האל [You are] the Almighty by virtue of Your strength, the Great by virtue of the glory of Your Name, the Powerful for eternity and the Awesome by virtue of Your awe-inspiring deeds. The King who sits on a lofty and exalted throne.

1. *Psalms* 35:10. 2. *Psalms* 103:1.

---

ent on anyone's assistance. 2) He is "The Great" by virtue of the glory of His Name — it is lauded and honored by all creatures. 3) He is "The Powerful" by virtue of His strength — human strength decreases with age while His is eternal. 4) He is "The Awesome" by virtue of His awe-inspiring deeds — the entire universe recognizes that His doings are Divinely and supernatural.

Incidentally, in all Sephardic *siddurim*, the prayer of *Nishmat* appears without the four descriptions which distinguish Hashem, and thus the prayer of *"Ha'Ei-l beta'azumot"* is omitted as well.

(סידור אוצר התפלות בפי' עץ יוסף, ועי' כתר שם טוב לר' שם טוב ז"ל גאנין)

שׁוֹכֵן עַד מָרוֹם וְקָדוֹשׁ שְׁמוֹ. וְכָתוּב רַנְּנוּ צַדִּיקִים
בַּיהוָֹה לַיְשָׁרִים נָאוָה תְהִלָּה: בְּפִי יְשָׁרִים תִּתְרוֹמָם.
וּבְשִׂפְתֵי צַדִּיקִים תִּתְבָּרֵךְ. וּבִלְשׁוֹן חֲסִידִים תִּתְקַדָּשׁ
וּבְקֶרֶב קְדוֹשִׁים תִּתְהַלָּל:
וּבְמַקְהֲלוֹת רִבְבוֹת עַמְּךָ בֵּית יִשְׂרָאֵל בְּרִנָּה יִתְפָּאֵר
שִׁמְךָ מַלְכֵּנוּ בְּכָל דּוֹר וָדוֹר שֶׁכֵּן חוֹבַת כָּל־הַיְצוּרִים.
לְפָנֶיךָ יְהוָֹה אֱלֹהֵינוּ וֵאלֹהֵי אֲבוֹתֵינוּ לְהוֹדוֹת לְהַלֵּל
לְשַׁבֵּחַ לְפָאֵר לְרוֹמֵם לְהַדֵּר לְבָרֵךְ לְעַלֵּה וּלְקַלֵּס עַל
כָּל־דִּבְרֵי שִׁירוֹת וְתִשְׁבְּחוֹת דָּוִד־בֶּן יִשַׁי עַבְדְּךָ מְשִׁיחֶךָ:
וּבְכֵן יִשְׁתַּבַּח שִׁמְךָ לָעַד מַלְכֵּנוּ הָאֵל הַמֶּלֶךְ הַגָּדוֹל
וְהַקָּדוֹשׁ בַּשָּׁמַיִם וּבָאָרֶץ. כִּי לְךָ נָאֶה יְהוָֹה אֱלֹהֵינוּ
וֵאלֹהֵי אֲבוֹתֵינוּ לְעוֹלָם וָעֶד שִׁיר וּשְׁבָחָה הַלֵּל וְזִמְרָה
עֹז וּמֶמְשָׁלָה נֶצַח גְּדֻלָּה וּגְבוּרָה תְּהִלָּה וְתִפְאֶרֶת קְדֻשָּׁה
וּמַלְכוּת. בְּרָכוֹת וְהוֹדָאוֹת לְשִׁמְךָ הַגָּדוֹל וְהַקָּדוֹשׁ
וּמֵעוֹלָם עַד־עוֹלָם אַתָּה אֵל: בָּרוּךְ אַתָּה יְהוָֹה אֵל מֶלֶךְ
גָּדוֹל וּמְהֻלָּל בַּתִּשְׁבָּחוֹת אֵל הַהוֹדָאוֹת אֲדוֹן הַנִּפְלָאוֹת
בּוֹרֵא כָּל־הַנְּשָׁמוֹת רִבּוֹן כָּל־הַמַּעֲשִׂים. הַבּוֹחֵר בְּשִׁירֵי
זִמְרָה. מֶלֶךְ יָחִיד חֵי הָעוֹלָמִים:

"By the mouth of the upright shall
You be exalted, and by the lips of
the righteous shall You be blessed.
By the tongue of the pious shall
You be sanctified, and among the
holy shall You be praised."

בפי ישרים תתרוֹמם
ובשפתי צדיקים תתברך
ובלשון חסידים תתקדש
ובקרב קדושים תתהלל

QUESTION: In some *siddurim* this statement is written in four
lines of three words each to show that the first letter of the second
word of each line forms an acrostic of the name "Yitzchak."
Additionally, the third letter of the final word of each line forms
an acrostic of the name "Rivkah."

What is the significance of this?

שוכן He who lives for eternity, exalted and holy is His Name. And it is written:[1] "Sing joyously to *Adonai*, you righteous; it befits the upright to offer praise." By the mouth of the upright shall You be exalted, and by the lips of the righteous shall You be blessed. By the tongue of the pious shall You be sanctified, and among the holy shall You be praised.

ובמקהלות And in the assemblies of the myriads of Your people, the House of Israel, with joyous song Your Name shall be glorified, our King, in every generation, for this is the duty of all creatures before You, *Adonai*, our God, and God of our fathers: to thank, laud, praise, glorify, exalt, beautify, bless, raise high, and to acclaim; even beyond the words of songs and praises of David, the son of Yishai, Your servant, Your anointed.

ובכן And therefore, may your Name be praised forever, our King — the Almighty, the King, the Great, the Holy — in heaven and on earth. For to You, *Adonai*, our God, and God of our fathers, it is fitting forever: song and praise, laud and hymn, power and dominion, victory, greatness and might, praise and splendor, holiness, and sovereignty, blessings and thanksgivings to Your great and holy Name, and from the [highest] world to the [lowest] world, You are Almighty. Blessed are You, *Adonai*, Almighty King, great and extolled with praises, Almighty worthy of thanksgiving, Master of wonders, Creator of all souls, Ruler of all creatures, Who chooses [to take pleasure] in songs of praise, the only King, the Life of all the worlds.

1. *Psalms* 33:1.

ANSWER: The combined numerical value of Yitzchak and Rivkah (יצחק רבקה) is 515, which is also the numerical value of the word *Tefillah* — prayer (תפלה). They are the only couple that the Torah mentions praying together (see *Bereishit* 24:2 Rashi).

* * *

Prayer is song and praise to Hashem, and it should be recited with joy and happiness. Our Sages (*Taanit* 2a) in explanation of the verse "to serve Him with all your heart" (*Devarim* 11:13) have defined prayer as the "service of Hashem performed in the heart." It is elementary that mental and emotional concentration is an essential component of prayer (Rambam, *Tefillah* 4:15).

It is interesting to note that the word "*shirah*" (שירה) — "song" — and also the words "*bekavanat haleiv*" (בכונת הלב) — "concentration of the heart" — have the same numerical value as the word "*tefillah*" (515).

בָּרוּךְ אַתָּה יְהֹוָה אֱלֹהֵינוּ מֶלֶךְ הָעוֹלָם בּוֹרֵא פְּרִי הַגָּפֶן: ושותה בהסיבה

ברכה אחרונה על הגפן:

בָּרוּךְ אַתָּה יְהֹוָה אֱלֹהֵינוּ מֶלֶךְ הָעוֹלָם עַל הַגֶּפֶן
וְעַל פְּרִי הַגֶּפֶן וְעַל תְּנוּבַת הַשָּׂדֶה וְעַל־אֶרֶץ חֶמְדָּה
טוֹבָה וּרְחָבָה שֶׁרָצִיתָ וְהִנְחַלְתָּ לַאֲבוֹתֵינוּ לֶאֱכוֹל
מִפִּרְיָהּ וְלִשְׂבּוֹעַ מִטּוּבָהּ רַחֶם נָא יְהֹוָה אֱלֹהֵינוּ עַל־
יִשְׂרָאֵל עַמֶּךְ וְעַל־יְרוּשָׁלַיִם עִירֶךְ וְעַל־צִיּוֹן מִשְׁכַּן
כְּבוֹדֶךְ וְעַל־מִזְבְּחֶךְ וְעַל־הֵיכָלֶךְ. וּבְנֵה יְרוּשָׁלַיִם עִיר
הַקֹּדֶשׁ בִּמְהֵרָה בְיָמֵינוּ וְהַעֲלֵנוּ לְתוֹכָהּ. וְשַׂמְּחֵנוּ בָהּ
וּנְבָרֶכְךָ בִּקְדֻשָּׁה וּבְטָהֳרָה. (בשבת: וּרְצֵה וְהַחֲלִיצֵנוּ בְּיוֹם
הַשַּׁבָּת הַזֶּה): וְזָכְרֵנוּ לְטוֹבָה בְּיוֹם חַג הַמַּצּוֹת הַזֶּה. כִּי
אַתָּה יְהֹוָה טוֹב וּמֵטִיב לַכֹּל וְנוֹדֶה לְךָ עַל הָאָרֶץ וְעַל
פְּרִי הַגָּפֶן: בָּרוּךְ אַתָּה יְהֹוָה עַל הָאָרֶץ וְעַל פְּרִי הַגָּפֶן.

ברכת בנר על שאר משקין:

בָּרוּךְ אַתָּה יְהֹוָה אֱלֹהֵינוּ מֶלֶךְ הָעוֹלָם בּוֹרֵא
נְפָשׁוֹת רַבּוֹת וְחֶסְרוֹנָן עַל כֹּל מַה שֶּׁבָּרָאתָ לְהַחֲיוֹת
בָּהֶם נֶפֶשׁ כָּל־חָי. בָּרוּךְ חֵי הָעוֹלָמִים:

Those who have a custom to recite hymns, after the *Seder* (see supplement p. 223) should not do so now, between this blessing and the one for the fourth cup. One must recite the blessing for the fourth cup immediately now.

The recitation of hymns is not mentioned in the *Gemara (Pesachim 117b),* as a part of the *Seder.* It is merely a custom which started many years later in some communities (see *Orach Chaim* 580).

It is not the prevailing Lubavitch custom to recite them.

ברוך Blessed are You, *Adonai*, our God, Who created the fruit of the vine.

We drink the fourth cup of wine **while reclining on our left side.** It is customary to drink the entire cup, but at the very least, a *revi'it* (3.5 fluid ounces) must be drunk to justify the recitation of the blessing that follows drinking wine.

One should not drink afterwards. Leniency is granted with regard to drinking water, but the custom is to refrain from drinking even that. The blessing after drinking wine is recited:

ברוך Blessed are You, *Adonai*, our God, King of the universe, for the vine, and the fruit of the vine, for the produce of the field, for the desirous, good, and spacious land that You favored to give as a heritage to our fathers, to eat of its fruits and be satiated with its goodness. Have mercy, we beg you, *Adonai*, our God, on Israel Your people, on Jerusalem, Your city, on Zion the dwelling place of Your glory, on Your altar, and on Your Sanctuary. And rebuild Jerusalem, the holy city, speedily in our days, and bring us up into it, and make us rejoice in it, and we will bless You in holiness and purity (on *Shabbat:* and may it please You to strengthen us on this *Shabbat* day) and remember us for good on this day of the Festival of *Matzot*. For You, *Adonai*, are good and do good to all, and we thank You for the land and for the fruit of the vine. Blessed are You, *Adonai*, for the land and for the fruit of the vine.

A person who is not able to drink wine and instead used mead or other beverages for the four cups (see *Shulchan Aruch Harav* 472:28) should recite the following blessing:

ברוך Blessed are You, *Adonai*, our God, King of the universe, Who created numerous living beings and their needs, for all the things You have created with which to sustain the soul of every living being. Blessed is He Who is the Life of all the worlds.

ואח״כ יאמר:

לְשָׁנָה הַבָּאָה בִּירוּשָׁלָיִם:

"לשנה הבאה בירושלים"
"Next year in Jerusalem."

QUESTION: Why "next year"?

ANSWER: The intent is not that we should wait until next year to be in Jerusalem. We are asking Hashem to take us out of exile immediately, and thus, next year when we celebrate *Pesach*, we will be in Jerusalem.

(ספר השיחות תש״ה)

* * *

Rabbi Shneur Zalman of Liadi did not include the passage, *"Chasal Siddur Pesach"* — "The *Pesach Seder* has been completed" — in his *Haggadah* because the *Pesach Seder* never truly ends. Instead, it continues throughout the year.

The Hebrew word for Egypt is *Mitzrayim* (מצרים), which can also be read as *"meitzarim"* — "limitations and boundaries." The *Pesach* experience is constant, for every day, a Jew must leave Egypt — *Mitzrayim* — transcend his previous *meitzarim* — limitations — and reach higher levels of holiness.

(ספר השיחות תש״ג ע׳ 83)

Afterwards say:

Next Year in Jerusalem!

L'shanah habaah is recited only once. It is not the prevailing Lubavitch custom to recite the concluding hymns which are to be found in most *Siddurim* and *Haggadot*.

After saying "Next year in Jerusalem!" the prevailing Lubavitch custom is for the wine from the Cup of Eliyahu to be poured back into the bottle. All those present sing *"Keili atah ve'odeka"* — "You are my A-lmighty and I will thank You" — to the melody composed by Rabbi Shneur Zalman of Liadi, founder of *Chabad Chassidut*, known as the *Alter Rebbe*.

* * *

Before retiring to bed, it is customary to recite only the first portion of *Shema* and the *berachah* of *Hamapil*.

(שו"ע הרב, תפ"א:ב)

On the second night of *Pesach*, the prevailing Lubavitch custom is to recite the entire prayer before going to bed as on any *Yom Tov*.

(היום יום ט"ז ניסן)

הוספה

Supplement

The recital of the *Haggadah* of *Pesach* concludes with either the recital of *Yishtabach* or *Yehalelucha* (see *Shulchan Aruch Harav* 580:1).

Some *(Ashkenazi)* communities have a custom to recite certain *piyutim* — liturgical hymns — after the completion of the *Haggadah* (see *Magen Avraham* 580:2, ibid. 580:3). For their convenience these are included in this *Haggadah* as a supplement together with commentary.

חֲסַל סִדּוּר פֶּסַח כְּהִלְכָתוֹ. כְּכָל מִשְׁפָּטוֹ וְחֻקָּתוֹ. כַּאֲשֶׁר זָכִינוּ לְסַדֵּר אוֹתוֹ. כֵּן נִזְכֶּה לַעֲשׂוֹתוֹ: זָךְ שׁוֹכֵן מְעוֹנָה. קוֹמֵם קְהַל עֲדַת מִי מָנָה. בְּקָרוֹב נַהֵל נִטְעֵי כַנָּה. פְּדוּיִם לְצִיּוֹן בְּרִנָּה:

לְשָׁנָה הַבָּאָה בִּירוּשָׁלָיִם

בליל ראשון אומרים פיוט זה ובליל שני מתחילים ובכן אמרתם (עמוד 228).

וּבְכֵן וַיְהִי בַּחֲצִי הַלַּיְלָה:

אָז רוֹב נִסִּים הִפְלֵאתָ	בַּלַּיְלָה.
בְּרֹאשׁ אַשְׁמוּרוֹת זֶה	הַלַּיְלָה.
גֵּר צֶדֶק נִצַּחְתּוֹ כְּנֶחֱלַק לוֹ	לַיְלָה.

וַיְהִי בַּחֲצִי הַלַּיְלָה:

"חסל סדר פסח...פדוים לציון ברנה"
**"The Pesach Seder has been completed...
bringing them redeemed to Zion in joyous song"**

QUESTION: Who composed this statement?

ANSWER: In some communities on *Shabbat Hagadol* certain *Yotzrot* — liturgical prayers — are said in the *Shacharit*. One is *Elokei haruchot lechol basar* — "G-d Who knows the spirit of all beings" — which contains many of the *halachot* — laws — related to *Pesach*, and concludes with *"Chasal sidur Pesach"* and the sentence which follows it in the *Haggadah*.

It was composed by Rabbeinu Yosef ben Shmuel Tov Elem. He was a great Torah scholar who lived in France around 4800. Some say that he was one of Rashi's teachers.

(הגש״פ מר׳ שבח ז״ל קנעביל)

"חסל סדר פסח"
"The Pesach Seder has been completed."

QUESTION: Since the rest of the statement is in *Lashon Hakodesh* — Hebrew — why is the first word, *"chasal"* — "has been completed" — in Aramaic?

ANSWER: When the letters of the word *"chasal"* are written out in full, i.e. חיי״ת — סמי״ך - למ״ד — their numerical value is six hundred and twelve, which is also the numerical value of the word *"brit"* (ברית) — "circumcision."

In the Torah (*Shemot* 12:48) it is written, "No uncircumcised male may eat of it [the *Pesach*-offering]." Thus, with the word *"chasal"* we are alluding that all the males present are halachically eligible to be participants. (See p. 194.)

(הגש״פ עם פי׳ ילקוט שמעוני בשם ריח דודאים)

The *Pesach Seder* has been completed in accordance with its law, with all its rules and statutes; just as we merited to observe it, so may we merit to perform it again. Pure One, Who dwells on high, raise up the congregation that is without number! Soon may You lead the stock You have planted, redeemed to Zion in joyous song.

Next year in Jerusalem!

The following is said on the first night:

And thus it came to pass at midnight!

Then most of the miracles You wondrously performed were at night. At the beginning of the watches on this night. To the righteous convert [Avraham] You granted victory when divided was the night.[1] And it came to pass at midnight!

1. *Bereishit* 14:15.

"ובכן ויהי בחצי הלילה. אז רוב נסים..."

"It came to pass at midnight. Then most of the miracles..."

QUESTION: Who composed this hymn?

ANSWER: The author was Rabbi Yannai, who was one of the early composers of liturgical hymns and the teacher of the renown liturgical poet Rabbi Elazar Hakalir. It is also recited in some communities on *Shabbat Hagadol* during the *Shacharit* prayer.

(הגש"פ מר' שבח ז"ל קנעביל)

"ובכן ויהי בחצי הלילה"

"It came to pass at midnight."

QUESTION: In this poem we mention many miracles and salvations that Hashem has performed for the Jewish people throughout history on the night of *Pesach*. What is the significance of their occurrence in the middle of the night?

ANSWER: The light of day symbolizes times of glory and success, and the darkness of night symbolizes times of exile and tribulation. People usually sleep during the dark hours and are deeply asleep at midnight. The poet is stressing that Hashem watches over His beloved people at all times. However, at times it is revealed and obvious, and at times not. Metaphorically, when it is dark (in the time of *galut*) and the Jewish people are in the depth of their sleep and see no relief for their misery and suffering, unexpectedly Hashem reveals Himself, and in a miraculous way the darkness of the night is converted to light and the Jewish people see a new horizon.

* * *

דָּנְתָּ מֶלֶךְ גְּרָר בַּחֲלוֹם — הַלַּיְלָה.
הִפְחַדְתָּ אֲרַמִּי בְּאֶמֶשׁ — לַיְלָה.
וַיָּשַׂר יִשְׂרָאֵל לְמַלְאָךְ וַיּוּכַל לוֹ — לַיְלָה.
וַיְהִי בַּחֲצִי הַלַּיְלָה:

זֶרַע בְּכוֹרֵי פַתְרוֹס מָחַצְתָּ בַּחֲצִי — הַלַּיְלָה.
חֵילָם לֹא מָצְאוּ בְּקוּמָם — הַלַּיְלָה.
טִיסַת נְגִיד חֲרוֹשֶׁת סִלִּיתָ בְּכוֹכְבֵי — לַיְלָה.
וַיְהִי בַּחֲצִי הַלַּיְלָה:

יָעַץ מְחָרֵף לְנוֹפֵף אִוּוּי הוֹבַשְׁתָּ פְּגָרָיו — בַּלַּיְלָה.
כָּרַע בֵּל וּמַצָּבוֹ בְּאִישׁוֹן — לַיְלָה.
לְאִישׁ חֲמוּדוֹת נִגְלָה רָז חֲזוֹת — לַיְלָה.
וַיְהִי בַּחֲצִי הַלַּיְלָה:

מִשְׁתַּכֵּר בִּכְלֵי קֹדֶשׁ נֶהֱרַג בּוֹ — בַּלַּיְלָה.
נוֹשַׁע מִבּוֹר אֲרָיוֹת פּוֹתֵר בְּעִתּוּתֵי — לַיְלָה.
שִׂנְאָה נָטַר אֲגָגִי וְכָתַב סְפָרִים — בַּלַּיְלָה.
וַיְהִי בַּחֲצִי הַלַּיְלָה:

עוֹרַרְתָּ נִצְחֲךָ עָלָיו בְּנֶדֶד שְׁנַת — לַיְלָה.
פּוּרָה תִדְרוֹךְ לְשׁוֹמֵר מַה — מִלַּיְלָה.
צָרַח כַּשּׁוֹמֵר וְשָׂח אָתָא בֹקֶר וְגַם — לַיְלָה.
וַיְהִי בַּחֲצִי הַלַּיְלָה:

קָרֵב יוֹם אֲשֶׁר הוּא לֹא יוֹם וְלֹא — לַיְלָה.
רָם הוֹדַע כִּי לְךָ הַיּוֹם אַף לְךָ — הַלַּיְלָה.
שׁוֹמְרִים הַפְקֵד לְעִירְךָ כָּל הַיּוֹם וְכָל — הַלַּיְלָה.
תָּאִיר כְּאוֹר יוֹם חֶשְׁכַת — לַיְלָה.
וַיְהִי בַּחֲצִי הַלַּיְלָה:

Incidentally, the words *"bachatzi halayelah"* (בחצי הלילה) — "at midnight" — have the numerical value of 190. The refrain of the poem emphasizes Hashem's redeeming us from Egypt one hundred and ninety years earlier than it was originally destined to happen.

(הגש"פ מוצל מאש - בית אהרן - בפי' פאר אהרן)

"גר צדק נצחתו כנחלק לו לילה"
"To the righteous convert [Avraham] You granted victory when divided was the night. And it came to pass at midnight"

QUESTION: What is the connection between the miracle performed for Avraham in the middle of the night and the miracle performed for his descendants in Egypt in the middle of the night?

ANSWER: Regarding Avraham's pursuit of the enemy kings the Torah says, *"Vayeichaleik aleihem laylah"* — "He deployed

You judged the king of Gerar (Avimelech) in a dream at night.[1] You frightened the Aramean [Lavan] in the dark of the night.[2] Israel struggled with the angel and overcame him by night.[3] And it came to pass at midnight!

The Egyptian firstborn children You crushed at midnight.[4] They could not find their fortune when they awoke at night. The forces of the prince of Charoshet [Sisra] You swept away with the stars of night.[5] And it came to pass at midnight!

The blasphemer [Sanchereb] planned to raise his hand [against Jerusalem], You withered his corpses at night. Bel and his pedestal were overthrown in the darkness of night.[6] To the beloved man [Daniel] You revealed secret visions in the night.[7] And it came to pass at midnight!

He who became drunk [Balshatzar] using the holy vessels was slain on that very night.[8] From the lions' den was rescued [Daniel] the interpreter of nightmares.[9] The Agagite [Haman] bore hatred in his heart and wrote letters at night. And it came to pass at midnight!

You roused Your victory over him when You disturbed [Achashveirosh's] sleep by night.[10] You will tread the wine-press[11] to help those who ask the watchman: "When will there be an end to the night [exile]." He will proclaim like a watchman and say: "Morning will come [for the Jews] and also the night [for the tormentores]."[12] And it came to pass at midnight!

Bring near the day (the messianic age) that is neither day nor night. Most High! Show that Yours is the day as well as the night. Appoint watchmen to guard Your city (Jerusalem) the entire day and the entire night. Illuminate as the light of day the darkness of night. And it came to pass at midnight!

1. *Bereishit* 20:3. 2. 31:24. 3. 32:25. 4. *Shemot* 12:29. 5. Judges 5:20. 6. II Kings 19:35. 7. Daniel ch. 2. 8. 5:30. 9. Ch. 7. 10. Esther 6:1. 11. Isaiah 63:3. 12. 21:11-12.

---

against them at night" (*Bereishit* 14:15). Rashi in the name of the *Midrash* explains *"vayeichaleik"* to mean "He divided" — [the night]. During the first half of the night He performed a miracle for Avraham, and He reserved the second half for His miraculous revelation in Egypt.

This night is referred to in the Torah (*Shemot* 12:42) as *"leil shimurim,"* a night of protection [for the Jewish people throughout the generations]. It says *"shimurim"* — "protections" — in plural, because this night was designated as one of protection and salvation throughout the generations.

(אברבנאל, תפארת שלמה,
ועי' מסכת ר"ה י"א ע"ב שלילה זה משומר משושת ימי בראשית לגאולה)

וּבְכֵן וַאֲמַרְתֶּם זֶבַח פֶּסַח:

בַּפֶּסַח. אֹמֶץ גְּבוּרוֹתֶיךָ הִפְלֵאתָ

פֶּסַח. בְּרֹאשׁ כָּל מוֹעֲדוֹת נִשֵּׂאתָ

פֶּסַח. גִּלִּיתָ לְאֶזְרָחִי חֲצוֹת לֵיל

וַאֲמַרְתֶּם זֶבַח פֶּסַח:

בַּפֶּסַח. דְּלָתָיו דָּפַקְתָּ כְּחוֹם הַיּוֹם

בַּפֶּסַח. הִסְעִיד נוֹצְצִים עֻגוֹת מַצּוֹת

פֶּסַח. וְאֶל הַבָּקָר רָץ זֵכֶר לְשׁוֹר עֵרֶךְ

וַאֲמַרְתֶּם זֶבַח פֶּסַח:

בַּפֶּסַח. זוֹעֲמוּ סְדוֹמִים וְלוֹהֲטוּ בָּאֵשׁ

פֶּסַח. חֻלַּץ לוֹט מֵהֶם וּמַצּוֹת אָפָה בְּקֵץ

בַּפֶּסַח. טִאטֵאתָ אַדְמַת מוֹף וְנוֹף בְּעָבְרְךָ

וַאֲמַרְתֶּם זֶבַח פֶּסַח:

פֶּסַח. יָהּ רֹאשׁ כָּל אוֹן מָחַצְתָּ בְּלֵיל שִׁמּוּר

פֶּסַח. כַּבִּיר עַל בֵּן בְּכוֹר פָּסַחְתָּ בְּדַם

בַּפֶּסַח. לְבִלְתִּי תֵּת מַשְׁחִית לָבֹא בִּפְתָחַי

וַאֲמַרְתֶּם זֶבַח פֶּסַח:

פֶּסַח. מִסְגֶּרֶת סֻגָּרָה בְּעִתּוֹתֵי

פֶּסַח. נִשְׁמְדָה מִדְיָן בִּצְלִיל שְׂעוֹרֵי עֹמֶר

פֶּסַח. שׂוֹרְפוּ מִשְׁמַנֵּי פּוּל וְלוּד בִּיקַד יְקוֹד

וַאֲמַרְתֶּם זֶבַח פֶּסַח:

"קָרֵב יוֹם אֲשֶׁר הוּא לֹא יוֹם וְלֹא לַיְלָה"
"Bring near the day that is neither day nor night."

QUESTION: If it is neither day nor night, what is it?

ANSWER: Originally, when Hashem created the world, the light was extremely powerful. Not wanting the wicked to benefit from it, He hid it for the future to be used by the righteous (*Chagigah* 12a). The prophet says that in the days of *Mashiach*, "The light of the moon will be like the (present) light of the sun, and the light of the sun will [then be] seven times as strong, like the light of seven days" [of creation] — (Isaiah 30:26 — see Rashi).

Thus, we are beseeching Hashem to hasten the arrival of the day "that is neither day" — not like our present day, but many times brighter — "nor night" — whose night, too, will not be as dark as the present night, but much brighter, like the day at present.

(כתנות אור פ' בא מר' מאיר ז"ל מק"ק אייזן שטאט פיורדא תקכ"ו, מח"ס שו"ת פנים מאירות)

On the second night:

And You Shall Say: "This is the *Pesach* Feast!"

The power of Your might, you wondrously displayed on *Pesach*. Above all Festivals You exalted *Pesach*.[1] You revealed to the Easterner [Avraham] what would happen at midnight on *Pesach*.[2] And you shall say: "This is the *Pesach* feast!"

On his doors You knocked on the heat of the day on *Pesach*. He served the brilliant ones [the angels] cakes of *matzah* on *Pesach*. He ran to the herd, recalling the ox prepared on *Pesach*.[3] And you shall say: "This is the *Pesach* feast!"

The Sodomites angered God and were consumed by fire on *Pesach*.[4] Lot was saved from among them; he baked *matzot* [for the angels] on *Pesach*.[5] You swept clean [the cities] Mof and Nof when You passed through Egypt on *Pesach*. And you shall say: "This is the Pesach feast!"

God, You crushed the firstborn of On [Egypt's god] on the guarded night of *Pesach*. Mighty One, Your firstborn You passed over because of the blood of the *Pesach*. Without allowing the destroyer to enter my doors on *Pesach*.[6] And you shall say: "This is the *Pesach* feast!"

The besieged and beleaguered city [Jericho] trembled on *Pesach*.[7] Midian was destroyed with a barley cake of the *Omer* of *Pesach*.[8] The fat of Pul and Lud [Sanchereb's armies] were burned in a blazing flame on *Pesach*.[9] And you shall say: "This is the *Pesach* feast!"

1. *Vayikra* 23:5.   2. *Bereishit* 15:14.   3. 18:1, 6-7.   4. 19:24.   5. 19:3.   6. *Shemot* ch. 12.   7. Joshua 6:1, 5:10. 8. Judges 7:13.   9. Isaiah 66:19, II Kings ch. 19.

"אומץ גבורתיך..."
"The power of Your might..."

QUESTION: Who composed this hymn?

ANSWER: The author was the very famous liturgical poet Rabbi Elazar Hakalir who lived in *Eretz Yisrael* in the city of *Kiryat Sefer*. He is mentioned by Rashi and *Tosafot* in the Babylonian Talmud (see *Yoma* 67a, *Rosh Hashanah* 27a).

There are different opinions as to when he lived. Some say that he was the Tanaic sage Rabbi Elazar the son of Rabbi Shimon (bar Yochai). There is also an opinion that he was Rabbi Elazar ben Arach. The most popular opinion is that he lived in the tenth century during the era of the *Ga'onim*.

(עי' שו"ע אדמו"ה"ז סי' ס"ח:ב, הגש"פ מר' שבח ז"ל קנעביל,

ועי' שו"ת תשובה מאהבה מר' אלעזר נ' דוד ז"ל פלעקלס - מפראג, סי' א)

פֶּסַח.	עוֹד הַיּוֹם בְּנֹב לַעֲמוֹד עַד גָּעָה עוֹנַת
בַּפֶּסַח.	פַּס יָד כָּתְבָה לְקַעֲקֵעַ צוּל
בַּפֶּסַח.	צָפֹה הַצָּפִית עָרוֹךְ הַשֻּׁלְחָן

וַאֲמַרְתֶּם זֶבַח פֶּסַח:

בַּפֶּסַח.	קָהָל כִּנְּסָה הֲדַסָּה צוֹם לְשַׁלֵּשׁ
בַּפֶּסַח.	רֹאשׁ מִבֵּית רָשָׁע מָחַצְתָּ בְּעֵץ חֲמִשִּׁים
בַּפֶּסַח.	שְׁתֵּי אֵלֶּה רֶגַע תָּבִיא לְעוּצִית
פֶּסַח.	תָּעֹז יָדְךָ וְתָרוּם יְמִינְךָ כְּלֵיל הִתְקַדֶּשׁ חַג

וַאֲמַרְתֶּם זֶבַח פֶּסַח:

כִּי לוֹ נָאֶה. כִּי לוֹ יָאֶה.

אַדִּיר בִּמְלוּכָה. בָּחוּר כַּהֲלָכָה. גְּדוּדָיו יֹאמְרוּ לוֹ. לְךָ וּלְךָ. לְךָ כִּי לְךָ. לְךָ אַף לְךָ. לְךָ יְיָ הַמַּמְלָכָה. כִּי לוֹ נָאֶה. כִּי לוֹ יָאֶה.

"עוֹד הַיּוֹם בְּנֹב לַעֲמוֹד"

"While it was yet day, he wanted to be standing in Nov."

QUESTION: Why was Sancherev so anxious to be in Nov that day (*Erev Pesach*)?

ANSWER: When David was fleeing from King Shaul, he came to the priestly city of Nov and persuaded the *Kohanim* there to give him a supply of food and ammunition. When Shaul learned of their aiding David, he had them all killed. The heavenly court then held the entire Jewish community responsible for this murder, and the Jews thus became vulnerable to attack and defeat.

Many years later Sancherev, the Assyrian king, thought to exploit the Jews' loss of heavenly protection in his lust to conquer Jerusalem. His astrologers told him that they saw the day before *Pesach* as the last opportunity to take advantage of the Jews' culpability for the annihilation of Nov. Therefore, they advised him that if he would go that day and attack Jerusalem, he would be victorious.

Determined to reach Jerusalem that very same day, he traveled with his troops in one day a distance that normally takes ten, and arrived in Nov, from where he was able to see Jerusalem. When he gazed at Jerusalem, it appeared small to him, and he arrogantly exclaimed, "Is this the city of Jerusalem, for which I utilized all my armies and conquered all the countries between here and my native Assyria?" He then contemptuously shook his head and waved his hand at the Temple Mount in Zion.

While it was yet day he [Sanchereb] wanted to be standing in Nov[1] until there came the season of *Pesach*. A fragment of a hand inscribed the destruction of Tzul on *Pesach*. They prepared the watch and set the table on *Pesach*. And you shall say: "This is the *Pesach* feast!"

Hadassah [Esther] gathered a congregation for a three-day fast on *Pesach*. You crushed the head of an evil house [Haman] on a fifty-cubit gallows on *Pesach*.[2] Two punishments, You will suddenly bring on Utz [Rome] on *Pesach*.[3] Strengthen Your hand, and raise Your right Hand as on the night that has sanctified the holiday of *Pesach*. And you shall say: "This is the *Pesach* feast!"

To Him, praise is proper; to Him, praise is fitting!

Mighty in Kingship, truly distinguished, His legions say to Him: To You and only You, to You and just for You, to You, yes, only You, to You, God, Kingship is due, to Him, praise is proper; to Him, praise is fitting.

1. Isaiah 10: 32.   2. Esther 4:12, 7:10.   3. Isaiah 47:9.

His soldiers wanted to immediately attack the city, but Sancherev told them, "You are tired, so let us wait till tomorrow, and we shall destroy it." They went to sleep, and during the night an angel came and killed 185,000 men. When the survivors arose in the morning, they saw their camp filled with corpses.

Through delaying his attack by one day, Sancherev allowed the Jews' culpability for the sin of Nov to expire, and his campaign against Jerusalem ended in utter defeat.

(מסכת סנהדרין דף צ"ה ע"א)

"אדיר במלוכה בחור כהלכה...דגול במלוכה הדור כהלכה"
"Mighty in Kingship, truly distinguished...
Pre-eminent in Kingship, truly glorious."

QUESTION: *"Bachur"* literally means "a young man" and *"hadur"* is usually associated with an elderly person (see *Vayikra* 19:32). How are these terms relative to Hashem?

ANSWER: Hashem appears in different forms. At *Kriat Yam Suf* — the splitting of the sea — He appeared as a young powerful warrior. At the giving of the Torah on Mt. Sinai, He appeared in the form of a merciful sage (*Yalkut Shimoni Shemot* 246).

According to the *Arizal*, the different forms of revelation depend on the mission to be accomplished. *Kriat Yam Suf* was against the laws of nature: Water, which normally flows continuously, stood as a pillar. To emphasize that Hashem governs nature, He appeared as a powerful, conquering warrior.

דָּגוּל בִּמְלוּכָה. הָדוּר כַּהֲלָכָה. וָתִיקָיו יֹאמְרוּ לוֹ. לְךָ וּלְךָ. לְךָ כִּי לְךָ. לְךָ
אַף לְךָ. לְךָ יְיָ הַמַּמְלָכָה. כִּי לוֹ נָאֶה. כִּי לוֹ יָאֶה.

זַכַּאי בִּמְלוּכָה. חָסִין כַּהֲלָכָה. טַפְסְרָיו יֹאמְרוּ לוֹ. לְךָ וּלְךָ. לְךָ כִּי לְךָ.
לְךָ אַף לְךָ. לְךָ יְיָ הַמַּמְלָכָה. כִּי לוֹ נָאֶה. כִּי לוֹ יָאֶה.

יָחִיד בִּמְלוּכָה. כַּבִּיר כַּהֲלָכָה. לִמּוּדָיו יֹאמְרוּ לוֹ. לְךָ וּלְךָ. לְךָ כִּי לְךָ.
לְךָ אַף לְךָ. לְךָ יְיָ הַמַּמְלָכָה. כִּי לוֹ נָאֶה. כִּי לוֹ יָאֶה.

מוֹשֵׁל בִּמְלוּכָה. נוֹרָא כַּהֲלָכָה. סְבִיבָיו יֹאמְרוּ לוֹ. לְךָ וּלְךָ. לְךָ כִּי לְךָ.
לְךָ אַף לְךָ. לְךָ יְיָ הַמַּמְלָכָה. כִּי לוֹ נָאֶה. כִּי לוֹ יָאֶה.

עָנָיו בִּמְלוּכָה. פּוֹדֶה כַּהֲלָכָה. צַדִּיקָיו יֹאמְרוּ לוֹ. לְךָ וּלְךָ. לְךָ כִּי לְךָ. לְךָ
אַף לְךָ. לְךָ יְיָ הַמַּמְלָכָה. כִּי לוֹ נָאֶה. כִּי לוֹ יָאֶה.

קָדוֹשׁ בִּמְלוּכָה. רַחוּם כַּהֲלָכָה. שִׁנְאַנָּיו יֹאמְרוּ לוֹ. לְךָ וּלְךָ. לְךָ כִּי לְךָ.
לְךָ אַף לְךָ. לְךָ יְיָ הַמַּמְלָכָה. כִּי לוֹ נָאֶה. כִּי לוֹ יָאֶה.

תַּקִּיף בִּמְלוּכָה. תּוֹמֵךְ כַּהֲלָכָה. תְּמִימָיו יֹאמְרוּ לוֹ. לְךָ וּלְךָ. לְךָ כִּי לְךָ.
לְךָ אַף לְךָ. לְךָ יְיָ הַמַּמְלָכָה. כִּי לוֹ נָאֶה. כִּי לוֹ יָאֶה.

אַדִּיר הוּא. יִבְנֶה בֵיתוֹ בְּקָרוֹב. בִּמְהֵרָה בִּמְהֵרָה בְּיָמֵינוּ בְּקָרוֹב. אֵל
בְּנֵה. אֵל בְּנֵה. בְּנֵה בֵיתְךָ בְּקָרוֹב:

The giving of the Torah was not an act contrary to nature, and therefore he appeared as a merciful sage.

In this hymn one phrase relates to His taking us out of Egypt and the splitting of the sea, and the following phrase refers to the giving of the Torah. This pattern repeats itself throughout the eight phrases of the hymn.

Thus, the poet is saying that at *Kriat Yam Suf* Hashem demonstrated His mighty Kingship when He appeared as *"bachur kahalachah"* — a young man in the prime of his strength. And the pre-eminence of His Kingship was evident when at the giving of the Torah, He appeared *"hadur kahalachah"* — like a majestic sage — among the myriads of holy angels.

(הגש״פ מעשה נסים לר׳ יעקב ז״ל מליסא)

"במהרה במהרה בימינו בקרוב"
"Quickly, quickly, in our days soon."

QUESTION: Why is the word *"bimeheirah"* — "quickly" — repeated?

Pre-eminent in royalty, truly glorious, His faithful say to Him: To You and only You, to You and just for You, to You, yes, only You, to You, God, Kingship is due, To Him, praise is proper; to Him, praise is fitting.

Pure in Kingship, truly powerful, His angels say to Him: to You and only You, to You and just for You, to You, yes, only You to You, God, Kingship is due, to Him, praise is proper; to Him, praise is fitting.

Alone in Kingship, truly powerful, His learned ones say to Him: To You and only You, to You and just for You, to You, yes, only You, to You, God, Kingship is due, to Him, praise is proper; to Him, praise is fitting.

Dominant in Kingship, truly awesome, Those around Him say to Him: To You and only You, to You and just for You, to You, yes, only You, to You, God, Kingship is due, to Him, praise is proper; to Him, praise is fitting.

Humble in Kingship, truly redeeming, His righteous say to Him: To You and only You, to You and just for You, to You, yes, only You, to You, God, Kingship is due, to Him, praise is proper; to Him, praise is fitting.

Holy in Kingship, truly merciful, His peaceful ones say to Him: To You and only You, to You and just for You, to You, yes, only You, to You, God, Kingship is due, to Him, praise is proper; to Him, praise is fitting.

Forceful in Kingship, truly supporting, His true ones say to Him: To You and only You, to You and just for You, to You, yes, only You, to You, God, Kingship is due, to Him, praise is proper; to Him, praise is fitting.

He is Mighty. May He build His House soon. Quickly, quickly, soon in our days, Almighty build, Almighty build, build Your House soon.

ANSWER: Hashem told the Jewish people that "When you will beget children and grandchildren, *venoshantem* — and you will have been a long time — in the land, you will grow corrupt ... *avod toveidun maheir* — you will surely perish quickly — from the land which you are crossing the Jordan to possess" (*Devarim* 4:25, 26).

The *Gemara* (*Sanhedrin* 38a) says that the word *"venoshantem"* (ונושנתם) — "and you will have been a long time" — has the numerical value of 852 and that it alludes to the number of years the Jews would be in the land before the prophecy of destruction would take place. Since the prophecy is that the Jews would "surely perish *maheir* — quickly" — the *Gemara* concludes that in Hashem's measuring of time, *"meheirah"* — "quickly" — means 852 years. In reality, Hashem compassionately exiled the Jews two years before the dread prophecy of destruction was set to go into effect (after they had occupied the land for 850 years).

בָּחוּר הוּא. גָּדוֹל הוּא. דָּגוּל הוּא. יִבְנֶה בֵיתוֹ בְּקָרוֹב. בִּמְהֵרָה בִּמְהֵרָה בְּיָמֵינוּ בְּקָרוֹב. אֵל בְּנֵה. אֵל בְּנֵה. בְּנֵה בֵיתְךָ בְּקָרוֹב:

הָדוּר הוּא. וָתִיק הוּא. זַכַּאי הוּא. חָסִיד הוּא. יִבְנֶה בֵיתוֹ בְּקָרוֹב. בִּמְהֵרָה בִּמְהֵרָה בְּיָמֵינוּ בְּקָרוֹב. אֵל בְּנֵה. אֵל בְּנֵה. בְּנֵה בֵיתְךָ בְּקָרוֹב:

טָהוֹר הוּא. יָחִיד הוּא. כַּבִּיר הוּא. לָמוּד הוּא. מֶלֶךְ הוּא. נוֹרָא הוּא. סַגִּיב הוּא. עִזּוּז הוּא. פּוֹדֶה הוּא. צַדִּיק הוּא. יִבְנֶה בֵיתוֹ בְּקָרוֹב. בִּמְהֵרָה בִּמְהֵרָה בְּיָמֵינוּ בְּקָרוֹב. אֵל בְּנֵה. אֵל בְּנֵה. בְּנֵה בֵיתְךָ בְּקָרוֹב:

קָדוֹשׁ הוּא. רַחוּם הוּא. שַׁדַּי הוּא. תַּקִּיף הוּא. יִבְנֶה בֵיתוֹ בְּקָרוֹב. בִּמְהֵרָה בִּמְהֵרָה בְּיָמֵינוּ בְּקָרוֹב. אֵל בְּנֵה. אֵל בְּנֵה. בְּנֵה בֵיתְךָ בְּקָרוֹב:

בליל שני של פסח,

אלו שעדיין לא קיימו מצות ספירת העומר אומרים כאן:

בָּרוּךְ אַתָּה יְהֹוָה אֱלֹהֵינוּ מֶלֶךְ הָעוֹלָם. אֲשֶׁר קִדְּשָׁנוּ בְּמִצְוֹתָיו וְצִוָּנוּ עַל סְפִירַת הָעוֹמֶר:

הַיּוֹם יוֹם אֶחָד, לָעֹמֶר:

Thus, when we pray that Hashem rebuild His house "*meheirah*" — "quickly" — we emphasize that the "quickly" we are referring to is not His "quickly" — 852 years — but *"bimeheirah beyameinu"* — quickly according to our understanding of time, so that it will be very soon, in our days. (פון אונזער אלטען אוצר)

"א-ל בנה, א-ל בנה, בנה ביתך בקרוב"
"Al-mighty build, Al-mighty build, build Your house soon."

QUESTION: There seems to be a contradiction. *"Ei-l b'neih"* means that He should build immediately, and *"B'neih beitecha bekarov"* — "build Your house *soon*" — means not necessarily immediately, but soon?

ANSWER: In the *Gemara* (*Rosh Hashanah* 11a) Rabbi Yehoshua states that just as the redemption from Egypt was in the month of *Nissan*, so too, the final redemption will be in *Nissan*. Rabbi Eliezer opines that the final redemption will be in *Tishrei*.

Our prayers are geared according to both opinions. Since we are now celebrating *Pesach*, which is in the month of *Nissan*. We pray *"Ei-l b'neh"* — "Al-mighty build Your house immediately." However, if the final redemption is destined to take place in *Tishrei*, then "build Your house *soon*" — we cannot wait any longer.

(הגש״פ תוספות בנימין לר׳ בנימין אליהו ז״ל מזאלשין)

* * *

He is chosen, He is great, He is supreme. May He build His House soon. Quickly, quickly, soon in our days, Almighty build, Almighty build, build Your House soon.

He is glorious, He is faithful, He is pure, He is pious. May He build His House soon. Quickly, quickly, soon in our days, Almighty build, Almighty build, build Your House soon.

He is immaculate, He is unique, He is powerful, He is learned, He is the King, He is awesome, He is sublime, He is strong, He is the Redeemer, He is righteous. May He build His House soon. Quickly, quickly, soon in our days, Almighty build, Almighty build, build Your House soon.

He is holy, He is merciful, He is Almighty, He is Forceful. May He build His House soon. Quickly, quickly, soon in our days, Almighty build, Almighty build, build Your House soon.

On the second night of *Pesach*, those who did yet count the *Omer* do so now.

Blessed are You, *Adonai*, our God, King of the Universe, Who has sanctified us by His commandments and commanded us about the counting of the *Omer*.

Today is the first day of the *Omer*.

QUESTION: Since the construction of the *Beit Hamikdash* does not supersede *Yom Tov*, and it also can be only during the day (Rambam, *Beit Habechirah* 1:12), why do we pray for the immediate rebuilding (even tonight)?

ANSWER: These laws only apply when the *Beit Hamikdash* is constructed by human hands. Our prayer is "Al-mighty — *You* — build." Thus, none of these restrictions are relative to Him.

(הגש״פ נפתלי שבע רצון מר׳ נפתלי הירץ ז״ל גינזבורג,

ועי׳ רש״י בר״ה דף ל׳ ע״א דבנין השלישי בידי שמים הוא ויכול להיות גם בשבת ויו״ט ובלילה)

"וצונו על ספירת העומר"
"Commanded us about the counting of the *Omer*"

QUESTION: Why do we count *Sefirah* between *Pesach* and *Shavuot*?

ANSWER: The ultimate purpose of leaving Egypt was to receive the Torah on Mount Sinai. Every Jew is required to occupy himself as much as possible with the study of Torah, but unfortunately people do not appreciate the value of time and frequently waste time that could be used for Torah study. Counting *Sefirah* before *Shavuot* is a preparation for *kabbalat haTorah*, and it empha-

הָרַחֲמָן. הוּא יַחֲזִיר לָנוּ עֲבוֹדַת בֵּית הַמִּקְדָּשׁ לִמְקוֹמָהּ בִּמְהֵרָה בְיָמֵינוּ. אָמֵן סֶלָה:

לַמְנַצֵּחַ בִּנְגִינֹת מִזְמוֹר שִׁיר: אֱלֹהִים יְחָנֵּנוּ וִיבָרְכֵנוּ יָאֵר פָּנָיו אִתָּנוּ סֶלָה: לָדַעַת בָּאָרֶץ דַּרְכֶּךָ בְּכָל גּוֹיִם יְשׁוּעָתֶךָ: יוֹדוּךָ עַמִּים אֱלֹהִים יוֹדוּךָ עַמִּים כֻּלָּם: יִשְׂמְחוּ וִירַנְּנוּ לְאֻמִּים כִּי תִשְׁפֹּט עַמִּים מִישֹׁר וּלְאֻמִּים בָּאָרֶץ תַּנְחֵם סֶלָה: יוֹדוּךָ עַמִּים אֱלֹהִים יוֹדוּךָ עַמִּים כֻּלָּם: אֶרֶץ נָתְנָה יְבוּלָהּ יְבָרְכֵנוּ אֱלֹהִים אֱלֹהֵינוּ: יְבָרְכֵנוּ אֱלֹהִים וְיִירְאוּ אוֹתוֹ כָּל אַפְסֵי אָרֶץ:

אָנָּא בְכֹחַ. גְּדֻלַּת יְמִינְךָ. תַּתִּיר צְרוּרָה:	אב"ג ית"ץ
קַבֵּל רִנַּת עַמְּךָ. שַׂגְּבֵנוּ טַהֲרֵנוּ נוֹרָא:	קר"ע שט"ן
נָא גִבּוֹר. דּוֹרְשֵׁי יִחוּדְךָ. כְּבָבַת שָׁמְרֵם:	נג"ד יכ"ש
בָּרְכֵם טַהֲרֵם. רַחֲמֵם. צִדְקָתְךָ תָּמִיד גָּמְלֵם:	בט"ר צת"ג
חֲסִין קָדוֹשׁ. בְּרוֹב טוּבְךָ. נַהֵל עֲדָתֶךָ:	חק"ב טנ"ע
יָחִיד גֵּאֶה. לְעַמְּךָ פְּנֵה. זוֹכְרֵי קְדֻשָּׁתֶךָ:	יג"ל פז"ק
שַׁוְעָתֵנוּ קַבֵּל. וּשְׁמַע צַעֲקָתֵנוּ. יוֹדֵעַ תַּעֲלוּמוֹת:	שק"ו צי"ת

בָּרוּךְ שֵׁם כְּבוֹד מַלְכוּתוֹ לְעוֹלָם וָעֶד:

רִבּוֹנוֹ שֶׁל עוֹלָם. אַתָּה צִוִּיתָנוּ עַל יְדֵי מֹשֶׁה עַבְדֶּךָ לִסְפּוֹר סְפִירַת הָעוֹמֶר כְּדֵי לְטַהֲרֵנוּ מִקְּלִפּוֹתֵינוּ וּמִטֻּמְאוֹתֵינוּ. כְּמוֹ שֶׁכָּתַבְתָּ בְּתוֹרָתֶךָ. וּסְפַרְתֶּם לָכֶם מִמָּחֳרַת הַשַּׁבָּת מִיּוֹם הֲבִיאֲכֶם אֶת עוֹמֶר הַתְּנוּפָה שֶׁבַע שַׁבָּתוֹת תְּמִימוֹת תִּהְיֶינָה: עַד מִמָּחֳרַת הַשַּׁבָּת הַשְּׁבִיעִית תִּסְפְּרוּ חֲמִשִּׁים יוֹם. כְּדֵי שֶׁיִּטָּהֲרוּ נַפְשׁוֹת עַמְּךָ יִשְׂרָאֵל מִזֻּהֲמָתָם. וּבְכֵן יְהִי רָצוֹן מִלְּפָנֶיךָ יְיָ אֱלֹהֵינוּ וֵאלֹהֵי אֲבוֹתֵינוּ שֶׁבִּזְכוּת סְפִירַת הָעוֹמֶר שֶׁסָּפַרְתִּי הַיּוֹם יְתֻקַּן מַה שֶּׁפָּגַמְתִּי בִּסְפִירָה (חֶסֶד שֶׁבְּחֶסֶד). וְאֶטָּהֵר וְאֶתְקַדֵּשׁ בִּקְדֻשָּׁה שֶׁל מַעְלָה. וְעַל יְדֵי זֶה יֻשְׁפַּע שֶׁפַע רַב בְּכָל הָעוֹלָמוֹת וּלְתַקֵּן אֶת נַפְשׁוֹתֵינוּ וְרוּחוֹתֵינוּ וְנִשְׁמוֹתֵינוּ מִכָּל סִיג וּפְגָם. וּלְטַהֲרֵנוּ וּלְקַדְּשֵׁנוּ בִּקְדֻשָּׁתְךָ הָעֶלְיוֹנָה. אָמֵן סֶלָה:

---

sizes the importance of time and its value. It serves as a reminder that we should use every free moment for the study of Torah.

(לקוטי שיחות ח"ז ע' 280)

The famous Chassidic Rebbe, Rabbi Avraham Mordechai of Ger (known as the "Imrei Emet") once said that the reason for the custom of giving a *chatan* a golden watch is to teach him that every minute is "wrapped in gold" and should not be wasted.

(שמעתי מהרב אליהו משה ז"ל ליס)

Another lesson we learn from *Sefirah* is the following: When counting *Sefirah*, we recite a *berachah* every night, yet when an entire day goes by and a person forgets to count, he can no longer recite the *berachah* on the following days. This teaches us that although each day is an independent entity, it also makes a unique contribution to all other days. Thus, the counting of *Sefirah* before *Shavuot* emphasizes the importance of each day and that one wasted day of Torah learning also affects the future.

"בָּרוּךְ אַתָּה ה' ... וְצִוָּנוּ עַל סְפִירַת הָעוֹמֶר"
"Blessed are You ... and commanded us about the counting of the *omer*"

QUESTION: Since *Sefirah* is a *mitzvah* which is not performed throughout the entire year, why don't we recite the *berachah* of "*Shehecheyanu*" when we begin counting?

May the Merciful One restore for us the service of the *Beit Hamikdash* to its place, speedily in our days; *Amein, Selah*.

We cannot answer by saying that in our times *Sefirat HaOmer* is only Rabbinic, since we do recite *"Shehecheyanu"* on the reading of the *Megillah*, which is also Rabbinic.

ANSWER: The Torah *(Vayikra 23:15)* connects the *mitzvah* of *Sefirah* to the *Omer*-offering on *Pesach*. Since we no longer have a *Beit Hamikdash* and cannot bring the *Omer*-offering, when we count *Sefirah* we are saddened and recite a special prayer: "May the Merciful One restore for us the service of the *Beit Hamikdash* to its place." Since a *"Shehecheyanu"* is only recited when one is in a happy and joyous mood, we do not recite it at the beginning of the *Sefirah*.

(כל בו, ועי' ילקוט יצחק מר' יצחק ז"ל זאלער על פ' אמור)

"היום יום אחד לעומר"
"Today is the first day of the *Omer*"

QUESTION: In the Diaspora we celebrate two days of *Yom Tov* because in the times of the *Beit Hamikdash* it was not immediately known if the previous month consisted of 29 days or 30 days. If so, on the first night when we start counting the *omer*, why don't we say, "Today is the first day, today is the second day," and on the next night why don't we say, "Today is the second day, today is the third day" etc.?

ANSWER: The purpose of counting is for clarification and verification. A person with an undetermined amount of money counts it to determine the exact amount. If after counting he is still in doubt, he counts it again until he verifies the exact amount. Since the *mitzvah* is to *count* the *Omer*, counting and remaining with a doubt as to the exact number of days would be contradictory to the entire concept of counting, and it would be improper to make a *berachah* for such an activity.

* * *

With this explanation we can also understand a *halachah* in *Shulchan Aruch (Orach Chaim* 489:1), which superficially is enigmatic. The *Magen Avraham* writes that if one recites the *Omer* counting in Hebrew and does not know the meaning of what he is saying, he has not fulfilled the *mitzvah*. Why is counting the *Omer* different than other prayers or blessings which one may say in Hebrew, even if he does not know the meaning of the words?

אֶחָד מִי יוֹדֵעַ. אֶחָד אֲנִי יוֹדֵעַ. אֶחָד אֱלֹהֵינוּ שֶׁבַּשָּׁמַיִם וּבָאָרֶץ:

שְׁנַיִם מִי יוֹדֵעַ. שְׁנַיִם אֲנִי יוֹדֵעַ. שְׁנֵי לֻחוֹת הַבְּרִית. אֶחָד אֱלֹהֵינוּ שֶׁבַּשָּׁמַיִם וּבָאָרֶץ:

שְׁלֹשָׁה מִי יוֹדֵעַ. שְׁלֹשָׁה אֲנִי יוֹדֵעַ. שְׁלֹשָׁה אָבוֹת. שְׁנֵי לֻחוֹת הַבְּרִית. אֶחָד אֱלֹהֵינוּ שֶׁבַּשָּׁמַיִם וּבָאָרֶץ:

אַרְבַּע מִי יוֹדֵעַ. אַרְבַּע אֲנִי יוֹדֵעַ. אַרְבַּע אִמָּהוֹת. שְׁלֹשָׁה אָבוֹת. שְׁנֵי לֻחוֹת הַבְּרִית. אֶחָד אֱלֹהֵינוּ שֶׁבַּשָּׁמַיִם וּבָאָרֶץ:

חֲמִשָּׁה מִי יוֹדֵעַ. חֲמִשָּׁה אֲנִי יוֹדֵעַ. חֲמִשָּׁה חֻמְשֵׁי תוֹרָה. אַרְבַּע אִמָּהוֹת. שְׁלֹשָׁה אָבוֹת. שְׁנֵי לֻחוֹת הַבְּרִית. אֶחָד אֱלֹהֵינוּ שֶׁבַּשָּׁמַיִם וּבָאָרֶץ:

שִׁשָּׁה מִי יוֹדֵעַ. שִׁשָּׁה אֲנִי יוֹדֵעַ. שִׁשָּׁה סִדְרֵי מִשְׁנָה. חֲמִשָּׁה חֻמְשֵׁי תוֹרָה. אַרְבַּע אִמָּהוֹת. שְׁלֹשָׁה אָבוֹת. שְׁנֵי לֻחוֹת הַבְּרִית. אֶחָד אֱלֹהֵינוּ שֶׁבַּשָּׁמַיִם וּבָאָרֶץ:

In light of the above — that the purpose of counting is for clarification and verification and valueless otherwise — if one recites the counting without knowing the meaning, the purpose of counting is not accomplished.

(שו״ת דבר אברהם ח״א סי׳ ל״ד, ועי׳ לקוטי שיחות ח״ז ע׳ 296)

"אחד מי יודע" — "Who knows one?"

QUESTION: What is the intent of this hymn?

ANSWER: This poem, composed in question and answer format, gives thirteen reasons that we merited to be redeemed from Egyptian bondage. The leader of the *Seder* asks the questions, and the participants respond, and through its challenging style, all remain alert till the conclusion of the *Seder*.

The name of the author is unknown, but in a *Siddur* of 1406 is stated that this and the *Chad Gadya* were found written on a parchment in the *Beit Medrash* of Rabbi Eliezer Rokeach of Worms (1176-1238).

(מבוא להגש״פ מהר״מ ז״ל כשר)

"אחד מי יודע...שלש עשר מי יודע"
"Who knows one...Who knows thirteen?"

QUESTION: Why do we go from one to thirteen and not higher?

ANSWER: The true *Echad* — One and Only — is Hashem, and the word *"echad"* (אחד) has the numerical value of thirteen. Hence, by commencing with His Oneness and concluding with thirteen,

Who knows one? I know one. One is our God in the heavens and on the earth.

Who knows two? I know two. Two are the Tablets of the Covenant (the Ten Commandments). One is our God in the heavens and on the earth.

Who knows three? I know three. Three are the Patriarchs. Two are the Tablets of the Covenant. One is our God in the heavens and on the earth.

Who knows four? I know four. Four are the Matriarchs. Three are the Patriarchs. Two are the Tablets of the Covenant. One is our God in the heavens and on the earth.

Who knows five? I know five. Five are the books of the Torah. Four are the Matriarchs. Three are the Patriarchs. Two are the Tablets of the Covenant. One is our God in the heavens and on the earth.

Who knows six? I know six. Six are the orders of the *Mishnah*. Five are the books of the Torah. Four are the Matriarchs. Three are the Patriarchs. Two are the Tablets of the Covenant. One is our God in the heavens and on the earth.

---

which is also an allusion to His Oneness, we are proclaiming that He is the One and Only from beginning to end.

* * *

In each stanza we repeat that which was previously enumerated. Thus, the overall total of all the items mentioned throughout the poem is ninety-one. The number ninety-one has great mystical significance. It is the combined numerical value of Hashem's holy four letter Name י-ה-ו-ה — the Tetragrammaton — and also the Name א-ד-נ-י. The Tetragrammaton emphasizes that he transcends past, present, and future, and the Name *A-donai* accentuates that He is the Master of the universe and above the limitations of time.

It is also the numerical value of *"amein"* (אמן) — which is an acronym for א-ל מלך נאמן — A-mighty, trustworthy King (see *Shulchan Aruch Harav* 124:12).

(הגש״פ מוצל מאש - בית אהרן - בפי׳ פאר אהרן)

"אחד מי יודע...שלשה עשר מי יודע"
"Who knows one...Who knows thirteen?"

QUESTION: The relevance of some of the items to the redemption from Egypt begs explanation, for instance *"Echad mi yodea... Echad hu Elokeinu"* — "Who knows one...One is our G-d...."

שִׁבְעָה מִי יוֹדֵעַ. שִׁבְעָה אֲנִי יוֹדֵעַ. שִׁבְעָה יְמֵי שַׁבַּתָּא. שִׁשָׁה סִדְרֵי
מִשְׁנָה. חֲמִשָׁה חֻמְשֵׁי תוֹרָה. אַרְבַּע אִמָּהוֹת. שְׁלֹשָׁה אָבוֹת. שְׁנֵי לֻחוֹת
הַבְּרִית. אֶחָד אֱלֹהֵינוּ שֶׁבַּשָּׁמַיִם וּבָאָרֶץ:

שְׁמוֹנָה מִי יוֹדֵעַ. שְׁמוֹנָה אֲנִי יוֹדֵעַ. שְׁמוֹנָה יְמֵי מִילָה שִׁבְעָה יְמֵי
שַׁבַּתָּא. שִׁשָׁה סִדְרֵי מִשְׁנָה. חֲמִשָׁה חֻמְשֵׁי תוֹרָה. אַרְבַּע אִמָּהוֹת. שְׁלֹשָׁה
אָבוֹת. שְׁנֵי לֻחוֹת הַבְּרִית. אֶחָד אֱלֹהֵינוּ שֶׁבַּשָּׁמַיִם וּבָאָרֶץ:

תִּשְׁעָה מִי יוֹדֵעַ. תִּשְׁעָה אֲנִי יוֹדֵעַ. תִּשְׁעָה יַרְחֵי לֵידָה. שְׁמוֹנָה יְמֵי
מִילָה שִׁבְעָה יְמֵי שַׁבַּתָּא. שִׁשָׁה סִדְרֵי מִשְׁנָה. חֲמִשָׁה חֻמְשֵׁי תוֹרָה. אַרְבַּע
אִמָּהוֹת. שְׁלֹשָׁה אָבוֹת. שְׁנֵי לֻחוֹת הַבְּרִית. אֶחָד אֱלֹהֵינוּ שֶׁבַּשָּׁמַיִם וּבָאָרֶץ:

עֲשָׂרָה מִי יוֹדֵעַ. עֲשָׂרָה אֲנִי יוֹדֵעַ. עֲשָׂרָה דִּבְּרַיָּא. תִּשְׁעָה יַרְחֵי לֵידָה.
שְׁמוֹנָה יְמֵי מִילָה שִׁבְעָה יְמֵי שַׁבַּתָּא. שִׁשָׁה סִדְרֵי מִשְׁנָה. חֲמִשָׁה חֻמְשֵׁי
תוֹרָה. אַרְבַּע אִמָּהוֹת. שְׁלֹשָׁה אָבוֹת. שְׁנֵי לֻחוֹת הַבְּרִית. אֶחָד אֱלֹהֵינוּ
שֶׁבַּשָּׁמַיִם וּבָאָרֶץ:

True, Hashem is the One and only, but how did this merit us
the redemption?

ANSWER: When Moshe and Aharon came to Egypt to meet
with the Jewish people and discuss their mission, the Torah states,
"And the people believed...and they bowed their heads and
prostrated themselves" (*Shemot* 4:31). In merit of their *emunah* —
faith — in Hashem, the One and only G-d in the heavens and on
the earth, they merited the redemption.

"שבעה ימי שבתא"
"Seven are the days of the week."

QUESTION: If this refers to the fact that the Jewish people
observed *Shabbat* even in Egypt, why mention the *seven* days of
the week?

ANSWER: Not only did they merit to be redeemed because
they rested on *Shabbat*; during the entire week they also
anticipated and longed for the *Shabbat* day.

"שמונה ימי מילה"
"Eight days of circumcision."

QUESTION: A *brit* — circumcision — is performed on the
eighth day and not on a daily basis for eight days?

ANSWER: Regardless of Pharoah's decree to kill the Jewish
male babies, the parents held onto them for eight days so that

Who knows seven? I know seven. Seven are the days of week. Six are the orders of the *Mishnah*. Five are the books of the Torah. Four are the Matriarchs. Three are the Patriarchs. Two are the Tablets of the Covenant. One is our God in the heavens and on the earth.

Who knows eight? I know eight. Eight are the days of circumcision. Seven are the days of the week. Six are the orders of the *Mishnah*. Five are the books of the Torah. Four are the Matriarchs. Three are the Patriarchs. Two are the Tablets of the Covenant. One is our God in the heavens and on the earth.

Who knows nine? I know nine. Nine are the months of pregnancy. Eight are the days of circumcision. Seven are the days of the week. Six are the orders of the *Mishnah*. Five are the books of the Torah. Four are the Matriarchs. Three are the Patriarchs. Two are the Tablets of the Covenant. One is our God in heavens and on the earth.

Who knows ten? I know ten. Ten are the Ten Commandments. Nine are the months of pregnancy. Eight are the days of circumcision. Seven are the days of the week. Six are the orders of the *Mishnah*. Five are the books of the Torah. Four are the Matriarchs. Three are the Patriarchs. Two are the Tablets of the Covenant. One is our God in the heavens and on the earth.

---

they could be circumcised before being killed. For the dedication and eagerness they demonstrated for eight days to perform the *mitzvah* of circumcision, they merited redemption.

"תשעה ירחי לידה"
"Nine months of pregnancy."

QUESTION: Nine months of pregnancy is a law of nature for a Jew and non-Jew alike?

ANSWER: The *Gemara* (*Sotah* 11b) states, "In the merit of the righteous women, our fathers were redeemed." Though the Egyptians endeavored to disrupt family life by making the Jewish men work nights, and decreed that the newborns should be killed, the Jewish women encouraged their husbands to procreate and happily endured the difficulties of pregnancy for nine months.

אֶחָד עָשָׂר מִי יוֹדֵעַ. אֶחָד עָשָׂר אֲנִי יוֹדֵעַ. אֶחָד עָשָׂר כּוֹכְבַיָּא. עֲשָׂרָה
דִּבְּרַיָּא. תִּשְׁעָה יַרְחֵי לֵידָה. שְׁמוֹנָה יְמֵי מִילָה שִׁבְעָה יְמֵי שַׁבַּתָּא. שִׁשָּׁה
סִדְרֵי מִשְׁנָה. חֲמִשָּׁה חֻמְשֵׁי תוֹרָה. אַרְבַּע אִמָּהוֹת. שְׁלֹשָׁה אָבוֹת. שְׁנֵי
לֻחוֹת הַבְּרִית. אֶחָד אֱלֹהֵינוּ שֶׁבַּשָּׁמַיִם וּבָאָרֶץ:

שְׁנֵים עָשָׂר מִי יוֹדֵעַ. שְׁנֵים עָשָׂר אֲנִי יוֹדֵעַ. שְׁנֵים עָשָׂר שִׁבְטַיָּא. אֶחָד
עָשָׂר כּוֹכְבַיָּא. עֲשָׂרָה דִּבְּרַיָּא. תִּשְׁעָה יַרְחֵי לֵידָה. שְׁמוֹנָה יְמֵי מִילָה שִׁבְעָה
יְמֵי שַׁבַּתָּא. שִׁשָּׁה סִדְרֵי מִשְׁנָה. חֲמִשָּׁה חֻמְשֵׁי תוֹרָה. אַרְבַּע אִמָּהוֹת.
שְׁלֹשָׁה אָבוֹת. שְׁנֵי לֻחוֹת הַבְּרִית. אֶחָד אֱלֹהֵינוּ שֶׁבַּשָּׁמַיִם וּבָאָרֶץ:

שְׁלֹשָׁה עָשָׂר מִי יוֹדֵעַ. שְׁלֹשָׁה עָשָׂר אֲנִי יוֹדֵעַ. שְׁלֹשָׁה עָשָׂר מִדַּיָּא.
שְׁנֵים עָשָׂר שִׁבְטַיָּא. אֶחָד עָשָׂר כּוֹכְבַיָּא. עֲשָׂרָה דִּבְּרַיָּא. תִּשְׁעָה יַרְחֵי לֵידָה.
שְׁמוֹנָה יְמֵי מִילָה שִׁבְעָה יְמֵי שַׁבַּתָּא. שִׁשָּׁה סִדְרֵי מִשְׁנָה. חֲמִשָּׁה חֻמְשֵׁי
תוֹרָה. אַרְבַּע אִמָּהוֹת. שְׁלֹשָׁה אָבוֹת. שְׁנֵי לֻחוֹת הַבְּרִית. אֶחָד אֱלֹהֵינוּ
שֶׁבַּשָּׁמַיִם וּבָאָרֶץ:

"אחד עשר כוכביא"
"Eleven are the stars."

QUESTION: How did this bring about the redemption?

ANSWER: In Yosef's second dream eleven stars bowed to him (*Bereishit* 37:9). This alluded to his brothers coming down to Egypt. Of stars it is said, "To all of them [Hashem] assigns names" (Psalms 147:4). The *Midrash* (*Shir Hashirim* 4:12) says that the eleven stars, i.e. brothers, went down to Egypt with Hebrew names and went up from it with the same Hebrew names. For maintaining their identity and not adopting Egyptian names, the Jews merited redemption.

"שנים עשר שבטיא"
"Twelve are the tribes."

QUESTION: How did this cause the redemption?

ANSWER: When a census of each tribe was taken in the wilderness, the nations reviled the Jews, saying, "How can the Jews trace their genealogy according to their tribes? If the Egyptian controlled their bodies, surely they had the power to violate their wives!" To this Hashem replied, in effect, that He added the letters "*hei*" and "*yud*" from His own Name as a prefix

Who knows eleven? I know eleven. Eleven are the stars [in Yoseph's dream]. Ten are the Ten Commandments. Nine are the months of pregnancy. Eight are the days of circumcision. Seven are the days of the week. Six are the orders of the *Mishnah*. Five are the books of the Torah. Four are the Matriarchs. Three are the Patriarchs. Two are the Tablets of the Covenant. One is our God in the heavens and on the earth.

Who knows twelve? I know twelve. Twelve are the tribes [of Israel]. Eleven are the stars. Ten are the Ten Commandments. Nine are the months of pregnancy. Eight are the days of circumcision. Seven are the days of the week. Six are the orders of the *Mishnah*. Five are the books of the Torah. Four are the Matriarchs. Three are the Patriarchs. Two are the Tablets of the Covenant. One is our God in the heavens and on the earth.

Who knows thirteen? I know thirteen. Thirteen are God's attributes [of mercy]. Twelve are the tribes. Eleven are the stars. Ten are the Ten Commandments. Nine are the months of pregnancy. Eight are the days of circumcision. Seven are the days of the week. Six are the orders of the *Mishnah*. Five are the books of the Torah. Four are the Matriarchs. Three are the Patriarchs. Two are the Tablets of the Covenant. One is our God in the heavens and on the earth.

---

and suffix respectively to their family names to attest to their chastity in Egypt (*Bamidbar* 26:5, Rashi) (as in "Hachanochi" החנוכי — the Chanochites). Thus, thanks to the twelve tribes not being affected by the immorality that prevailed in Egypt, they merited the redemption.

"שלשה עשר מדיא"
"Thirteen attributes of mercy"

In conclusion we state that the redemption from Egypt occurred thanks to His thirteen attributes of mercy, and hopefully very quickly He will have mercy on us again and send *Mashiach*, who will take us out of the current exile, lead us to our Holy land, and rebuild the *Beit Hamikdash*.

(הפירושים הנ"ל מיוסדים על הגש"פ אפוד בד מר' בנימין דוד ז"ל ראבינאוויץ וווארשא תרל"ב, הגש"פ זכרון נפלאות מר' אליעזר בן זאב וואלף הכהן ז"ל מסכאטשאב, וווארשא תר"מ, הגש"פ עטרת ישועה מר' חיים ז"ל טויביש, דראהאביטש תרנ"ו)

חַד גַּדְיָא. חַד גַּדְיָא. דְּזַבִּין אַבָּא בִּתְרֵי זוּזֵי. חַד גַּדְיָא. חַד גַּדְיָא:
וְאָתָא שׁוּנְרָא וְאָכְלָה לְגַּדְיָא. דְּזַבִּין אַבָּא בִּתְרֵי זוּזֵי. חַד גַּדְיָא. חַד גַּדְיָא:

"חד גדיא חד גדיא דזבין אבא בתרי זוזי"
"An only kid, an only kid, which father bought for two *zuzim*."

QUESTION: Who is the "kid," and what are the "two *zuzim*"?

ANSWER: This song is not merely a simple folksong. It is an allegory which conveys an important message.

The kid is an allusion to the Jewish people, and the father is Hashem. In Aramaic currency a *shekel* equals four *zuzim*, and two *zuzim* are a half-*shekel*; (*Shemot* 30:12, Rashi). Thus, the two *zuzim* are a reference to the half-*shekel*, which was given as *kofer nefesh* — atonement for the soul (ibid. 30:12-16). Through the giving of the half-*shekel*, Hashem acquired the Jewish people and it was used for the making of the *Mishkan* — Sanctuary — in which He dwelt among them. (הגש"פ מגדל עדר החדש בפי' מגן דוד)

Alternatively, the two *zuzim* are the two *luchot* — Tablets. Just as the *chatan* gives the *kallah* a ring under the *chupah* and thereby acquires her to be betrothed to him, likewise, under the suspended mountain (*chupah*), Hashem, the *chatan*, acquired the *kallah* (*K'lal Yisrael*) through the giving of the Tablets. (כסא דוד להחיד"א)

Alternatively, the "kid" represents the *Beit Hamikdash*, and the two coins represent the two golden pieces King David collected from each of the tribes to purchase the Temple Mount from Aravnah the Jebusite (see II Samuel 24 — *Zevachim* 116b, *Tosafot*). (הגש"פ - מעשה נסים)

According to these interpretations the poem then goes on to enumerate allegorically the trials and suffering we have encountered throughout our history as we have been subjugated by various nations. The poem ends with our ultimate redemption by Hashem.   * * *   (הגש"פ - מעשה נסים)

Alternatively, the "kid" is a reference to Yosef. After the brothers sold him, they slaughtered a young goat and dipped his tunic in its blood in order to convince Yaakov that he was devoured and remove any suspicion from themselves. His sale was an outcome of the jealousy which was aroused by his father's making him a tunic of

An only kid! An only kid! That father bought for two *zuzim*. An only kid, an only kid!

Then along came a cat and ate the kid that father bought for two *zuzim*. An only kid, an only kid!

---

fine wool, which according to the *Gemara* (*Shabbat* 10b) weighed the equivalent of *two sela* (Aramaic currency).

Accordingly, the poem allegorically discusses the experience of the Jewish people in Egypt (starting with the sale of Yosef) and other events throughout Jewish history until the time when Hashem will slaughter Satan and the kingdom will be Hashem's.

(הגש"פ ברכת השיר להרא"ל ז"ל צונץ)

* * *

Incidentally, in *mispar katan* — single numericals (not counting tens and hundreds) — Yosef (יוסף) adds up to 21, as does *Chad Gadya* (חד גדיא).

(הגש"פ ברכת השיר להרא"ל ז"ל צונץ)

"חד גדיא דזבין אבא ... ואתא הקדוש ברוך הוא"

"An only kid which father bought ... the Holy One Blessed be He came..."

QUESTION: To whom is this being told?

ANSWER: The *Chad Gadya* narrative is a dialogue between a Jew and an Egyptian. Prior to leaving Egypt the Jews were instructed about the *Pesach*-offering. When the Egyptians saw the Jews preparing the animals and learnt that they were planning to slaughter them and celebrate with the meat, they were horrified. "How can you do this? This is the god we worship!" they exclaimed.

The song begins with a Jew's response. He teases his former Egyptian slave master, saying, "An inexpensive goatling that father buys for two *zuzim* is your god? Even a cat is stronger than it." The Egyptian is dumbfounded and says, "You are right; perhaps I should begin worshipping the cat?" The Jew responds, "You are so foolish; don't you know that the dog bit the cat, and it is afraid of him?" "If so," says the Egyptian, "perhaps I should make the dog my god." The dialogue continues on until the Jew tells the Egyptian that the Holy One Blessed be He is the one true G-d whom all humanity should worship.

(הגש"פ מהר' טעבעלה ז"ל באנדי, פרנקפורט תרנ"ח)
ובמד"ר בראשית ל"ח י"ג יש ויכוח כעי"ז בין אברהם ונמרוד)

וְאָתָא כַלְבָּא וְנָשַׁךְ לְשׁוּנְרָא. דְּאָכְלָה לְגַדְיָא. דְּזַבִּין אַבָּא בִּתְרֵי זוּזֵי. חַד גַּדְיָא. חַד גַּדְיָא:

וְאָתָא חוּטְרָא וְהִכָּה לְכַלְבָּא. דְּנָשַׁךְ לְשׁוּנְרָא. דְּאָכְלָה לְגַדְיָא. דְּזַבִּין אַבָּא בִּתְרֵי זוּזֵי. חַד גַּדְיָא. חַד גַּדְיָא:

וְאָתָא נוּרָא וְשָׂרַף לְחוּטְרָא. דְּהִכָּה לְכַלְבָּא. דְּנָשַׁךְ לְשׁוּנְרָא. דְּאָכְלָה לְגַדְיָא. דְּזַבִּין אַבָּא בִּתְרֵי זוּזֵי. חַד גַּדְיָא. חַד גַּדְיָא:

וְאָתָא מַיָּא וְכָבָה לְנוּרָא. דְּשָׂרַף לְחוּטְרָא. דְּהִכָּה לְכַלְבָּא. דְּנָשַׁךְ לְשׁוּנְרָא. דְּאָכְלָה לְגַדְיָא. דְּזַבִּין אַבָּא בִּתְרֵי זוּזֵי. חַד גַּדְיָא. חַד גַּדְיָא:

וְאָתָא תוֹרָא וְשָׁתָה לְמַיָּא. דְּכָבָה לְנוּרָא. דְּשָׂרַף לְחוּטְרָא. דְּהִכָּה לְכַלְבָּא. דְּנָשַׁךְ לְשׁוּנְרָא. דְּאָכְלָה לְגַדְיָא. דְּזַבִּין אַבָּא בִּתְרֵי זוּזֵי. חַד גַּדְיָא. חַד גַּדְיָא:

וְאָתָא הַשּׁוֹחֵט וְשָׁחַט לְתוֹרָא. דְּשָׁתָה לְמַיָּא. דְּכָבָה לְנוּרָא. דְּשָׂרַף לְחוּטְרָא. דְּהִכָּה לְכַלְבָּא. דְּנָשַׁךְ לְשׁוּנְרָא. דְּאָכְלָה לְגַדְיָא. דְּזַבִּין אַבָּא בִּתְרֵי זוּזֵי. חַד גַּדְיָא. חַד גַּדְיָא:

וְאָתָא מַלְאַךְ הַמָּוֶת וְשָׁחַט לְשׁוֹחֵט. דְּשָׁחַט לְתוֹרָא. דְּשָׁתָה לְמַיָּא. דְּכָבָה לְנוּרָא. דְּשָׂרַף לְחוּטְרָא. דְּהִכָּה לְכַלְבָּא. דְּנָשַׁךְ לְשׁוּנְרָא. דְּאָכְלָה לְגַדְיָא. דְּזַבִּין אַבָּא בִּתְרֵי זוּזֵי. חַד גַּדְיָא. חַד גַּדְיָא:

וְאָתָא הַקָּדוֹשׁ בָּרוּךְ הוּא וְשָׁחַט לְמַלְאַךְ הַמָּוֶת. דְּשָׁחַט לְשׁוֹחֵט. דְּשָׁחַט לְתוֹרָא. דְּשָׁתָה לְמַיָּא. דְּכָבָה לְנוּרָא. דְּשָׂרַף לְחוּטְרָא. דְּהִכָּה לְכַלְבָּא. דְּנָשַׁךְ לְשׁוּנְרָא. דְּאָכְלָה לְגַדְיָא. דְּזַבִּין אַבָּא בִּתְרֵי זוּזֵי. חַד גַּדְיָא. חַד גַּדְיָא:

"חַד גַּדְיָא...וְאָתָא הַקָּדוֹשׁ בָּרוּךְ הוּא"

"An only kid...The Holy One Blessed be He came...."

QUESTION: In the *Chad Gadya* narrative who was right and who was wrong?

ANSWER: Rabbi Yehonatan Eibeshitz (1690-1764) was a renowned child prodigy. At a very young age he was asked the following: On the surface it appears that the cat was wrong in devouring the innocent kid. Thus, the dog was right for biting him, and the stick that hit him was wrong. Further, the fire was right in burning the stick, and the water that extinguished the fire was wrong. Consequently, the ox was right when he drank the water, and the *shochet* — slaughterer — was wrong for killing him. If so, the angel was right when he killed the *schochet* and Hashem was wrong?! How could it be?

The young genius responded the cat had indeed done a terribly wrong thing. A cat has no right to harm an innocent kid. However, regardless of whether it was right or not, it was in no

Then along came a dog and bit the cat, that ate the kid that father bought for two *zuzim*. An only kid, an only kid!

Then along came a stick and beat the dog, that bit the cat, that ate the kid that father bought for two *zuzim*. An only kid, an only kid!

Then along came a fire and burned the stick, that beat the dog, that bit the cat, that ate the kid that father bought for two *zuzim*. An only kid, an only kid!

Then along came the water and put out the fire, that burned the stick, that beat the dog, that bit the cat, that ate the kid that father bought for two *zuzim*. An only kid, an only kid!

Then along came an ox and drank the water, that put out the fire, that burned the stick, that beat the dog, that bit the cat, that ate the kid that father bought for two *zuzim*. An only kid, an only kid!

Then along came a *shochet* and slaughtered the ox, that drank the water, that put out the fire, that burned the stick, that beat the dog, that bit the cat, that ate the kid that father bought for two *zuzim*. An only kid, an only kid!

Then came the angel of death and killed the *shochet*, who slaughtered the ox, that drank the water, that put out the fire, that burned the stick, that beat the dog, that bit the cat, that ate the kid that father bought for two *zuzim*. An only kid, an only kid!

Then came the Holy Blessed One, and killed the angel of death, who killed the *shochet*, who slaughtered the ox, that drank the water, that put out the fire, that burned the stick, that beat the dog, that bit the cat, that ate the kid that father bought for two *zuzim*. An only kid, an only kid!

---

way the dog's business, and he had no right to take the law into his own hands and mete out justice. This is a matter for the authorities and not for a bystander. Thus, the stick was right for beating him, and the fire was wrong. The water was right and the ox wrong. Consequently, the *schochet* was right and the angel was wrong. Thus, the ultimate judge, Hashem, was right.

* * *

The message of the hymn is that no one has any right to harm the *Chad Gadya* — the Jewish people. Even when they are exiled, the "angels of death" — nations of the world — do not oppress the Jews in the interest of justice or virtue, but rather, motivated by hatred and enmity. In the end of days, Hashem will take us out of exile and mete out punishment to all the nations who tortured His beloved kid.

* * *

The hymn starts and concludes with the words *"Chad Gadya"* — an only kid — to emphasize that from beginning to end, we were, are, and will be His only kid — chosen people.

שיר השירים

(א) שִׁיר הַשִּׁירִים אֲשֶׁר לִשְׁלֹמֹה: יִשָּׁקֵנִי מִנְּשִׁיקוֹת פִּיהוּ כִּי טוֹבִים דֹּדֶיךָ
מִיָּיִן: לְרֵיחַ שְׁמָנֶיךָ טוֹבִים שֶׁמֶן תּוּרַק שְׁמֶךָ עַל כֵּן עֲלָמוֹת אֲהֵבוּךָ: מָשְׁכֵנִי אַחֲרֶיךָ
נָּרוּצָה הֱבִיאַנִי הַמֶּלֶךְ חֲדָרָיו נָגִילָה וְנִשְׂמְחָה בָּךְ נַזְכִּירָה דֹדֶיךָ מִיַּיִן מֵישָׁרִים
אֲהֵבוּךָ: שְׁחוֹרָה אֲנִי וְנָאוָה בְּנוֹת יְרוּשָׁלָם כְּאָהֳלֵי קֵדָר כִּירִיעוֹת שְׁלֹמֹה: אַל תִּרְאֻנִי
שֶׁאֲנִי שְׁחַרְחֹרֶת שֶׁשֱּׁזָפַתְנִי הַשָּׁמֶשׁ בְּנֵי אִמִּי נִחֲרוּ בִי שָׂמֻנִי נֹטֵרָה אֶת הַכְּרָמִים כַּרְמִי
שֶׁלִּי לֹא נָטָרְתִּי: הַגִּידָה לִּי שֶׁאָהֲבָה נַפְשִׁי אֵיכָה תִרְעֶה אֵיכָה תַּרְבִּיץ בַּצָּהֳרָיִם
שַׁלָּמָה אֶהְיֶה כְּעֹטְיָה עַל עֶדְרֵי חֲבֵרֶיךָ: אִם לֹא תֵדְעִי לָךְ הַיָּפָה בַּנָּשִׁים צְאִי לָךְ
בְּעִקְבֵי הַצֹּאן וּרְעִי אֶת גְּדִיֹּתַיִךְ עַל מִשְׁכְּנוֹת הָרֹעִים: לְסֻסָתִי בְּרִכְבֵי פַרְעֹה דִּמִּיתִיךְ
רַעְיָתִי: נָאווּ לְחָיַיִךְ בַּתֹּרִים צַוָּארֵךְ בַּחֲרוּזִים: תּוֹרֵי זָהָב נַעֲשֶׂה לָּךְ עִם נְקֻדּוֹת הַכָּסֶף:
עַד שֶׁהַמֶּלֶךְ בִּמְסִבּוֹ נִרְדִּי נָתַן רֵיחוֹ: צְרוֹר הַמֹּר דּוֹדִי לִי בֵּין שָׁדַי יָלִין: אֶשְׁכֹּל הַכֹּפֶר
דּוֹדִי לִי בְּכַרְמֵי עֵין גֶּדִי: הִנָּךְ יָפָה רַעְיָתִי הִנָּךְ יָפָה עֵינַיִךְ יוֹנִים: הִנְּךָ יָפֶה דוֹדִי אַף
נָעִים אַף עַרְשֵׂנוּ רַעֲנָנָה: קֹרוֹת בָּתֵּינוּ אֲרָזִים רַהִיטֵנוּ בְּרוֹתִים:

"שיר השירים אשר לשלמה"
"The song that excels all songs [lit. 'which is Shlomo's' i.e. he authored it] dedicated to Hashem, the King to Whom peace belongs." (1:1)

QUESTION: Rashi quotes Rabbi Akiva that "All the songs [in the Torah] are holy, but *Shir Hashirim* — the Song of Songs — is the holy of holies." Why is it even holier than the *Az Yashir*, which Moshe and the Jews sang when they crossed the sea and witnessed the great miracles?

ANSWER: During the period of courtship, the prospective *chatan* and *kallah* eagerly await two very important events. The first is *eirusin* — betrothal — and the second is *nissuin* — marriage — the happiest moment in one's life. The redemption from Egyptian bondage and the giving of the Torah soon thereafter were the *eirusin* — betrothal — between Hashem, the *chatan*, and *K'lal Yisrael*, the *kallah*.

The wealth of the Egyptians which the Jews were given upon their departure from Egypt, together with the even greater wealth they acquired at the sea, was the money Hashem used to commence the *"eirusin"* (see 1:11 Rashi). It was conditional upon their acceptance of the Torah, which was the culmination of the *eirusin* (see *Devarim* 33:4, *Pesachim* 49b, *Sefer Igra Debei Hiluli* p. 34).

(ב) אֲנִי חֲבַצֶּלֶת הַשָּׁרוֹן שׁוֹשַׁנַּת הָעֲמָקִים: כְּשׁוֹשַׁנָּה בֵּין הַחוֹחִים כֵּן רַעְיָתִי
בֵּין הַבָּנוֹת: כְּתַפּוּחַ בַּעֲצֵי הַיַּעַר כֵּן דּוֹדִי בֵּין הַבָּנִים בְּצִלּוֹ חִמַּדְתִּי וְיָשַׁבְתִּי וּפִרְיוֹ
מָתוֹק לְחִכִּי: הֱבִיאַנִי אֶל בֵּית הַיַּיִן וְדִגְלוֹ עָלַי אַהֲבָה: סַמְּכוּנִי בָּאֲשִׁישׁוֹת רַפְּדוּנִי
בַּתַּפּוּחִים כִּי חוֹלַת אַהֲבָה אָנִי: שְׂמֹאלוֹ תַּחַת לְרֹאשִׁי וִימִינוֹ תְּחַבְּקֵנִי: הִשְׁבַּעְתִּי
אֶתְכֶם בְּנוֹת יְרוּשָׁלַם בִּצְבָאוֹת אוֹ בְּאַיְלוֹת הַשָּׂדֶה אִם תָּעִירוּ וְאִם תְּעוֹרְרוּ אֶת
הָאַהֲבָה עַד שֶׁתֶּחְפָּץ: קוֹל דּוֹדִי הִנֵּה זֶה בָּא מְדַלֵּג עַל הֶהָרִים מְקַפֵּץ עַל הַגְּבָעוֹת:
דּוֹמֶה דוֹדִי לִצְבִי אוֹ לְעֹפֶר הָאַיָּלִים הִנֵּה זֶה עוֹמֵד אַחַר כָּתְלֵנוּ מַשְׁגִּיחַ מִן הַחַלֹּנוֹת
מֵצִיץ מִן הַחֲרַכִּים: עָנָה דוֹדִי וְאָמַר לִי קוּמִי לָךְ רַעְיָתִי יָפָתִי וּלְכִי לָךְ: כִּי הִנֵּה
הַסְּתָיו עָבָר הַגֶּשֶׁם חָלַף הָלַךְ לוֹ: הַנִּצָּנִים נִרְאוּ בָאָרֶץ עֵת הַזָּמִיר הִגִּיעַ וְקוֹל הַתּוֹר
נִשְׁמַע בְּאַרְצֵנוּ: הַתְּאֵנָה חָנְטָה פַגֶּיהָ וְהַגְּפָנִים סְמָדַר נָתְנוּ רֵיחַ קוּמִי לָךְ רַעְיָתִי יָפָתִי
וּלְכִי לָךְ: יוֹנָתִי בְּחַגְוֵי הַסֶּלַע בְּסֵתֶר הַמַּדְרֵגָה הַרְאִינִי אֶת מַרְאַיִךְ הַשְׁמִיעִנִי אֶת
קוֹלֵךְ כִּי קוֹלֵךְ עָרֵב וּמַרְאֵיךְ נָאוֶה: אֶחֱזוּ לָנוּ שֻׁעָלִים שֻׁעָלִים קְטַנִּים מְחַבְּלִים כְּרָמִים
וּכְרָמֵינוּ סְמָדַר: דּוֹדִי לִי וַאֲנִי לוֹ הָרֹעֶה בַּשּׁוֹשַׁנִּים: עַד שֶׁיָּפוּחַ הַיּוֹם וְנָסוּ הַצְּלָלִים
סֹב דְּמֵה לְךָ דוֹדִי לִצְבִי אוֹ לְעֹפֶר הָאַיָּלִים עַל הָרֵי בָתֶר:

The *nissuin* — marriage — will take place in the glorious period of the Messianic Era when all Israel will enjoy *Olam Haba* — the World to Come.

The Jews sang the *Az Yashir* to express their gratitude to Hashem for the betrothal, but in *Shir Hashirim* a yearning is expressed for the forthcoming *nissuin* — marriage — at which time there will be unparalleled love between Hashem and the Jewish people (see *Berachot 34b*).

Upon completing the *Seder* some read the *Shir Hashirim* since it talks of *yetziat mitzrayim*, and the splendor of the World to Come. In it we also beseech Hashem to hasten the time of the ultimate redemption so that we will be able to experience this exalted period.

(פתיחה לשיר השירים מר' יעקב ז"ל מליסא, ועי' בפירושו צרור המור)

"הנך יפה עיניך יונים"
"You are beautiful, your eyes are as doves." (1:15)

QUESTION: Rashi quotes the *Gemara* (*Taanit 24a*), "If a *kallah* — bride — has ugly eyes, her entire body should be examined, but if her eyes are beautiful, there is no need to investigate any further."

Why is so much emphasis placed on the eyes?

(ג) עַל מִשְׁכָּבִי בַּלֵּילוֹת בִּקַּשְׁתִּי אֵת שֶׁאָהֲבָה נַפְשִׁי בִּקַּשְׁתִּיו וְלֹא מְצָאתִיו:
אָקוּמָה נָּא וַאֲסוֹבְבָה בָעִיר בַּשְּׁוָקִים וּבָרְחֹבוֹת אֲבַקְשָׁה אֵת שֶׁאָהֲבָה נַפְשִׁי בִּקַּשְׁתִּיו
וְלֹא מְצָאתִיו: מְצָאוּנִי הַשֹּׁמְרִים הַסֹּבְבִים בָּעִיר אֵת שֶׁאָהֲבָה נַפְשִׁי רְאִיתֶם: כִּמְעַט
שֶׁעָבַרְתִּי מֵהֶם עַד שֶׁמָּצָאתִי אֵת שֶׁאָהֲבָה נַפְשִׁי אֲחַזְתִּיו וְלֹא אַרְפֶּנּוּ עַד שֶׁהֲבֵיאתִיו
אֶל בֵּית אִמִּי וְאֶל חֶדֶר הוֹרָתִי: הִשְׁבַּעְתִּי אֶתְכֶם בְּנוֹת יְרוּשָׁלַם בִּצְבָאוֹת אוֹ בְּאַיְלוֹת
הַשָּׂדֶה אִם תָּעִירוּ וְאִם תְּעוֹרְרוּ אֶת הָאַהֲבָה עַד שֶׁתֶּחְפָּץ: מִי זֹאת עֹלָה מִן הַמִּדְבָּר
כְּתִימֲרוֹת עָשָׁן מְקֻטֶּרֶת מוֹר וּלְבוֹנָה מִכֹּל אַבְקַת רוֹכֵל: הִנֵּה מִטָּתוֹ שֶׁלִּשְׁלֹמֹה שִׁשִּׁים
גִּבֹּרִים סָבִיב לָהּ מִגִּבֹּרֵי יִשְׂרָאֵל: כֻּלָּם אֲחֻזֵי חֶרֶב מְלֻמְּדֵי מִלְחָמָה אִישׁ חַרְבּוֹ עַל
יְרֵכוֹ מִפַּחַד בַּלֵּילוֹת: אַפִּרְיוֹן עָשָׂה לוֹ הַמֶּלֶךְ שְׁלֹמֹה מֵעֲצֵי הַלְּבָנוֹן: עַמּוּדָיו עָשָׂה
כֶסֶף רְפִידָתוֹ זָהָב מֶרְכָּבוֹ אַרְגָּמָן תּוֹכוֹ רָצוּף אַהֲבָה מִבְּנוֹת יְרוּשָׁלָם: צְאֶינָה וּרְאֶינָה
בְּנוֹת צִיּוֹן בַּמֶּלֶךְ שְׁלֹמֹה בָּעֲטָרָה שֶׁעִטְּרָה לוֹ אִמּוֹ בְּיוֹם חֲתֻנָּתוֹ וּבְיוֹם שִׂמְחַת לִבּוֹ:

ANSWER: Our Sages are not referring to the physical eyes, but speaking allegorically. Good and ugly "eyes" are an allusion to a person's outlook and perspective. When seeking a partner in life, one should explore her priorities. How does she view the spiritual and the material? If a bride's eyes — outlook — are beautiful, i.e. in accordance with Torah guidelines, one can unhesitatingly take her for a wife and there is no need to inquire or probe any further.

(עי' כלי יקר בראשית כ"ד: י"ד, בענין כלה שעיניה יפות)

"כְּשׁוֹשַׁנָּה בֵּין הַחוֹחִים כֵּן רַעְיָתִי בֵּין הַבָּנוֹת"
"As a rose among the thorns is
My beloved among the daughters [nations]" (2:2)

QUESTION: In what way are the Jewish people analogous to a rose?

ANSWER: When a rose is among thorns, a north wind goes forth and bends her toward the south and a thorn pricks her, then a south wind goes forth and bends her toward the north and a thorn pricks her; yet, for all that, her core is directed upwards. The same is true with the Jewish people. Although they are oppressed and tortured from all sides by the nations, their hearts are directed towards their Father in Heaven.

(מדרש רבה ויקרא כג:ה)

* * *

Once, while the Ramban (Nachmanides) and a priest were taking a stroll together in a garden, the priest said, "You Jews must be a terrible people; otherwise, why do all the nations of the world torture and despise you?" The Ramban took him to a

(ד) הִנָּךְ יָפָה רַעְיָתִי הִנָּךְ יָפָה עֵינַיִךְ יוֹנִים מִבַּעַד לְצַמָּתֵךְ שַׂעְרֵךְ כְּעֵדֶר
הָעִזִּים שֶׁגָּלְשׁוּ מֵהַר גִּלְעָד: שִׁנַּיִךְ כְּעֵדֶר הַקְּצוּבוֹת שֶׁעָלוּ מִן הָרַחְצָה שֶׁכֻּלָּם
מַתְאִימוֹת וְשַׁכֻּלָה אֵין בָּהֶם: כְּחוּט הַשָּׁנִי שִׂפְתוֹתַיִךְ וּמִדְבָּרֵךְ נָאוֶה כְּפֶלַח הָרִמּוֹן
רַקָּתֵךְ מִבַּעַד לְצַמָּתֵךְ: כְּמִגְדַּל דָּוִיד צַוָּארֵךְ בָּנוּי לְתַלְפִּיּוֹת אֶלֶף הַמָּגֵן תָּלוּי עָלָיו כֹּל
שִׁלְטֵי הַגִּבּוֹרִים: שְׁנֵי שָׁדַיִךְ כִּשְׁנֵי עֳפָרִים תְּאוֹמֵי צְבִיָּה הָרֹעִים בַּשּׁוֹשַׁנִּים: עַד שֶׁיָּפוּחַ
הַיּוֹם וְנָסוּ הַצְּלָלִים אֵלֶךְ לִי אֶל הַר הַמּוֹר וְאֶל גִּבְעַת הַלְּבוֹנָה: כֻּלָּךְ יָפָה רַעְיָתִי וּמוּם
אֵין בָּךְ: אִתִּי מִלְּבָנוֹן כַּלָּה אִתִּי מִלְּבָנוֹן תָּבוֹאִי תָּשׁוּרִי מֵרֹאשׁ אֲמָנָה מֵרֹאשׁ שְׂנִיר
וְחֶרְמוֹן מִמְּעֹנוֹת אֲרָיוֹת מֵהַרְרֵי נְמֵרִים: לִבַּבְתִּנִי אֲחֹתִי כַלָּה לִבַּבְתִּנִי בְּאַחַת
מֵעֵינַיִךְ בְּאַחַד עֲנָק מִצַּוְּרֹנָיִךְ: מַה יָּפוּ דֹדַיִךְ אֲחֹתִי כַלָּה מַה טֹּבוּ דֹדַיִךְ מִיַּיִן וְרֵיחַ
שְׁמָנַיִךְ מִכָּל בְּשָׂמִים: נֹפֶת תִּטֹּפְנָה שִׂפְתוֹתַיִךְ כַּלָּה דְּבַשׁ וְחָלָב תַּחַת לְשׁוֹנֵךְ וְרֵיחַ
שַׂלְמֹתַיִךְ כְּרֵיחַ לְבָנוֹן: גַּן נָעוּל אֲחֹתִי כַלָּה גַּל נָעוּל מַעְיָן חָתוּם: שְׁלָחַיִךְ פַּרְדֵּס
רִמּוֹנִים עִם פְּרִי מְגָדִים כְּפָרִים עִם נְרָדִים: נֵרְדְּ וְכַרְכֹּם קָנֶה וְקִנָּמוֹן עִם כָּל עֲצֵי
לְבוֹנָה מֹר וַאֲהָלוֹת עִם כָּל רָאשֵׁי בְשָׂמִים: מַעְיַן גַּנִּים בְּאֵר מַיִם חַיִּים וְנֹזְלִים מִן
לְבָנוֹן: עוּרִי צָפוֹן וּבוֹאִי תֵימָן הָפִיחִי גַנִּי יִזְּלוּ בְשָׂמָיו יָבֹא דוֹדִי לְגַנּוֹ וְיֹאכַל פְּרִי
מְגָדָיו:

---

section in the garden where there were beautiful rose bushes in
the midst of thorns, and said to him, "Does the fact that these
roses are pricked by the thorns and bitten by insects depict the
superiority of the thorns and the insects, and the inadequacy of
the rose? Of course not; it is merely that the refined and tender
rose is incapable of standing up to the strong and vicious thorns.
Likewise, their persecuting us is no proof of their superiority and
our inadequacy. They are coarse and rough, and we are physically
weak and delicate."

(פון אונזער אלטען אוצר)

"נפת תטפנה שפתותיך כלה, דבש וחלב תחת לשונך"
"The sweetness of Torah drops from your lips,
like honey and milk it lies under your tongue." (4:11)

QUESTION: What is the significance of comparing Torah to
honey and milk?

ANSWER: Honey is made by the bee, which is a forbidden
creature, and milk is a byproduct of blood (see *Bechorot* 6b).

Thus, both milk and honey originate from a source which is
tamei — contaminated — although after the product is developed
it is *tahor* — halachically pure for human consumption.

(ה) בָּאתִי לְגַנִּי אֲחֹתִי כַלָּה אָרִיתִי מוֹרִי עִם בְּשָׂמִי מוֹרִי יַעְרִי עִם דִּבְשִׁי
שָׁתִיתִי יֵינִי עִם חֲלָבִי אִכְלוּ רֵעִים שְׁתוּ וְשִׁכְרוּ דּוֹדִים: אֲנִי יְשֵׁנָה וְלִבִּי עֵר קוֹל דּוֹדִי
דוֹפֵק פִּתְחִי לִי אֲחֹתִי רַעְיָתִי יוֹנָתִי תַמָּתִי שֶׁרֹאשִׁי נִמְלָא טָל קְוֻצּוֹתַי רְסִיסֵי לָיְלָה:
פָּשַׁטְתִּי אֶת כֻּתָּנְתִּי אֵיכָכָה אֶלְבָּשֶׁנָּה רָחַצְתִּי אֶת רַגְלַי אֵיכָכָה אֲטַנְּפֵם: דּוֹדִי שָׁלַח
יָדוֹ מִן הַחוֹר וּמֵעַי הָמוּ עָלָיו: קַמְתִּי אֲנִי לִפְתֹּחַ לְדוֹדִי וְיָדַי נָטְפוּ מוֹר וְאֶצְבְּעֹתַי מוֹר
עֹבֵר עַל כַּפּוֹת הַמַּנְעוּל: פָּתַחְתִּי אֲנִי לְדוֹדִי וְדוֹדִי חָמַק עָבָר נַפְשִׁי יָצְאָה בְדַבְּרוֹ
בִּקַּשְׁתִּיהוּ וְלֹא מְצָאתִיהוּ קְרָאתִיו וְלֹא עָנָנִי: מְצָאֻנִי הַשֹּׁמְרִים הַסֹּבְבִים בָּעִיר הִכּוּנִי
פְצָעוּנִי נָשְׂאוּ אֶת רְדִידִי מֵעָלַי שֹׁמְרֵי הַחֹמוֹת: הִשְׁבַּעְתִּי אֶתְכֶם בְּנוֹת יְרוּשָׁלָ͏ִם אִם
תִּמְצְאוּ אֶת דּוֹדִי מַה תַּגִּידוּ לוֹ שֶׁחוֹלַת אַהֲבָה אָנִי: מַה דּוֹדֵךְ מִדּוֹד הַיָּפָה בַּנָּשִׁים
מַה דּוֹדֵךְ מִדּוֹד שֶׁכָּכָה הִשְׁבַּעְתָּנוּ: דּוֹדִי צַח וְאָדוֹם דָּגוּל מֵרְבָבָה: רֹאשׁוֹ כֶּתֶם פָּז
קְוֻצּוֹתָיו תַּלְתַּלִּים שְׁחֹרוֹת כָּעוֹרֵב: עֵינָיו כְּיוֹנִים עַל אֲפִיקֵי מָיִם רֹחֲצוֹת בֶּחָלָב
יֹשְׁבוֹת עַל מִלֵּאת: לְחָיָו כַּעֲרוּגַת הַבֹּשֶׂם מִגְדְּלוֹת מֶרְקָחִים שִׂפְתוֹתָיו שׁוֹשַׁנִּים נֹטְפוֹת
מוֹר עֹבֵר: יָדָיו גְּלִילֵי זָהָב מְמֻלָּאִים בַּתַּרְשִׁישׁ מֵעָיו עֶשֶׁת שֵׁן מְעֻלֶּפֶת סַפִּירִים:
שׁוֹקָיו עַמּוּדֵי שֵׁשׁ מְיֻסָּדִים עַל אַדְנֵי פָז מַרְאֵהוּ כַּלְּבָנוֹן בָּחוּר כָּאֲרָזִים: חִכּוֹ מַמְתַקִּים
וְכֻלּוֹ מַחֲמַדִּים זֶה דוֹדִי וְזֶה רֵעִי בְּנוֹת יְרוּשָׁלָ͏ִם:

(ו) אָנָה הָלַךְ דּוֹדֵךְ הַיָּפָה בַּנָּשִׁים אָנָה פָּנָה דוֹדֵךְ וּנְבַקְשֶׁנּוּ עִמָּךְ: דּוֹדִי יָרַד
לְגַנּוֹ לַעֲרוּגוֹת הַבֹּשֶׂם לִרְעוֹת בַּגַּנִּים וְלִלְקֹט שׁוֹשַׁנִּים: אֲנִי לְדוֹדִי וְדוֹדִי לִי הָרֹעֶה
בַּשּׁוֹשַׁנִּים: יָפָה אַתְּ רַעְיָתִי כְּתִרְצָה נָאוָה כִּירוּשָׁלָ͏ִם אֲיֻמָּה כַּנִּדְגָּלוֹת: הָסֵבִּי עֵינַיִךְ
מִנֶּגְדִּי שֶׁהֵם הִרְהִיבֻנִי שַׂעְרֵךְ כְּעֵדֶר הָעִזִּים שֶׁגָּלְשׁוּ מִן הַגִּלְעָד: שִׁנַּיִךְ כְּעֵדֶר הָרְחֵלִים
שֶׁעָלוּ מִן הָרַחְצָה שֶׁכֻּלָּם מַתְאִימוֹת וְשַׁכֻּלָה אֵין בָּהֶם: כְּפֶלַח הָרִמּוֹן רַקָּתֵךְ מִבַּעַד
לְצַמָּתֵךְ: שִׁשִּׁים הֵמָּה מְלָכוֹת וּשְׁמֹנִים פִּילַגְשִׁים וַעֲלָמוֹת אֵין מִסְפָּר: אַחַת הִיא
יוֹנָתִי תַמָּתִי אַחַת הִיא לְאִמָּהּ בָּרָה הִיא לְיוֹלַדְתָּהּ רָאוּהָ בָנוֹת וַיְאַשְּׁרוּהָ מְלָכוֹת
וּפִילַגְשִׁים וַיְהַלְלוּהָ: מִי זֹאת הַנִּשְׁקָפָה כְּמוֹ שָׁחַר יָפָה כַלְּבָנָה בָּרָה כַּחַמָּה אֲיֻמָּה
כַּנִּדְגָּלוֹת: אֶל גִּנַּת אֱגוֹז יָרַדְתִּי לִרְאוֹת בְּאִבֵּי הַנָּחַל לִרְאוֹת הֲפָרְחָה הַגֶּפֶן הֵנֵצוּ
הָרִמֹּנִים: לֹא יָדַעְתִּי נַפְשִׁי שָׂמַתְנִי מַרְכְּבוֹת עַמִּי נָדִיב:

(ז) שׁוּבִי שׁוּבִי הַשּׁוּלַמִּית שׁוּבִי שׁוּבִי וְנֶחֱזֶה בָּךְ מַה תֶּחֱזוּ בַּשּׁוּלַמִּית
כִּמְחֹלַת הַמַּחֲנָיִם: מַה יָּפוּ פְעָמַיִךְ בַּנְּעָלִים בַּת נָדִיב חַמּוּקֵי יְרֵכַיִךְ כְּמוֹ חֲלָאִים
מַעֲשֵׂה יְדֵי אָמָּן: שָׁרְרֵךְ אַגַּן הַסַּהַר אַל יֶחְסַר הַמָּזֶג בִּטְנֵךְ עֲרֵמַת חִטִּים סוּגָה
בַּשּׁוֹשַׁנִּים: שְׁנֵי שָׁדַיִךְ כִּשְׁנֵי עֳפָרִים תָּאֳמֵי צְבִיָּה: צַוָּארֵךְ כְּמִגְדַּל הַשֵּׁן עֵינַיִךְ בְּרֵכוֹת
בְּחֶשְׁבּוֹן עַל שַׁעַר בַּת רַבִּים אַפֵּךְ כְּמִגְדַּל הַלְּבָנוֹן צוֹפֶה פְּנֵי דַמָּשֶׂק: רֹאשֵׁךְ עָלַיִךְ
כַּכַּרְמֶל וְדַלַּת רֹאשֵׁךְ כָּאַרְגָּמָן מֶלֶךְ אָסוּר בָּרְהָטִים: מַה יָּפִית וּמַה נָּעַמְתְּ אַהֲבָה
בַּתַּעֲנוּגִים: זֹאת קוֹמָתֵךְ דָּמְתָה לְתָמָר וְשָׁדַיִךְ לְאַשְׁכֹּלוֹת: אָמַרְתִּי אֶעֱלֶה בְתָמָר
אֹחֲזָה בְּסַנְסִנָּיו וְיִהְיוּ נָא שָׁדַיִךְ כְּאֶשְׁכְּלוֹת הַגֶּפֶן וְרֵיחַ אַפֵּךְ כַּתַּפּוּחִים: וְחִכֵּךְ כְּיֵין
הַטּוֹב הוֹלֵךְ לְדוֹדִי לְמֵישָׁרִים דּוֹבֵב שִׂפְתֵי יְשֵׁנִים: אֲנִי לְדוֹדִי וְעָלַי תְּשׁוּקָתוֹ: לְכָה

Torah is compared to milk and honey because of its power to
elevate and purify even one who has fallen into a state of spiritual
contamination.

(עוללות אפרים)

דּוֹדִי נֵצֵא הַשָּׂדֶה נָלִינָה בַּכְּפָרִים: נַשְׁכִּימָה לַכְּרָמִים נִרְאֶה אִם פָּרְחָה הַגֶּפֶן פִּתַּח הַסְּמָדַר הֵנֵצוּ הָרִמּוֹנִים שָׁם אֶתֵּן אֶת דֹּדַי לָךְ: הַדּוּדָאִים נָתְנוּ רֵיחַ וְעַל פְּתָחֵינוּ כָּל מְגָדִים חֲדָשִׁים גַּם יְשָׁנִים דּוֹדִי צָפַנְתִּי לָךְ:

(ח) מִי יִתֶּנְךָ כְּאָח לִי יוֹנֵק שְׁדֵי אִמִּי אֶמְצָאֲךָ בַחוּץ אֶשָּׁקְךָ גַּם לֹא יָבֻזוּ לִי: אֶנְהָגֲךָ אֲבִיאֲךָ אֶל בֵּית אִמִּי תְּלַמְּדֵנִי אַשְׁקְךָ מִיַּיִן הָרֶקַח מֵעֲסִיס רִמֹּנִי: שְׂמֹאלוֹ תַּחַת רֹאשִׁי וִימִינוֹ תְּחַבְּקֵנִי: הִשְׁבַּעְתִּי אֶתְכֶם בְּנוֹת יְרוּשָׁלָם מַה תָּעִירוּ וּמַה תְּעֹרְרוּ אֶת הָאַהֲבָה עַד שֶׁתֶּחְפָּץ: מִי זֹאת עֹלָה מִן הַמִּדְבָּר מִתְרַפֶּקֶת עַל דּוֹדָהּ תַּחַת הַתַּפּוּחַ עוֹרַרְתִּיךָ שָׁמָּה חִבְּלַתְךָ אִמֶּךָ שָׁמָּה חִבְּלָה יְלָדַתְךָ: שִׂימֵנִי כַחוֹתָם עַל לִבֶּךָ כַּחוֹתָם עַל זְרוֹעֶךָ כִּי עַזָּה כַמָּוֶת אַהֲבָה קָשָׁה כִשְׁאוֹל קִנְאָה רְשָׁפֶיהָ רִשְׁפֵּי אֵשׁ שַׁלְהֶבֶתְיָה: מַיִם רַבִּים לֹא יוּכְלוּ לְכַבּוֹת אֶת הָאַהֲבָה וּנְהָרוֹת לֹא יִשְׁטְפוּהָ אִם יִתֵּן אִישׁ אֶת כָּל הוֹן בֵּיתוֹ בָּאַהֲבָה בּוֹז יָבוּזוּ לוֹ: אָחוֹת לָנוּ קְטַנָּה וְשָׁדַיִם אֵין לָהּ מַה נַּעֲשֶׂה לַאֲחוֹתֵנוּ בַּיּוֹם שֶׁיְּדֻבַּר בָּהּ: אִם חוֹמָה הִיא נִבְנֶה עָלֶיהָ טִירַת כָּסֶף וְאִם דֶּלֶת הִיא נָצוּר עָלֶיהָ לוּחַ אָרֶז: אֲנִי חוֹמָה וְשָׁדַי כַּמִּגְדָּלוֹת אָז הָיִיתִי בְעֵינָיו כְּמוֹצְאֵת שָׁלוֹם: כֶּרֶם הָיָה לִשְׁלֹמֹה בְּבַעַל הָמוֹן נָתַן אֶת הַכֶּרֶם לַנֹּטְרִים אִישׁ יָבִא בְּפִרְיוֹ אֶלֶף כָּסֶף: כַּרְמִי שֶׁלִּי לְפָנָי הָאֶלֶף לְךָ שְׁלֹמֹה וּמָאתַיִם לְנֹטְרִים אֶת פִּרְיוֹ: הַיּוֹשֶׁבֶת בַּגַּנִּים חֲבֵרִים מַקְשִׁיבִים לְקוֹלֵךְ הַשְׁמִיעִנִי: בְּרַח דּוֹדִי וּדְמֵה לְךָ לִצְבִי אוֹ לְעֹפֶר הָאַיָּלִים עַל הָרֵי בְשָׂמִים:

"בְּרַח דּוֹדִי וּדְמֵה לְךָ לִצְבִי אוֹ לְעֹפֶר הָאַיָּלִים עַל הָרֵי בְשָׂמִים"

**"Flee my Beloved, be like a gazelle or a young hart [in Your swiftness
to redeem us from this exile and rest Your Presence] upon the
mountain of spices [Mount Moriah and the *Beit Hamikdash*]." (9:14)**

QUESTION: What is the intent of asking Hashem to be like a
gazelle?

ANSWER: Unlike all other animals, when a deer sleeps, it only
closes one eye and keeps the other one open. Also, while running,
it always turns its head to look back. Thus, we are beseeching
Hashem that even if our behavior is such that He wants, so to
speak, to sleep and close His eyes and not look after us, or if He
wants to run away from us, G-d forbid, He should always keep
one eye open and turn His head and look back, i.e. see our
affliction and redeem us.

(תרגום)

לעילוי נשמת זקני
הרה"ג החו"ב איש יר"א כו'
ר' **צבי הכהן** ע"ה **קפלן**
עסק בחינוך ז"ך שנה בישיבת תורה ודעת
ולפני זה בישיבת מיר שבמיר
והעמיד תלמידים הרבה
נפטר ו' מנחם אב תשכ"ט

לעילוי נשמת זקנתי
הרבנית החשובה והעדינה
יהודית ע"ה **קפלן**
נפטרה יום א' דחג הפסח תשכ"ה
זכתה לדור ישרים יבורך

לעילוי נשמת אבי
הרה"ג חו"ב סוע"ה וכו'
ר' **שמואל פסח** ב"ר **משה** ע"ה
באגאמילסקי
מחשובי תלמידי הגאונים
ר' שמעון זצ"ל שקאפ בגראדנא
ור' ברוך בער זצ"ל לייבאוויץ בקאמיניץ
ולבסוף בישיבת מיר שבמיר
כיהן ברבנות בארה"ב
נפטר מוצש"ק פ' שלח כ"ד סיון תרצ"ט

לעילוי נשמת אמי
הרבנית החשובה והעדינה
חסיא הדסה בת הרה"ג ר' **צבי הכהן** ע"ה
עשתה צדקה וחסד במסירה ונתינה
לטובת הכלל והפרט
נפטרה בשם טוב
יום השלישי, פרשת בא ערב ר"ח שבט תשנ"א

ת. נ. צ. ב. ה.